The Spiritual Side of Writing

The Spiritual Side of Writing

Releasing the Learner's Whole Potential

Edited by

Regina Paxton Foehr
Illinois State University
and
Susan A. Schiller
Central Michigan University

Boynton/Cook Publishers
HEINEMANN
Portsmouth, NH

Boynton/Cook Publishers, Inc.
A subsidiary of Reed Elsevier Inc.
361 Hanover Street
Portsmouth, NH 03801-3912
Offices and agents throughout the world

The editors and publisher would like to thank those who have given their permission to include material in this book:

Excerpts from *Meditations for Women Who Do Too Much* by Anne Wilson Schaef. Copyright © 1990 by Anne Wilson Schaef. Reprinted by permission of HarperCollins Publishers.

Library of Congress Cataloging-in-Publication Data
Spiritual empowerment in pedagogy / edited by Regina Paxton Foehr,
  Susan A. Schiller.
      p.   cm.
  Includes bibliographical references (p.   ).
  ISBN 0-86709-413-3
  1. Teaching. 2. Spirituality—Study and teaching. 3. Education—
Philosophy. I. Foehr, Regina Paxton. II. Schiller, Susan A.
LB1027.S67 1997
371.1'001—dc20   96–41585
                                                                CIP

Editor: Peter R. Stillman
Production: J. B. Tranchemontagne
Manufacturing: Louise Richardson
Cover design: Barbara Werden

Printed in the United States of America on acid-free paper
00 99 98 97 DA 1 2 3 4 5 6 7 8 9

Contents

Acknowledgments

We thank those who have made this book possible for their friendship and the ways they have widened our understanding of what it means to be spiritually empowered. We especially thank all the contributors for the originality and diversity of their articles and annotated bibliographies. We are grateful to Peter Stillman, our editor, for keen judgment, for sharing our vision for the book, and for invaluable direction.

We appreciate the special contributions of our professional colleagues: Dick Graves, for generous assistance, wisdom, and soundness of advice when responding to our questions; James Moffett, for continuous support and for the smiles he put on our faces when he was the first one to submit an article in response to our call for papers; Parker Palmer, for his body of work that has been a source of inspiration; John Bradshaw, Larry Dossey, M.D., and Thomas Moore for their willingness to share their insights on their writing processes; and Elaine Hughes, Nell Ann Pickett, Gabriele Rico, and Charles Suhor for letting us know they valued our work.

We appreciate the support of our colleagues in the National Council of Teachers of English (NCTE) Assembly for Expanded Perspectives on Learning (AEPL) and their shared interest and openness to research in topics traditionally considered beyond the cognitive domain.

Support from colleagues and friends has also made the journey into this book gratifying. Susan thanks Francis Molson, Ron Primeau, Ann Bardens, Stacy Jo Schiller, and Sandra Smith, who have been important sources of encouragement. Ruth Ray, Lisa Sandlin, Two Moons, and Barry Alford were helpful readers of draft work, and their wisdom facilitated our collaboration and growth. Two Moons, Mary Ann Wernette, Susan Forster, Eirene Kay, and Susan Corcoran also gave Susan a great deal of spiritual support.

Regina wishes to thank Ron Fortune, William Kraemer, and Anita Johnson, whose collaboration, creative insights, and direction were invaluable and inspiring. She thanks Helen Walker, Elizabeth Crowley, and Deborah Loest for important revision suggestions and Kim Lerette and Linda Meyer for transcribing interview tapes. She appreciates friends whose interest and enthusiasm buoyed her own: Annette Watkins, Elaine Kohsman, Doris Hill, Cathy Anderson, Diane White, Karen Turner, Sharon Thomson, Dan Bachman, and Pamela Yeast. She also values the support of colleagues, including Lee Brasseur, Heather Graves, Joel Haefner, Ron Strickland, and Roberta Trites. And she recognizes with gratitude the response and listening ear of Jim Kalmbach, Stan Renner, Russ Rutter, and Torri Thompson.

We are grateful to all of our students and former students and to the book's contributors and readers who have influenced our understanding of the nature of spiritual empowerment in pedagogy.

We offer our very special thanks to our spouses, John Foehr and Theopolis Gilmore. They have been extremely generous with time, ideas, patience, and encouragement.

Introduction

We've all experienced *spiritual empowerment* in learning. We may recognize it in sudden insight or awareness; in an instant when we understand with pristine clarity that evokes feelings of joy and a renewal of energy. We may know it by different names—*imagination, inspiration, intuition, kinesthetic knowledge, felt sense, passion for knowing, aha experience, archetypal energy, the collective unconscious.* We find it paradoxical—noncognitive but deeply known, inexplicable yet deeply felt, inexpressible in language yet familiar and trusted. It surprises us, it assures us, it transforms us; it makes us want to know more.

The Spiritual Side of Writing has to do with helping teachers and students discover ways to access the inner and transcendent spiritual power inherent in human beings. "Spirituality is," after all, "a fundamental condition of being human" according to University of Chicago psychologist and *"flow"* theorist, Mihaly Csikszentmihalyi (quoted in Henderson 1994, 40). It teaches people to trust their own abilities and creative processes—to move beyond their apprehension and self doubts. The processes that access this inner/transcendent power build self-confidence, create hope, and make one feel more connected to others and the world by engaging the mind *and* the spirit.

The Spiritual Side of Writing acknowledges that even in the academy intellectual and creative activity, like language itself, is spiritual. Spiritually open pedagogy, as the ancient Greeks suggested, can reintroduce balance while at the same time fostering lifelong learning. It recognizes that critical thinking and spirituality are not mutually exclusive but are mutually intertwined, complementary parts of the whole of knowing.

In fact, critical thinking, intellectual argument, and the interchange that occurs when people exchange ideas with one another can represent some of the highest forms of spiritual empowerment. Sharing ideas can create a connectedness to each other and represent a search toward truth. Likewise, critique and inquiry can help us on the journey toward a higher consciousness. Guiding students to think for themselves, to develop interpretive skills, and to learn to trust their ideas can also be acts of spiritual empowerment. For all of these ways of experiencing are spiritual, creating the exhilaration that comes when two ideas come together to create a fresh, new third idea. In these exchanges ideas and insights seem to come, not just from a place within, but from a place that transcends the self, a source that seems simultaneously deeply personal and universal. These exchanges can fill students with wonder, exhilaration, and an awe for learning. They can give students a new vision of their own power to understand and create meaning.

One college senior described spiritual empowerment as "a sense of radiance during my writing . . . a radiance that has grown in intensity over time . . . that grows intense during times of reading literature, criticism, and scholarly articles . . . and a source of awareness, intelligence and love." For this she credits a professor in whose class she felt spiritually empowered. As many of the contributors to this book have done for their students, her professor encouraged her to risk venturing into uncharted territory—to go to the edge, a vulnerable potentially frightening place. We never know what may lie beyond the edge. But when we take the leap into the unknown and unfamiliar, what we discover may be dazzling or energizing beyond what we could have imagined, offering growth, delight, and deep insight. The authors in this collection have gone to the edge and have let spiritual empowerment in the academy take flight. When we issued the call for these essays, the overwhelming response from professors across the nation revealed the depth of interest in spiritual empowerment within the teaching profession. We had expressly stated that this book was to be not about religion but about spiritual empowerment as defined by each contributor. Combining theory and practice, all of them write with concern and commitment to students' learning. With expertise and professionalism, they describe theories and philosophies and apply them in pedagogy. They link spiritual reform to education in natural ways that foster lifelong learning and they preserve the mandate to separate church and state. We thank them, for they have made it possible for us to present this collection.

R.P.F.
Bloomington, Illinois

S.A.S.
Mt. Pleasant, Michigan

Part One

Spiritual Philosophies for Teaching and Learning— Embracing the Paradox, Honoring the Whole

Whether we call it *"flow,"* *"inspiration,"* or *"creative insight,"* we cannot contain our experience of spiritual empowerment. It makes us smile—may even make us a bit giddy—as we experience it or witness our students marvel in its wonder, writing what they did not know they were capable of writing, interpreting literature they thought they could not understand, or solving problems that seemed beyond their ability. As teachers, individually, we value it, recognizing it intuitively as a crucial element in learning, a key to changing one's level of conscious awareness. But, ironically, although we are awed by its transformation potential, in the mainstream postmodern academy we have turned our backs on this source of power. Instead, as Regina Foehr argues in her article for this collection we have favored the safety of tradition and convention and have collectively chosen *alienation* from this spiritually nourishing reservoir of enlightenment, eschewing activities that activate the region of the psyche that is the source of courage, confidence, and new ideas. Institutionally, we have chosen alienation because of our error in interpreting *spirituality*. We understand it archetypally, from the personal and the collective unconscious, and we understand it metaphorically. But institutionally we have oversimplified our interpretation of spirituality.

We have reduced it to literal, linear, or one-dimensional levels instead of recognizing its paradoxical and metaphorical nature. This reductive interpretation has created a dichotomous split, a fragmentation of the whole. If we are to return to wholeness individually and collectively, we must reconceptualize the role of spirituality in language and learning, seeing its metaphorical power and embracing its paradox (42–47).

Though the spiritual dimension of learning has traditionally not been acknowledged in the academy, paradoxically it is the source of inspiration, enlightenment, and psychic sustenance in the life of the learner *and* the teacher. Cognition and spirituality are not *either/or* dichotomies but *both/and* complementary parts of the whole. To heal the fracture within the self and reclaim the whole in the academy, we need to honor the paradox of the spiritual. Spirituality in learning can be found in the mundane and in everyday duties. It can spring from silence or from nature or wonder or union with God. It can spring from addressing our shadow. It can be messy to deal with; it can come in scraps and fragments. But the fragment of an idea when developed can be the catalyst causing a student for the first time to see him- or herself as a writer, or it can bring illumination, touching the mind, the heart, or the psyche, giving life to the reader or the writer.

People, relationships, and all of life exemplify paradox. If we are to reconnect the fragmented self and return to wholeness, we need to embrace paradox. Contributing authors of the essays in this section of the book offer metaphorical interpretations of spirituality in teaching and learning, and they provide philosophies, arguments, and methods for activating the spiritual region of the psyche that embrace paradox and honor the whole.

James Moffett's essay centers on the theory that "people are here on earth to grow, not primarily to achieve or acquire except as doing so enhances inner growth," that we don't so much "learn to live as live to learn." Through a "soul school," an extended metaphor for the evolution of consciousness, he offers a spiritual framework for re-visioning education and teaching the whole person.

Richard Graves defines grace in pedagogy as "a place where all lines converge and everything relates to everything else in harmony." He discusses some qualities of grace in pedagogy, including its power to transform, to heal, to transcend the ego, to surprise, and to enhance creativity. Graves offers student and teacher examples that represent grace in pedagogy.

Kristie Fleckenstein employs Yeats's image from "The Second Coming" of a rough beast slouching into existence to herald the meaninglessness of a new age. The beast serves as a powerful metaphor for our present pedagogy. She argues that we have lost our spiritual center, and she calls for an exploratory pedagogy, based in a spiritual center—a center that holds.

Susan Schiller believes composition instruction can be improved by integrating spirituality-based pedagogy with composition theory. She points out that since professional writers frequently draw from their spirituality in order to create and find expression, so too can students in composition classes. By practicing a spirituality-based approach to composition, the academy can participate in and contribute to the whole-transition shift in reality that seems to be occurring.

Regina Foehr explores the effects of the academy's literal interpretation of spirituality and offers archetypal psychology as a metaphor for understanding the complex, paradoxical nature of spirituality. Her article features interviews with physician Larry Dossey and psychologists John Bradshaw and Thomas Moore, best-selling writers from other disciplines who speak about the spiritual forces that influence their writing.

1

Soul School

James Moffett

Suppose it is true, as spiritual traditions maintain, that people are here on earth to grow, not primarily to achieve or acquire except as doing so enhances inner growth. Since what we achieve and acquire mean little in the end, this inner cultivation seems a more likely purpose for life. Suppose we don't learn merely to be able to get by, get along, get around, or get ahead. These are all essential, but they fare better when education aims beyond them on the assumption that they are the means and education the end. Suppose we don't so much learn to live as live to learn. Once understood in this way, knowing becomes a different matter—and a much more important one. Making a living and making a life become part of making sense of life, so that everything in it has meaning.

Notoriously, people fall apart when they reach their goals. Someone struggles fanatically to become rich and famous, then, when successful, takes to alcohol or other drugs. Success breeds despair as much as does failure. Husband and wife work zestfully to build their dream house and then get divorced. Or plan and strive to make it big in the middleclass–white-collar jobs, a house and cars and friends that show their status, kids with straight teeth who go on to good colleges. Then they don't have a basis for action anymore, no motive or meaning. What do you do after you've achieved your goals, especially now that life expectancy is longer?

Some find new goals in time to regain meaning, but the problem is that the goals are too small. It's wrenching to see people constantly turning over jobs, hobbies, houses, mates, and friends looking for new stimuli, new gratifications, or new reasons to live. Actually, people are not as shallow as they seem. They want meaning, but they are fixated on small goals—to win this person, to make their bedroom look as stylish as those in *Better Homes and Gardens,* to fit an image of a sporty businessman, to impress professional peers with an article in the right journal. If you're trying to reduce suffering or explore the mysteries of life, you'll never run out of your goal. The big aims aren't reached in a lifetime, or if so, like making a scientific discovery that has taken many years, you can parlay the results into another long-range goal if you have overarching purposes. Indeed, there's nothing wrong with small goals if they are integrated into bigger ones. So goes holistic thinking.

Living to learn makes whatever happens useful and meaningful, but it takes a spiritual framework to keep learning experiences that are painful from becoming a mockery. Such lifelong learning is not idle, for its own sake, or even for the sake of curiosity. After all, native curiosity itself most likely represents an innate feeling that we are here to learn. Suppose growth is the master goal. Then the focus of public education and the purpose of life would be one and the same—inner growth for meaning. If so, one's talents and traits, predispositions and predilections would develop not merely for their own sake but as part of an individual's evolving toward spiritual fulfillment.

Soul School

What would this super goal be if not the full realization, at all levels of being, that one is a spirit, a part of Spirit, temporarily incarnated, exiled, and therefore in a state of amnesia? This purpose would be metaphysical or cosmological in that it would be part of some universal evolution. Fairy tales of urchins discovering they are princesses or princes may be taken as wish fulfillments of peasants longing for ease and opulence, but all literature is at bottom a secularization of holy lore.[1] Underneath the stories of rags to riches, of unknown inheritances, of mistaken identity, of high estate disguised as low, lie ancient gnostic myths of self-realization in its true meaning of Self-realization. The protagonist overcomes the amnesia, the forgetfulness of the River Styx separating the spirit world from the physical world.

Perhaps we develop ourselves not only because it's the most practical way to live on earth but because it's how we find out who we really are, which might be more than we think. According to this view, personal development is transpersonal development. Traditionally, enlightenment or awakening transforms one's life. But since one then actually recognizes—re-cognizes—one's true nature as Spirit, it would be more accurate to regard this transformation as a transfiguration. One's nature has not changed, had never changed, but now one sees through the material plane to the radiance within, as the three disciples and Arjuna were permitted to behold during the transfigurations of Christ and Krishna.

To realize oneself means to fulfill oneself, to bring all potentialities to realization. (The U.S. Army recruiting slogan, "Be all that you can be," typifies popular understanding, which unwittingly caricatures the spiritual truth it intuits by casting it in material terms.) "Realize" means both "become aware of" and "make real." That's exactly what happens, it's said, when

1. In Part Two of *Harmonic Learning* I explored this thesis.

enlightenment or self-realization occurs. One comes to know Spirit with the same sense of reality as we feel about the objects and events of daily life. In realizing the hidden nature of one's self as Self, one at once realizes also the hidden nature of the universe, the two being both Spirit, consubstantial. Thus realized also is the basic meaning of religion as rebonding.

The mysteries of antiquity provide the model for this experience of realizing in the double sense. The hierophant placed the initiate in a deep trance underground for three days, during which the spirit could disengage itself to go out of the body and be conducted on a tour of higher planes. As disembodied consciousness, the initiate then saw spiritual reality so directly and convincingly that henceforth no teaching or scripture was necessary, and the reality of the experience remained forever. Christ's and Lazarus's three-day entombments and resurrections represent this original born-again, out-of-body "witnessing," so debased in later exoteric misunderstanding. A vast, gradually secularizing literature has constantly attested to or reworked this breaking through to other planes of reality—from myths of being abducted underground, like Persephone through the entranced, spirit-guided revelations of other worlds in Vergil and Dante, to modern "night journeys," "underground" heroes, and "double" stories, to which may be added many science fiction stories voyaging to alternative realities (following the lead of *Alice in Wonderland*) as well as the recent clinical literature of near-death experiences and shamanistic drug "trips."

It has become commonplace to point out that "educate" means to "lead out," but lead out what? What is there in us to draw out and develop— "unfold"—besides the garbage of conditioning and the private wealth of narcissism? What seeds grow into what fruit? What of this inner world is to be made real in the outer? What is so great about fulfilling myself if I'm a rotten person? Or innately depraved? In the spiritual view, no one is rotten to the core, because at the core is the soul, the seed of Spirit planted in an incarnated individual that if fulfilled will decontaminate the garbage and transmute the narcissism from self-cultivation to Self-realization. What is led out—awakened—is this soul. Earth would be only the growing medium.

Continuing Higher Education

But if Earth is a soul school, why does it have so short a session—a mere blip in time for any one spirit, which is, after all, immortal? What in blazes is this spirit doing all the rest of the time, before and after its four score years or so on the physical plane? The answer from esoteric literature is that it is getting schooled on one of the other planes of reality engendered by the "successive emanations" that precipitate Spirit into increasingly denser manifestations. More-evolved spirits (the oldest of "old souls") never need return to the physical plane once they have learned all they have to learn here. Even as earthlings, it's said, we travel astrally out of the body at night (in a sort of minimystery initiation), and this is the purpose of sleep, still puzzling to scientists. (Asleep, we are "dead to the world," this world.) So Earth is only one school, and through either sleep, ecstasy, or other experiences that temporarily release our higher vehicles from the physical body, the soul divides its learning time between different planes during even its assignment to this terrestrial classroom.

Most religions assert or assume, as early Christianity did, and as the esoteric teaching makes most explicit, that individuals incarnate many times on the physical plane before they no longer need to return. What completes the concept of Earth as a soul school driven by spiritual evolution is an idea repugnant to modern sensibility, mostly because its early repression in Western culture caused it to be misunderstood and cast into ludicrous associations. Disregarding the inevitable debasements of popularization, the notion of reincarnation is inseparable from personal spiritual growth. Outside the whole spiritual framework in which it makes sense, it can seem bizarre and even ghoulish, but whether one believes in it or not, it stands as an excellent model of individualized learning.

Part of why it is hard to believe, the fact that we don't usually remember past lives, is explained in the very concept of it, which includes amnesia. Compare the plural lives of reincarnation to the plural selves in a psychiatric case of a multiple personality. If the multiple selves knew of each other, that would thwart the very function of the multiplicity, which is to permit conflicting aspects of the person to exist by keeping them from confronting each other. If an incarnated individual knew of its former lives, it would, for one thing, have to have access to a plane of consciousness higher than the physical one, since knowledge of those lives can reside not within the memories acquired in the present life but only in some vehicle of the person meta to the physical. Accessing higher planes from this one would mean that the person could also know the long-range spiritual reason for this incarnation and might try to avoid doing what is needed—likewise thwarting the whole point.

In other words, just as the healing of the multiple personality has to be conducted from a perspective meta to that of the patient, through some collaboration between the psychiatrist and the most inclusive self of the patient, soul growth is plotted between lives by the spirit while enjoying the higher consciousness of the discarnate state and the help of more evolved individuals present on that plane. Were the patient to know all selves at once, she or he would already be cured. Were the soul in one life to know of other lives, it would already have raised its consciousness beyond the physical plane. But the patient begins to learn of other selves, and the soul of other lives, while still in the restricted state, eventually integrating them into a new state.

Now compare both of these to a student. Reincarnation makes no sense without karma, which corresponds remarkably to the process of self-determining or individualized education. Karma refers to the experience an individual is logging inasmuch as it indicates patterns of the past and needs for the future. Commentators often define it by the biblical quotation, "As you sow, so shall ye reap," which is indeed pertinent but too compact and figurative to convey alone the whole concept unless you understand it already. It's not a statement about justice like "an eye for an eye" or "you get what you deserve." It means rather that each individual creates a history or pattern of action all his or her own that must ultimately be filled in, off-set, balanced, and otherwise amended until the soul has completed its experience on this plane and learned all it can. It is basic trial-and-error learning enabling the soul to live out or live through the physical plane, to outgrow materiality. Before reincarnating, the soul takes stock of past and future in its higher state of consciousness and in consultation with those more evolved, just as, between projects or phases of activity in an individualized learning environment, secular students periodically review and preview their work from the longer-range perspective of their total growth in order to decide with counselors their next action.

The main thing that the patient, soul, and student have in common is that what they do at each step depends on awareness of what they have done previously and on its meaning. This process is holistic and individual. It cannot be standardized, because current decisions depend on unique personal patterns of the past requiring unique future steps. Everyone's karma is different. Trying to save souls by general rules, formulas, and programs doesn't work any better than trying to heal emotions or educate minds by uniform procedures. Eventually churches, hospitals, and schools all have to learn this. Though I believe it's helpful to reflect on these parallel learning experiences, reason alone should tell us that, by the very nature of growth, it will always require individualizing. To grow is to change, and change has to proceed from wherever a person has fetched up at the time he or she starts to learn. The end may be generalizable as a common goal or desideratum, but each person starts toward it from unique circumstances and conditions in which he or she is enmeshed, like the spirit fallen into and involved in matter so idiosyncratically that only certain paths or means will work. Education consists of finding for oneself what these are.

A Self-Realizing Education

If life on Earth is one big soul school, it surely runs on an individualized curriculum. If there's anything to the spiritual view besides superstition and wish fulfillment, each exiled spirit has to wend its own way, because deconditioning oneself is different for each person. If we're all too involuted in matter to see straight, surely we have different labyrinths to unwind. We're not born with the same inheritances or into the same circumstances. Each life weaves its own web. To rejoin the One, we must travel back by different paths. But who knows the path for herself or himself, let alone for another? Does the state know which course each must pursue? If it cannot know how to select and order experiences for even material learning, as I would assert, but must allow for individuals to work out their own ways, how can it possibly know for spiritual revelation?

This is not a negative situation, unless you insist on the supremacy of the state. What the state can know is that learning of any sort, material or spiritual, occurs as part of some individual unfolding that varies from each of us to another and that efforts to standardize impair immeasurably. The same self-determining learning fields that the state can set up to prepare most effectively for employment in the workplace will foster mystical ecstasy if that's what an individual feels impelled toward. It's not the state's business to decide whether I'm to have either a secular or a spiritual education. As public schooling has been, the state has excluded the spiritual on grounds that "jobs, not religion, are our business—spiritualize on your own time."

But in requiring me to attend school all my youth, the state leaves me little time on my own and subjects me to conditions that work against my spiritual development. Most of my daily life is programmed not only from the outside but by people who take their marching orders from a policy that is far from impartial and that imposes, on the contrary, a fixed curriculum standardized for the lowest common denominator and based on a political notion of majority rule that should not apply to learning. And this is democracy? And education for democracy? Or are we to understand, as argued for the military, that public education constitutes a special exemption from democratic ideals such that you must check your civil rights at the door?

If there's any chance at all that the spiritual reality and purpose I've tried to describe exist, then absolutely nothing should be allowed to interfere with the self-realization that would align individuals with it. Nothing. The state does not have to decide whether it believes in it or not. It has only to organize resources so that people can find out that or anything else for themselves. It's much harder to determine who you are and what you may do even in the worldliest matters when others are constantly forcing things on you and planning everything for you—when you are reactive. It's essential to assert feeling and will and thought proactively enough to establish your own patterns of action. Then you have something of yourself out there for you and others to respond to so that with their help you can chart past and future.

We have to enact our conditioned being as we are now and at the same time draw on the unconditioned being that sleeps within. Then we command the personal and transpersonal material we need to work with for growth. This self-realizing sort of acting out replaces the self-destructive acting out occurring now from the rage and impotence of being manipulated and robbed of one's life. So long as we are only reacting to a predetermined curriculum, we are forced to construct our knowledge and to pattern our action according to public decision making and group consciousness. This interferes with each person's process of growing up, healing, and finding his or her best work, personal bonds, and social roles. It interferes with the flow of energy and intuition that the surface self should be able to tap from its central inner source. And, if spiritual teaching is true, it interferes with the growth of the soul toward real redemption, which would be "making good on" the Spirit it incarnates.

The Spiritual Evolution of Consciousness

State-set standardized learning programs also resist the evolution of individual consciousness that transformation of the culture awaits. Self-consciousness and self-determination have surely not evolved as far as they have only to self-destruct and ruin the culture in which they have grown. If this evolution is destined from without, then we should go with it, not fight it. If we ourselves can determine the course it takes, then we should see that it consummates individualism in a way best fitting all purposes. This would be the spiritual way. It alone allows for all needs, all possibilities, and all realities, because it embraces all.

The esoteric teaching says that Spirit ensouls animals collectively, each species having a group soul that beams to individual members of it their considerable knowledge, which we call instinct because they do not have to learn it personally. Human beings also partake of a group soul into which they are bonded genetically or culturally in addition to being individually ensouled. In keeping with both Richard Bucke's "simple consciousness" and Julian Jaynes's "bicameral mind," early human beings abided essentially within the group soul and only gradually developed a personal soul. People today scatter across a wide range of such development and so are at odds about how much to adhere to or depart from a common ethos, which is the cultural embodiment of a group soul. It may be useful to regard this conflict as the tug-of-war everyone feels between the group soul and the personal soul or, in secular terms, between one's collective and individual natures.

Individual souls must differentiate themselves from the group soul of the race and culture and identify, beyond them, with the All or One itself. But with rare exceptions we are balking desperately at doing this. Most of the strife in the world today is occurring between religions and ethnic groups, that is, between group souls that ferociously refuse to accept each other because each mistakes itself as Spirit instead of one localized manifestation of Spirit. The vicious intensity of the slaughter and rapine by religious people who are quite civilized and moral among their own kind is difficult to explain by ordinary psychology. Why such intransigent refusal to tolerate differences that are spiritually superficial? Why not live and prosper together rather than laying each other waste one generation after another? Such consuming hatred of "outsiders" can hardly be explained except by the malingering of individuals in group souls, by the great difficulty of "breaking away."

Like a clutching parent who fears self-elimination if truly successful in bringing children to maturity, the culture does not really want its members to "grow up," although it exists to do just that. So the culture and individuals have to coevolve. The reason that history shows a pattern of consciousness evolving from collective to individual may be that this direction does indeed fulfill a cosmic purpose. In any case, it seems sensible for a culture to undertake today to wean individuals from itself if only to halt the slaughter and strife. This means deliberately educating for self-direction and self-realization. A new cosmopolitan kind of citizen will result who feels psychologically and spiritually self-sufficient enough to transcend ethnic and religious boundaries and put union over difference, cosmos over country or culture. Only then will the wars end.

Regarding in-groups as group souls in an evolutionary context should help us think about conflicts even if we regard the spiritual account of them as merely mythical or metaphorical. In any case, people who fulfill themselves tend to quit making trouble. One can stop at this thought and still arrive at the need for a spiritual education. What I'm suggesting in addition is that considering the esoteric account seriously, with or without believing it, may improve the quality of our problem solving and will allow for whatever may prove to be true. Instead of keeping its members dependent, a culture must, like a good parent, ready them and release them to go forth as free souls. In the words of a popular song, "God bless the child that's got its own."

Homeward Bound

But why the evolution of consciousness in the first place? If an individual spirit did not incarnate, it would not become amnesic and need awakening and redemption. It's as if Spirit wishes to parcel itself into manifold manifestations (out of One, many), a sort of self-realization or self-expression of its own in the direction from energy to matter while of course also remaining as it was. This would proceed by global ensoulments such as the Solar Logos, Spiritus Mundi, Plato's Soul of the World, and the various group souls as of animal species and human races. This precipitation would culminate in individual incarnations and the materializing of all aspects or potentialities of Spirit. Whereas Spirit "realizes" itself by manifesting itself through a spectrum of successively denser emanations, its incarnations realize themselves by becoming conscious of Spirit as their true nature and of the incarnating process itself. What we feel as grace is the homeward pull of Spirit; what we do in prayer is "call home."

In this sense, that the Creator needs its creation, God is said to depend on us—divinity on humanity. Thus the real humanism is not secular. Anthropos was always considered in spiritual traditions as God on earth, by the very nature of incarnation. This is why Christ is referred to as both Son of God and Son of Man. Only by denying our inner divinity can we regard humanism as secular. Using our faculties to the fullest to create the arts and sciences and civilization is manifesting Spirit through our own incarnation. In fulfilling ourselves we are playing our part in the self-fulfillment of Spirit itself.

That is, the mission is to respiritualize oneself while one is matter and thus to spiritualize matter, transform the world. It's as if the cosmic goal is for Spirit to enjoy the best of all worlds at once. Simply being part of Spirit like a fetus in the womb contrasts with being individually conscious of being part of Spirit. Consciousness makes all the difference, and the purpose of evolution seems to be to bring about on the lowest plane total consciousness of the highest plane. Apotheosis, becoming God, models this process, exemplified in the lives of avatars like Moses, Buddha, Jesus, and Mohammed, who achieved cosmic consciousness while incarnated in mortal form.

Consummating individuals means bringing them home again. As they return to their common origin, they rejoin but in a new union beyond the old group souls. "Everything that rises must converge." For the individual to evolve from self-consciousness into cosmic consciousness, it must paradoxically lose itself, in keeping with the biblical idea that the seed must die in order to bear fruit. In shamanistic mythology, the initiate is dismembered and reassembled into a new being, like Orpheus. The individual cannot remain merely self-conscious and self-serving but, rather, must be reborn through an expansion of consciousness and identity that comprehends all other people on its way to comprising the cosmos. Being torn apart represents the deconditioning from heredity and environment that must precede the unconditioned state of pure, free being. It resembles the process of being wounded and healed, as to be expected, since some therapy will always have to prepare for spirituality. To be here is to be wounded, and recovering will hurt. But losing oneself leads to ecstasy, which means literally being outside oneself, "transported."

Of course the paradox, the "dual teaching," of finding oneself by losing oneself refers to the very nature of incarnation. The highest frequency is stepped down, via the successive emanations, to the lowest frequency—or heaviest "vibe"—in the form of some physical body. A human being partakes of all emanations or planes of reality at once, without knowing it, until it achieves cosmic consciousness, which is in fact defined by this realization or awakening. This is the esoteric meaning of "know thyself," which post-Freudian people are apt to understand as merely making the unconscious conscious, as psychological awareness. This meaning is indeed important and, like therapy, is a prerequisite or concomitant of spiritual consummation. But the ultimate meaning of "know thyself" seems to be "know thy Self," thy origin in Spirit, which is tantamount to comprehending the cosmos itself, since the interplay of these plural realities makes up both it and oneself.

The notion of correspondences between an individual and the universe explains much of spiritual thinking. It is the counterpart of some scientists' holographic conception of the universe, in which each part reflects the whole.[2] It underlies teachings such as "Man is the measure of all things,"

2. See Ken Wilbur, ed., *The Holographic Paradigm and Other Paradoxes* (Cambridge, MA: Shambhala, 1982).

which means "Understand how you are made, and you will know the nature of creation." From antiquity different cultures have transmitted the adages "Thou art That" and "As above, so below." You are a microcosm of the cosmos. It is in this sense that God is said to have made the world and humankind in its own image. If you know how you are composed, you know what the world is like.

This correspondence of course changes utterly how one interprets the idea that self-knowledge is the gateway to knowledge of other things. Otherwise, "know thyself" may seem to be a pious effort to make a case for the inner life or to justify self-cultivation for its own sake. Without understanding this relationship between identifying and learning—sympathy in its basic sense—it's also difficult to see why forms of meditation and trance-state attunement are primal learning methods. You don't have to subscribe to the esoteric view to see how much we learn of something outside by concentrating on it so raptly that counterparts within us give rise to thoughts, feelings, and images that inform us about it. This is the heart of intuition. It requires dissolving, through resonance, the boundaries between inner and outer. Raptness expands consciousness, which brings on rapture.[3]

Regarded as secular, soul school provides an education full of soul—spirited and loving. It is powered by the life force, like the African-American radio station I once heard identify itself as "broadcasting with 50,000 watts of soul." It is soulful also in that it works through deep feeling. It honors the experiencer, and the range and depth of experience is the key to growth. Regarded as sacred, soul school provides the material experience that, spiritualized, enables the exile to return, awake now to all worlds. In every sense of finding and fulfilling oneself, soul school is about coming home.

3. George Leonard had the right idea about thirty years ago in his *Education and Ecstasy* (New York: Delacorte Press, 1968), in which he was already drawing on spiritual disciplines and proposing counterculture practices for public education.

Mostly about the individual consciousness
evolution of individual consciousness with
to soul consciousness in education.
application

· We should get Moffett's book (see back).

2

Grace, in Pedagogy

Richard L. Graves

When it comes, the landscape listens,
Shadows hold their breath.

(Emily Dickinson)

If you can imagine a perfect place, a place where all lines converge and
everything relates in harmony to everything else, where the sense of peace is
so full that it seems beyond human understanding, then that place would be
called "grace." The popular understanding of grace is sometimes limited to
the theological realm and, for that reason, some may question whether or not
it is appropriate for school settings. I believe, to the contrary, that grace has
profound implications for pedagogy. The way I am using the word is more
akin to its physical and social connotations, as when we say "she dances with
grace" or "he acted with grace." Used in this manner, the term connotes harmony of movement, coordination, poise under pressure. But a hint of the
transcendent also pervades this meaning of the word. For the dancer spends
hours in practice, but when the moment of performance comes, some magic
takes over, some invisible force beyond the muscles themselves. This same
transcendent quality is present in Bill Ayers's description of "a life in teaching": "Surprising splashes of color can suddenly appear at its center; unexpected patterns can emerge and lend the whole affair a sense of grace and
purpose and possibility"(Ayers 1993).

Grace is a living reality, a force capable of touching all aspects of human
life. To be sure, grace is an invisible reality; some people can't see it, and
those who do can't prove its presence. Nevertheless, it's there, in much the
same way that Annie Dillard tells us the natural world is *there* but remains
invisible: "It's all a matter of keeping my eyes open. Nature is like one of

15

those line drawings that are puzzles for children: Can you find hidden in the tree a duck, a house, a boy, a bucket, a giraffe, and a boot?"(1988, 1183).

Grace does not live in some hothouse environment but in the ordinary experiences of daily life. Grace happens in everyday routines and habits, in buying and selling, in the sweat of the workplace, in conversations and transactions, in the small joys and disappointments of life. Moreover, it shows up in the most unlikely places. Grace lurks among the vegetables in the supermarket. Grace sits on a bar stool and smokes a cigarette. Grace roams the corridors of a big city hospital. Grace is always there, everywhere; we don't see it, but it changes our lives when we experience it.

The Coming of Grace

Grace is not something that can be called up at will, planned on, or included in a syllabus. Rather it is like some elusive being hiding in the shadows, camouflaged by its surroundings. From time to time, we catch a glimpse of it and in that moment detect something of its awe and magnitude. Yet the more determined we are to find it, the more it eludes us. Whenever I have tried to re-create moments of grace, they have always fallen flat. Grace comes at a specific moment, called up by the unique circumstances of that moment, not to be repeated again. And so we learn that grace moves to its own rhythm, follows its own agenda, and it is always beyond our power to control or manipulate.

A certain *accidental* quality of grace sometimes makes seeing it difficult for teachers, especially experienced teachers. The teacher who has followed the same syllabus for years may be mentally disconnected from the present moment. After following the same notes for so long, the mind easily slips into automatic pilot. When that happens, the small miracles of grace occurring before one's eyes go unseen, thus diminishing the quality of the present moment. The aware teacher senses the wonder of it all—when feeling the grace of sudden inspiration or when observing a student's sudden understanding for the first time.

Grace cannot be sought out directly, like some rare mushroom, nor does it come to the mind asleep. It is possible, however, to prepare for it. Once we know it's there, that awareness lingers in the back of the mind. To find grace—or better, *to be found by grace*—we must live not only in the immediate moment but let go of ego involvement in that moment, for grace comes in by the back door. Our attention must be focused on something else, immersed in the business at hand: reading, writing, thinking, creating. While the attention is elsewhere, grace is at work in the unconscious. Consequently, it's good to keep a little distance, stay busy creating, and refrain from saying too much about it. When the conditions are right, grace finds us.

On some occasions grace may be accompanied by a "message." Writer and teacher Elizabeth Neeld describes such an experience. Returning home after her husband's premature death, Neeld felt exhausted and almost paralyzed by the fear of being alone. Then suddenly, she says, "The unexplainable happened." She "heard" the words "Look outside. The sun is shining. Life is good" (1990, 23). Sometimes the manifestation of grace is so vivid that the recipient uses the word *heard* to describe the event, although we understand that the words heard may not actually be audible. Perhaps the voice of grace is the unconscious mind breaking through into the conscious life. The message is clear and direct: common words, simple sentences, plain language coming directly to the heart. Struck by the moment, the recipient may repeat the words silently, feel the truth in their coming, and embrace their fullness. The words are remembered and treasured for a lifetime.

Some Qualities of Grace

In order to understand how grace might find a place in pedagogy, it is appropriate that we look at some of its characteristics. What I describe, though, should not be considered as definitive but only suggestive. For grace continually defines and redefines itself, molding to the demands of specific situations and continually eluding human efforts to categorize and limit it.

Transforming. Although some may see schools generally as institutions for information processing, grace operates at a level much deeper than the acquisition of information. Grace touches emotions, beliefs, attitudes, values, perspectives, and the human will. Although social bureaucracy enforces the information function of schools, many teachers are aware of the role of the transformation of consciousness in the educational process—both inside and outside the classroom. Perhaps the greatest value of grace lies in its power to transform human consciousness. But since the transformation of consciousness has not had a prominent role in the culture of schools, those who experience such transformations themselves do not fully understand them and may be hesitant to discuss them within the school setting, in part because they are not able to explain them logically and fear that they will be derided by others. They often attribute their origin to some external source. People do not always see that grace often comes in small things. One classroom teacher shared her experience of suddenly overcoming depression after losing her husband and being left with small children and an enormous debt. She said:

> One day, looking out an upstairs window, I saw a rabbit in the front yard, and I knew that everything would be fine. Somehow I realized that if that rabbit, who seemed so full of peace and so much a part of nature, would be all right then I would be too. Soon I was back to normal.

What caused her changed attitude? Why at that moment did the young teacher begin the journey to overcome her depression? It is tempting to look to external sources, to provide easy intellectual answers, yet somehow for her, the real meaning of the event transcended the experience and intellectual explanation. Such is the work of grace.

Grace works in the most unlikely conditions and uses the common and ordinary in life and in nature to accomplish its goals. One is left to wonder about the invisible force behind the details of the teacher's story, the energy that eventually led to her recovery.

Healing. Moments of grace are invariably moments of healing. The stresses and anger of everyday life, left unresolved, turn into a constant, low-grade grief. How many people live out their lives with such grief, unaware of its presence? Their serious problems are obvious—not enough money; problems with health; addictions; violent, life-threatening environments—but even the ordinary problems of twentieth-century life can be stressful. In many classrooms, for example, the normal curve of distribution allows only ten percent of a given population to be classified as excellent. Thus the vast majority of American young people are reminded daily that they have not measured up. Competition, peer and social pressures, uncertainty about the future—all these take their toll on the human spirit. But paradoxically grace can be present even in such circumstances. The potential of grace is present in the face of death; in all that's rotten and decaying; in failure and loss; in stupid, misguided acts. Teachers have seen bright and creative young people overcome the most miserable home environments. Who can explain such situations? Grace teaches us not to despise that which is abhorrent but rather to look for the promise within it.

Transcending the Ego. Because grace operates in the specific rather than the abstract, its work is most apparent in the arena of the human personality. Over the years, within the lifetime of an individual, personal preference becomes habit, enabling one to carry out the routines of daily life without investing excessive energy into every minor decision. When habit becomes intertwined with ego, however, the results can be unfortunate. For example, when habit becomes entangled with feelings of inferiority, a pattern of thought emerges that is reflected in statements such as "I am just as good as you" and "Mine is better than yours." When habit becomes entangled with the desire for power and control, then ego, never listening, tries to define every situation with its own words. Sometimes habit becomes infatuated with materialism, hoping for self-enhancement, but the results are never as fulfilling or satisfying as expected.

Grace cuts through all this, going directly to the roots of the personality, shaking loose all the dead appendages of the ego. Grace returns us to our original home, to "our face before we were born." Once at home, though, grace leads us back again to the workaday world, providing the energy to sustain and carry out responsibilities. Grace provides the perspective to see ourselves in the larger context, not just as students and teachers but as individuals connected with each other and with a world beyond ourselves.

Opening the Possible. Grace makes "all things possible." Limited by family and community myths and personal life history, an individual cannot see what grace can see. Grace is infinite, opening up the possible. Grace cuts through the boundaries of culture, language, race, social class, economic level, age, handicaps, intelligence level, geography, and birth. Grace interrupts the expected and creates its own channel. This is not to say that grace is capricious but rather that it overcomes human limitations, working toward something good in positive, unexpected ways.

Pointing Toward What Is Right. Grace carries with it a certain moral and ethical tone, nudging the recipient toward what is just and right. Grace doesn't ignore the law, but seeks out its spirit rather than its letter. Grace is not didactic or legalistic, but works instead as a gentle nudger. It has its own internal wisdom and sense of justice, fulfilling some unseen law of order, balancing wrong with right, providing correction where needed.

This is not to deny the presence of evil, a corollary dark force that grace opposes. But in some cases grace works with the dark side to accomplish its own ends. Sometimes grace appears unexpectedly in the heart of darkness. Is it possible that grace is so comprehensive that it includes within its framework the shadow of darkness too?

Enhancing Creativity. On some occasions, as in art, all things converge. Color, line, proportion, rhythm, and tone come out just right as though some invisible wisdom beyond the artist guided the creation. Others look at the work, call it a masterpiece, and ask the artist to explain the vision that created it. But the artist cannot explain it; it is an act of grace. That same grace guides writing, thinking, and creating. Sometimes we cannot explain why a piece works, where an idea or inspiration came from, but we recognize it as transcendent.

Grace is manifested in all walks of life, but it is particularly striking in the primitive artist. This is the miracle of grace, coming unexpectedly, full of surprise. It is a truism that many artists are not accepted by those within their own country. Perhaps it is a gift of grace that allows others to recognize the spirit of creative genius in the primitive, in that rare, original vision ignored or ridiculed by its contemporaries.

Surprising. In one way or another, all the world's great religions have been touched by grace. Once touched, however, each tends to define grace in its own terms, through its own experience. Each religion believes its way is the only way, but grace is larger than any single religion. Religions die and new ones are born, but grace lives on. Not the exclusive property of this religion or that, grace is a powerful force available to the secular as well as to the religious world.

Rather than conform to fixed rules, grace continues to surprise. It shows up in unexpected places, in coincidences that prove to be extraordinary, and in synchronistic events. On one hand, the rational mind dismisses these as chance, but on the other, we are left to wonder. Turning aside from busyness and the routine of daily life, we are led by grace to enter another world. This is a world that is spontaneous rather than sequential, accidental rather than planned, random rather than linear, simultaneous rather than causal, and mystical rather than logical.

Sounds like expressivism

In view of this element of surprise, grace may seem to some to be inappropriate for educational institutions, whose charge they see as the transmission of information in a linear and logical fashion. But just as the world has passed through the industrial-technological revolution, it is now in the process of passing through the information revolution. On the horizon is the promise of yet another world, one in which the physical and the spiritual are blended into a single harmonic whole. This world is both richer and deeper than the worlds of technology or information. In this yet nameless new world, grace plays an important function, bringing new dimensions to the quality of our lives.

Grace and Pedagogy

Because grace is so fluid, always adapting to current conditions, it seems presumptuous even to suggest possible applications. So let this be the first caveat: Grace will always be larger than our feeble attempts to describe it. With this in mind, let us explore some possible intersections of grace and pedagogy.

Grace cannot be formally included in a syllabus or incorporated into a curriculum or mandated into a school system. Preferring the specific to the abstract, grace may not be as apparent in the planning stages as in the actual doing. Consequently, if grace ever comes into pedagogy, it will be there not because it was planned but because the conditions were right and because some sensitive soul had the wisdom not to thwart it. Since grace is fluid, the best way to encourage it is to leave space for it to happen. Teachers must believe that grace is possible—in their lives, in the lives of their students, in the daily transactions of the school experience.

For grace to occur within a classroom, it seems to me that the class should exhibit three qualities. It must be *authentic/ communal* (or *dialogic*)/ and *intuitive*. In an *authentic* classroom, common sense requires that teachers make good plans, but grace reminds us that the best-laid plans often go astray. Our success depends on how well we are able to grasp these two conflicting goals: on the one hand, to make the best plans possible and on the other, to be ready to abandon them. In other words, we must learn to be as disciplined as possible but at the same time be spontaneous. The most tempting and most dangerous path is to embrace one of the contraries and reject the other, which is really not a solution at all. The best path is to lay hold of both opposites, allowing the tension between the two to create the energy for living and learning.

An authentic learning experience is one that arises naturally and spontaneously in a specific time and place. It cannot be replicated; it is a unique event. Even though a teacher may have taught a given subject for a lifetime, each class is a new experience. The students are different, the subject matter is different (if ever so slightly), even the teacher is a different person from the last time he or she taught the subject. Thus the emerging dynamic within each class opens up an array of new possibilities. Teachers should look for grace at these living intersections of learning and seize opportunities for making it an ally in the learning process. We must keep in mind, however, that authentic situations cannot be fabricated or manufactured. Such events arise spontaneously out of the *living now*, those moments in time and space when lives intersect as a community of learners.

A classroom that exhibits *communal* qualities invites the presence of grace. The central feature of such a classroom is dialogue, acts of speaking with honesty and listening with respect. The word *communal* itself suggests something sacred, something beyond the ordinary experiences of daily life. Into such environments grace moves easily, for the number of personal transactions here is much greater than that in traditional classrooms. Moreover, a communal classroom addresses the problem of personal isolation and views learning in a broad, human context.

For this to occur, the classroom should rely upon an *intuitive* quality that works in unison with the structural content of a course. The role of the teacher in such a classroom is similar to that of a master chef watching a favorite creation baking in the oven. The chef watches carefully, observing every nuance of the baking, listening at the oven, and catching all the pungent aromas as the heat of the oven transforms the creation. The chef knows that he or she is not the energy doing the transforming, but merely the one watching the process occur. Yet in this watching there is a special kind of wisdom, a wisdom born of patience, loving care, and studied experience. In such a classroom environment, the possibilities of grace abound.

Over the years a number of events have occurred in my classes that I attribute to grace. Some of them are personal transformations that I know about only because my students have told me after the fact. Others have occurred publicly, involving several people. Below are two of those public events that I hope will illustrate something of the presence of grace.

Cathy

When giving a writing assignment in one of my classes, I ask my students to describe the single life experience that has been for them *their most powerful learning experience*. I tell them to put a pseudonym on their description, for their work will be published and distributed to the other class members. Some of these reveal an intensity or immediacy not often found in textbooks.

Cathy, then a college junior, described the experience that had haunted her since her freshman year when she had come to a large university and was trying to fit in. Cathy's story has a universal quality, holding both the promise and the pain of coming into adulthood. In an essay describing her experience of getting drunk at a party and realizing the next day that she had slept with a stranger, Cathy said, "I hated myself." She described how over the next two years she had become suicidal. She wrote about the moment when she was on the verge of taking her life.

> Something very strange happened that night. My plans were intervened by someone or something, I'm not really sure. Nevertheless, I believe that it was someone who was looking out for me. I heard a voice and it said, "You're too tired to do this right now. Get some sleep and wait until tomorrow." At that moment I felt a peace wash over me from head to toe. I was clean. It soothed my soul and for the first time in a long time, I felt good. It's hard for me to describe that feeling; it was nothing that I have ever felt in my life. A transformation took place that night, although I was unaware of it at the time. I once again had hope.

Cathy experienced grace on several levels—through the event itself, through the acts of writing about it and sharing it with the class, and through hearing the class's response to her experience. Her story illustrates that we need not know the name of grace in order to be touched by grace. She knew grace as "someone or something," metaphorically as "someone who was looking out for me." The name is not important. What is important is that during her time of greatest need, Cathy found a healing force that led her back to life.

But in writing about the event, Cathy found even more healing, for herself as well as for her classmates. The shame associated with such events encourages silence, which in turn intensifies feelings of loneliness, isolation, and despair. By having the courage to tell her story, Cathy invited others with similar experiences to tell their stories. All of us, both men and women, learned from Cathy's story, and in her story we found seeds of grace for our own lives. Grace can be found in an open, accepting audience that can itself be moved by grace.

Angie

Recently during the spring quarter, Angie, a graduating senior who had become a class leader, missed class for four successive days. Until that point she had perfect attendance and had made several contributions to the class. Efforts to reach her were unsuccessful, and several of her classmates expressed concern. Her class had become a community. When she returned she seemed quieter than usual and distracted. She asked if she might speak to the whole class to explain her absence. To the best of my memory, this is what she said:

> As you may know I am older than most of you. I am twenty-six years old, and in a few weeks I hope to walk across the stage and receive my degree. This has been my goal in life for a long time.
>
> It has not been an easy road. I grew up in a small town in north Alabama. All through high school my boyfriend and I had planned on coming to the university. However, the summer after my senior year I became ill. To my dismay, the doctor told me I was pregnant. When I told my boyfriend, his immediate response was that I should get an abortion. I asked him if he loved me, and he said, "I think I do."
>
> I was distraught. What should I do? That evening after talking to him, I happened to be watching television. It just so happened that a program came on that described, very vividly, what happened to the fetus during abortion. In that moment my decision was made: I would have the baby. From that point on, my boyfriend and I took separate paths. He went to the university as we had planned; I stayed home to have the baby.
>
> Up to that point I had not told my mother. My mother and father had divorced when I was younger, and even though I lived with my mother we were never close. In fact, we had our differences. I knew that I needed to bring her a gift when I broke the news to her. She loved music boxes, so I went to our local drug store to try to find one. I looked at several, but selected one that played "Amazing Grace," my mother's favorite song. The druggist told me the lid on that particular one was broken. That's perfect, I said to myself, for I am a broken woman.
>
> About the time I had the baby my mother remarried. The man she married, my stepfather, offered more support and encouragement than my real parents ever had. He was wonderful during those tough times. Fortunately, I found someone else who loved me and loved my baby, and we were married. For three years we saved everything we could because our goal was to come to the university.
>
> Now we are both graduating, but last week my stepfather died. I had so much wanted him to be present at my graduation. He meant so much to me, but he will not be there. During these days I have been absent, I have been helping my mother with the funeral.

When Angie finished her story, I looked around the room. Angie's classmates were stunned. Some had tears in their eyes.

"I am so overcome with Angie's story," I told the class, "that I cannot respond. Will someone please respond to her?" I wanted my students to have the experience of responding in an authentic way to the events that Angie revealed to us. The room was silent. I looked at the students, tried to make eye contact, but they were all looking down.

The silence in the room was heavy, but it gave us time to receive the depth of Angie's account as well as her courage in revealing it. Then came a voice, a few halting words full of emotion and sincerity: "Angie, I just want you to know that I reach out to you." The speaker was Martha, not the most outstanding student in class but in that moment more eloquent than any of us.

For a few moments that morning grace touched our lives. Grace was a better teacher than any of us. Very likely the students who were present that morning will always remember the poignancy, the charged atmosphere, the tone of Angie's voice as she described her recent grief. A week later, Angie brought her daughter to class. It was a kind of confirmation for all of us in the class, perhaps even more so for Angie, who was now so close to her goal of obtaining a college degree that had been at once so important and so elusive to her. Angie's telling of her story might not ordinarily be categorized as academic; yet the text of her experience touched the class as deeply and profoundly as the text of any short story, novel, or essay might have. Those of us who shared it felt its grace of *authenticity, intuition,* and *community.* Although these accounts illustrated for us the presence of grace in a clear and dramatic way, events do not have to be dramatic to be acts of grace. Everyday, routine events can be transformed by the presence of grace. Grace allows us to see ourselves in perspective, and the drive for power and ego is diminished. It causes us to live in the present moment, fully, attentively, creatively. It teaches us not to assume more wisdom than we should. Grace tells us that each day is new, each moment a living opportunity if we just open our hearts to it.

If we focus only on the dramatic, we might miss the miracles of grace occurring at our fingertips. Since grace always seems just beyond our reach, beyond our limited power of language and understanding, when I try to write about it, I wonder at times whether I have really driven it away—for myself as well as for others. Yet I am always reminded of its presence, in the stories I hear from others and in the small miracles I see all around me. Perhaps the best we can do is try to keep our hearts open. Then maybe, when we least expect it—at noon or in the morning or at some wildly surprising time—grace will come again. If it does, the day will be better for it.

About recognizing and receiving grace as a force in life and in the classroom. About creating a classroom that is authentic—which seems also to mean personal—in order to do this.

3

Creating a Center That Holds
Spirituality Through Exploratory Pedagogy

Kristie S. Fleckenstein

> Turning and turning in the widening gyre
> The falcon cannot hear the falconer;
> Things fall apart; the center cannot hold;
> —William Butler Yeats

In "The Second Coming," William Butler Yeats predicts the passing of an age in which the spiritual center that gave order and meaning to existence disintegrates. As a result of the loss of this spiritual anchor, order and meaning, even existence as we know it, career into chaos. The final image of the poem is that of a rough beast slouching into existence, a beast whose birth heralds the meaninglessness of a new age. Yeats's vision, while not specifically inspired by a postmodern, postprocess composition classroom, serves as a powerful metaphor for our present pedagogy. I fear that we too have lost our spiritual center and, in the process, have created a "rough beast" that threatens our existence.

We have become a culture dominated by the desire to quantify. As a result, we either dismiss or denigrate forces resistant to current methods of computation and analysis. Nowhere is such a cultural phenomenon more evident than in our classrooms, where we honor the material over the spiritual, the rational over the intuitive, the social over the self. Critical thinking is given supremacy with little thought to the *raison d'etre* for that thinking. Thus, the heart of teaching, the spiritual center, is lost and, as Yeats predicts, "things fall apart" (1962, 91).

How, then, can we recenter ourselves and our classrooms? In this paper I attempt to answer this question by, first, defining the nature of a spiritual center; second, describing the characteristics of a pedagogy designed to construct a spiritual center; and, third, arguing that exploratory pedagogy offers our best hope for creating a center that holds.

Peter Berger and Morris Berman offer insights into the definition of a spiritual center. According to Berger (1967), a social constructionist in sociology, a spiritual center is a culture's and an individual's ordering principle. Without that ordering principle, alienation of individuals from the self and from others occurs, resulting in an erosion of a meaningful existence. Thus, a spiritual center orders reality in such a way as to render it significant to a society's members. Without that center, society and its members are disconnected from themselves and from any sense of a congruent reality. The creation and maintenance of that center, for both individuals and their culture, are fragile processes that Berger compares to a conversation. An ordering principle is developed and maintained dialectically, through "conversations" between self and significant others. Disrupt the conversation, and the center is disrupted.

In addition to ordering, a spiritual center integrates. Morris Berman, an historian of science, contends that "an alienated consciousness" is the hallmark of the postmodern world. Dating such disconnectedness from the rise of sixteenth-century Cartesian dualism, Berman asserts that the artificial separation of mind and matter, with the privileging of mind, has divided human beings from their affective, or spiritual, basis of learning. The creation of meaning requires a participating, not an alienated, consciousness, one that emotionally identifies itself with the object being learned. Any act of learning thus requires the integration of subject and object, a process that creates and orders each simultaneously. Building on the work of Gregory Bateson, Berman claims that meaning-making is "ecological," which is the same metaphor Louise Rosenblatt uses to characterize her transactional theory of meaning-making (Berman 1990).

An ordering imperative created and maintained dialectically and an ecological integration affectively based—these elements seem to be the essence of spiritual centeredness. On the basis of this definition, a pedagogy that evokes a spiritual center must embrace five qualities.

1. The affective foundation of learning
2. The integration of the emotional and the cognitive, the material and the intuitive
3. The contribution of the subjective consciousness to an order-making endeavor, even though that consciousness may be socially encoded
4. The act of meaning-making as dialectic—a conversation that creates and maintains self and society
5. The creation of a participating consciousness

So how do we achieve such ordering and integrating? I wish to argue that our best hope for creating a spiritual center lies in exploratory pedagogy.

Exploratory pedagogy is a term I use to describe the growing, loosely coordinated work that integrates such nontraditional approaches to teaching as intuition, meditation, imagery, and somatic learning. It offers a crucial complement to social, liberatory, and cognitive approaches. The potential of exploratory pedagogy to create a spiritual center lies in its efforts to acknowledge the importance of affect in cognition, affirm the worth of personal experience, transform our concept of the self, and build meaning dialectically.

Restoring the Balance: The Affective Foundation

As an age careens out of balance, Yeats in "The Second Coming" envisions two equally dangerous stances: lack of conviction and passion without purpose. At the heart of both problems, as well as a host of others, lie emotions, feelings, moods, beliefs, personality traits, and so on—that loose aggregate that psychologists call *affect* (Aylwin 1985) and that is the spiritual basis of all learning (Berman 1990). As Lev Vygotsky contends, separating thinking from affect transforms thought into "meaningless epiphenomena incapable of changing anything" (1962, 8). Exploratory pedagogy, with its explicit acknowledgment of affect, allows us to accept, investigate, and incorporate the essential role affect plays in the act of writing and in our teaching of writing. It is an aspect of meaning-making and teaching that has been traditionally excluded from composition pedagogy. By moving beyond accepted cognitive and social boundaries, exploratory pedagogy attends to the heart, that is, the spiritual center, of any meaning-making process.

To illustrate more concretely, an exploratory orientation allows us to focus on forces that engender thought—"our desires and needs, our interests and emotions" (Vygotsky 1962, 150). It allows us to focus on that which "holds the last 'why' in the analysis of thinking" (Vygotsky 1962, 150). Such an affective orientation includes motivation, impetus, exigency, engagement, and commitment—all of which refer to elements that drive a writer to begin and continue writing. In a writing classroom that incorporates affect, topics such as a writer's self-image, a student's personal history with writing (including childhood and family experiences), and the writer's personal as well as rhetorical goals obtain legitimacy.

Deeply intertwined with motivation is anxiety (Daly and Hailey 1984) and writer's block (Rose 1984), both of which, within an exploratory classroom, are reenvisioned as affective as well as cognitive phenomena. For example, through exploratory pedagogy, new attention is given to such highly emotional factors as the writer's comfort level with a topic or an orientation. If a topic is highly evocative, then students experience greater difficulty transforming felt meaning into discursive language (de Beaugrande 1984). Although highly emotional topics may engage a writer more intensely, rhetorical sophistication may suffer in reverse proportion to that

intensity. An affective orientation encourages teachers to address this phenomenon by examining the emotional nature of anxiety.

In addition, exploratory pedagogy allows us to investigate anxiety as a
manifestation of alienation, the disconnectedness that Berger cites as characteristic of disrupted cultural conversations and that Berman claims is a result
of Cartesian dualism. Thus, writing anxiety, within this context, can be re-
conceptualized as a product of spiritual decentering—a loss of the ability to
order and integrate. Alleviating the anxiety requires alleviating the sense of
alienation.

Teaching the Arcane: The Cognitive-Affective Fusion

Spiritual centeredness requires more than just a new focus on affect, important
though that may be. It requires an *integration* of cognition and affect, as does
successful writing. For instance, writing is in many ways an arcane endeavor.
Unfortunately, a predominantly cognitive orientation denies or ignores those
aspects of writing not accessible to empirical analysis. At the other extreme,
if we laud affect to the exclusion or subordination of cognition, we risk a return
to the concept of writing as inaccessible and unteachable except to those who
already possess innate genius. A synthesis of cognition and affect is required,
and exploratory pedagogy provides just such an integration.

Exploratory pedagogy recognizes the unquantifiable aspects of meaning-
making: intuition, values, felt sense, moods, emotions. Then it develops
strategies that allow us access to these slippery areas. Thus, something as
mystical as inspiration is no longer a matter of chance or genius but accessible through more conscious strategies. As Sondra Perl has illustrated, students can be taught to attend to a felt sense, to use a felt sense, and to enrich
their meaning-making process. Similarly, students can be trained to evoke
mental images as a means to enhance their writing processes (Worley 1994).
Finally, the explosive union of metaphor and emotion can hone a writer's
ability to transform the presentational into the discursive (H. Miller 1994).
Felt sense, intuition, imagery are unquantifiable, perhaps even arcane, areas
that exploratory pedagogy transforms into the teachable, thus moving them
from the margins of pedagogy to the center. Simultaneously, such integration
in writing complements the need for integration in spiritual centeredness.

Similarly, the sense of panic and exhilaration that writing evokes in many
also becomes more understandable through the affective-cognitive union of
exploratory pedagogy. Much of writing consists of explosive moments of
conflict in which the inexpressible is pressed into expression, balanced—if we
are lucky—by mystifying moments of flow (Csikszentmihalyi 1990) when
writing seems to proceed by itself. Thus, writing mysteriously elicits the
Janus-faced responses of fear, perhaps even loathing, and of heady joy. Given
the affective-cognitive balance in exploratory pedagogy, both responses are
open to teaching. We teach our students to court the conflict, invite the panic,

and open the door to flow, which results when effort and ability balance. For instance, the creation and instantiation of personal goals that challenge the writer intellectually and emotionally (Langston 1989) enhance a writer's ability to experience flow. Deliberate evocation of and sensitivity to mental imagery achieve a similar effect (Fleckenstein 1991). Thus, a critically balanced exploratory pedagogy transforms conflict into creativity and encourages writers to experience the magic of unimpeded flow.

Enlarging a Theory of Meaning: The Material-Intuitive Fusion

Such a crucial integration of cognition and affect also furthers our efforts to recenter spiritually by expanding the very nature of knowing. The affective-cognitive fusion, essential to spiritual centeredness, highlights the inseparability of emotion, language, and image. Underlying current conceptualizations of thinking is a reductive view of knowledge as exclusively language-based. For instance, poststructuralist thought envisions human beings as essentially discursive creatures, created by their languages. Thinking is seen as internalized talk (Vygotsky 1962; Bruffee 1986) and emotion as the outcome of cognitive evaluation (Harre 1986). Schema theory, which informs much of the cognitive approach to both reading and writing, is also based on a view of thinking as a language-based, propositional process. However, this view of thinking is simplistic and, as Berman contends, alienating. Exploratory pedagogy, however, acknowledges a more complex web of meaning-making—for instance, that which is encompassed by dual-coding theory.

Mark Sadoski, Ernest Goetz, and Allan Paivio have written persuasively suggesting that a dual-coding theory provides a powerful alternative to the flawed schema theory. Imagery, as well as language, is at the heart of Allan Paivio's dual-coding theory. According to Paivio, people handle phenomena by means of two functionally and structurally distinct systems: a visual system for nonverbal objects and events and a verbal system for language. The visual system organizes information synchronously in a type of visual nested set in which smaller units are embedded in larger parts and the entire configuration is available for use more or less at once, like elements of a fabric. The verbal system, on the other hand, is organized sequentially into larger structures, like the links of a chain. Imagery functions as a conceptual peg around which related information is clustered. Thus, images can become ideational nodes for conceptual development (Paivio 1986). Sir Frederic Bartlett's original work in schema theory and, more recently, George Lakoff and Mark Johnson's work with metaphors similarly suggest the need to reconceptualize thinking as something more than a solely linguistic process (Bartlett 1932; Lakoff and Johnson 1980).

For exploratory pedagogy, as for spiritual centeredness, thinking is more than just a language-based propositional process. It fuses language, emotion, and image. A reflectively balanced exploratory pedagogy acknowledges this fusion and builds on the multifaceted nature of truth making. It embraces language as well as emotion and imagery as important elements in creating the web of meaning. Exploratory pedagogy's growing attention to metaphor and metaphorical thinking (Miller 1994) exemplifies one way in which language, emotion, and image are incorporated within writing. Thus, through efforts to redress the marginalization of affect without rejecting cognition, exploratory pedagogy embraces the "affective-volitional basis" (Vygotsky 1962, 150) of all thought and reflects the integrative and affective nature of a spiritual center.

Reclaiming the Self: The Subjective Consciousness

One of the unfortunate repercussions of a poststructuralist orientation is the despair resulting from the erosion of self and meaningfulness. Selfhood and believing are frequently victims of an extreme social perspective: Nihilism subjugates hopefulness; determinism makes an illusion of choice. In Yeats's words, "the ceremony of innocence is drowned" (1962, 91). To Berger, this is the essence of alienation. Thus, perhaps the most striking element of spiritual centeredness is its renewed emphasis on the self, in stark contrast to an era that heralded the death of author and agency (Barthes 1989). Centering spiritually requires us to refocus our attention on the quality of experiential truth and the power of personal narrative to create our realities. Regardless of the way in which our sense of reality is constructed, we experience it as both a personal and a shared construct (Berger 1967). By continuously insisting on only the social or shared nature of our world view, we strip our students of their belief in the validity and worth of their personal experiences. We destroy their selfhood and leave nothing in its place, thus creating the very alienation we should fear. For any learning to occur, which includes increasing our students' critical consciousness, it is necessary to honor the ways in which students create a sense of experienced, as well as shared, reality.

Exploratory pedagogy—honoring intuition (Holman 1994), illustrating the power of meditation (Gallehr), and somatic learning (Klein and Hecker 1994)—restores belief in and respect for the self. Examine for a moment the potential of such an emphasis for helping students construct a spiritual center. This orientation focuses students' attention directly on their conviction of a personally experienced reality. It requires them to confront their sense of being while demanding that we as teachers subordinate our own sense of being in order to enter their reality. Techniques such as meditation and silence implicitly honor the authority of individual experience. Such a process restores respect for and appreciation of each writer's personal ordering of life. On the basis of this confidence and respect, we can then move classes into more complex investigations of the ways in which personal reality becomes a shared reality that, in turn, becomes itself personal reality. What is important in this movement is the restoration of writers' confidence in their own sense of being, or self, before we ask them to reexamine that self critically.

Reclaiming Self and Society: The Dialectic

Just as the integration of affect and cognition is a central characteristic of spiritual centeredness, so is the integration of self and society. For as Berger explains, our fragile sense of a concrete reality and self is dialectic: It is maintained through the myriad faces of conversation between self and significant others. Self is not isolated; it gains identity and creates order by means of an other. Self and culture are dialectic and conversational.

Reflectively implemented, the reclamation of self within an exploratory classroom simultaneously embraces the dialectical nature of self and society because every rhetorical act is perceived as dialectic. Writing does not take place within a vacuum. It is always writing something for someone, even if that someone is a projection of one's self. Never is it only internal or only external but a convoluted combination of both, an intricate *pas de deux* between a writer persona and a reader persona. Exploratory pedagogy does not fall victim to the extreme expressionist perspective that fosters the growth and authority of a self by denigrating and excluding the presence of an other. Nor does it accede to an extreme social perspective that undermines the importance of writer agency and self-authority. In both extreme situations, the necessity of navigating the fluid waters created by the evolution of writer, text, and readers is lost.

A critically balanced exploratory pedagogy avoids the isolationism of self-glorification and the nullification of an extreme social perspective. It integrates both into a center. The personal is not glorified but problematized in an exploratory classroom, thus creating an amalgamation of the social and the personal. A manifestation of this fusion is the range of writing roles that we find in an exploratory pedagogy. For instance, to use James Britton's terminology, exploratory pedagogy valorizes writing in the participant role, in which writers and readers transact to achieve something within a shared world; in the spectator role, in which writers focus on creating a personally experienced vision of the world; and in both roles simultaneously, in which writers shift between experienced and shared realities. Transactional, poetic, and expressive writing problematizes the role of the self by constantly shifting the locus of authority and stability. This range of roles also emphasizes the ways in which the personal and social are environmentally linked, with each mutually transforming the other.

Recreating Self: Participating Consciousness

Poststructuralist thinking has forced us to redefine the concept of the self; however, replacing the traditional Freudian concept of a unified, contained

self with the poststructuralist concept of a fragmented, discursive self is neither our only nor our strongest option. Too much is lost in each case, including especially our ability to strike a balance and navigate our way through
the disparate voices that comprise self. Our ability to increase the number
and range of the voices within is truncated by these two options, Recentering spiritually, however, necessitates a reconceptualization of the self, one
that is neither isolated nor sociohistorically determined. Instead, creating a
spiritual center is an outgrowth of developing within ourselves and our students a participating consciousness, which, in turn, is based on the idea of
learning as ecological (Berman 1990).

According to Berman, the act of knowing can never occur without individual consciousness identifying with the unknown. The process of knowing
requires that we turn toward something human or nonhuman without any
desire to appropriate the other for some pragmatic use. We do not appropriate it. Instead, we try to be the other somatically and emotionally. In such an
act, Berman asserts, there is no loss of self but rather a heightened feeling of
life and awareness through identification with another. Thus, participating
consciousness requires a reordering of our understanding of the relationship
between self and other. It implies an environmental or transactional self, one
that becomes or exists only in relationship to an other: not a self, not an
other, but a selfother (Berman 1990). The self is neither fragmented nor
unified, but centered within the act of participation. We become more ourselves as we identify with an other. It is not an interaction but a transaction,
in Rosenblatt's sense of the term: an environmental relationship in which
forces mutually create each other (Rosenblatt 1978, Chapter Two).

Exploratory pedagogy offers the hope of fostering that participating consciousness in a writing classroom among students and teachers. Notably, the
growing importance of empathy in an exploratory setting (Teich 1994) supports the growth of a participating consciousness. For example, participating
consciousness requires a merging through which we imagine another's life,
while simultaneously recognizing our individual upbringing, beliefs, and
emotions. We extend ourselves in a physical sense by trying to understand
within the body what it is like to step into another's shoes. We embed ourselves in an other, neither managing nor restraining disparate selves, but dissolving them in "an affirmative quality of kinship that no longer allows for
privileged status" (Hershusius 1994, 19). Empathy, a process by which we
experience the emotions of another (see Hoffman 1984), creates this participating consciousness.

Creating a Center That Holds

Exploratory pedagogy in our composition classrooms offers the most opti-
mistic hope of spiritually centering ourselves and our methodology. We are,
after all, creatures in whom spirit and flesh, chaos and order, feeling and

rationality continually merge and re-form in a bewildering "innerscape" of shifting boundaries. We are creatures in whom self is transformed by our being in and of the world, our being a self and an other. We need a pedagogy that joyously embraces specious contraries. Within the purview of exploratory pedagogy critically pursued, writing and learning are no longer that beast with the head of a man and the body of a lion that Yeats so fears in "The Second Coming." Instead, both writing and learning become a fluid amalgamation of mystery and realization, and something once arcane becomes meaningful and accessible to everyone. It is spiritual. It is centered.

Advocates 'exploratory pedagogy" - sort of a reaction against poststructuralist attacks on the self and the unquantifiable. The experience of "self" has to be recognized an honored before it can be critically considered. Exploratory pedagogy sounds similar to Graves' "authentic" classroom.

4

Writing
A Natural Site for Spirituality
Susan A. Schiller

The Dream

I was a new student. Sitting in the classroom I could sense a difference. All the students could enter or depart the room at any moment—whenever the urge struck. It was obvious that specific class enrollment was outdated. A tacit understanding and respect for others' learning and teaching filled the air, and most students stayed for an hour to participate in the experience.

I was in an English class, still as Dr. Schiller, but as a student. Dr. Jasper, a woman my age, was talking about poetry in film. She had just introduced a new book on film, yet this was a poetry class, and students came to write poetry. We all kept notebooks for our poems and randomly, sympathetically shared our work with one another. Everyone expressed interest in each other's work. As the hour ended, a new teacher came into the room; some of the students stayed, some left. I left, walking down the hall in search of a German class that I had signed up to take.

I could see I was walking on the second floor and, down below, the hallway opened onto a mezzanine. The space was circular, bright, spacious, and full of excitement. People were milling around. Some sat eating snacks. Some sat in front of TV monitors. Some sat in lounge areas talking. Some were headed for other classrooms. At one point, I stood with four other people outside a large lecture hall where people were discussing paleontology. One or two of the others took seats in the room, but I did not, since I needed to be somewhere else. In the classroom next door, a teacher was showing slides about brain research and the way sound is manifested in our brains. This interested me, but I was trying to find the German class. I went down the stairs and, as I started to walk across the mezzanine, I was drawn to a table near a lounge area where a large screen was showing a film. I suddenly changed my focus away from the German class; now I was pulled in a different direction, and I clearly had permission to follow my intuition.

I stood at the table with a young man who had been watching the film in the lounge area. A young woman came up and asked him, "Did you have fun in the film?" He said, "Yes." I looked at them oddly because I was stunned. I suddenly understood that these students could maintain passive and active positions in the learning process. They could jump into the film as an actor, actress, producer, or director at the same time as they sat in the audience watching the film and their own involvement in it. The film required their participation, but they also had to observe themselves in the learning. They had to see, not just with their eyes, but with their bodies. They had to feel the spirit in the learning so that the learning could reciprocate and feed their spirit.

Finally, I saw that this was an experiential school in which spirit guided learning. Lecture time was minimized. Its usefulness was noted, but a reliance on it was considered outdated. Its purpose was understood and utilized, but experience was given the premium value. I looked around and felt everyone's thirst for knowing and discerned their collaborative habits. In this school, particularly apparent on the mezzanine, students and teachers blended into one learning body. In the teaching, teachers learned, too. Students knew this, helped it along, and could stand and assume the teacher role whenever it became necessary for learning. As a result, distinctions between student and teacher were practically nonexistent. Tests were thought to be harmful, curriculum requirements were abandoned, and the four-year degree belonged to schools from the past. Instead, people relied on their natural interests to shape and eventually develop a core of instruction that would lead to career choices. People could drop out but could also return to school at any time, pick up where they had left off, or start afresh. This type of educational system was accepted by the culture, was valued for its reliance on intuition, and was regarded as superior to all systems that had gone before it. Learning reigned. With authority ascribed to learning rather than to people or systems, spirit caused a thirst for sharing and growing together, and it was good that way.

Is this just an idealistic dream? Perhaps. But as educators, we must dream; for if we do not, realities do not shift. That student in the back row who cannot envision success would still sleep if not for our efforts to reach out, to show the power in vision. That idea that needs exposure would be unheard if not for our attempts to get it published. That paradigm of thought would stagnate if not for our questions and ways of reseeing. Dreams realized, manifested into action, shape our culture. Our actions can begin quite simply, but our dreams are powerful with imagination, powerful in challenge. In today's age of educational reform, we are just now beginning to dream toward a spirit-based education, which I define as an education that honors affect, intuition, inner knowing, and connections to God, to the Earth, and to human beings. If we let it, if we are open to its power, spirit-based education can guide us and can foster change. Where does it start? It starts in our hopes, in our idealism, in our courage to live as spiritual beings. It starts today, in our classrooms. The easiest, most natural place to begin is in the composition classroom.

In the Academy

Writing is a natural site for spirituality. Every time we pick up a pen to express language, sometimes language that stretches our reach, we push inward to discover new realms of experience. The journey inward automatically imposes a quest for connections between the known and the unknown, between the cognitive and the intuitive, between the self and the other. We know that through writing we construct our worldview, that we encourage ourselves to accept new ideas and life habits. Many writers have already made this connection and rely on spirit to guide their work. Those of us who teach composition can follow these writers' lead as we define and develop spirit-based writing assignments/environments for ourselves and for our students.

Fortunately, today, a growing number of people want to inculcate a spirit-based approach. Still in the inchoate stages, their efforts to introduce change through carefully planned pedagogy and composition theory are contributing to the way we talk about composition studies. But to create spirit-based teaching, as educational reformer Parker Palmer advises, "we must cultivate personal experience of that which we need to profess" (1993, 113). We must invite and develop a spirit-based life. It begins with centering on what it means to be spiritual.

First, we need to accept and value the fact that spirituality can be defined in myriad ways because it is mysterious. The infinite potential offered to us by such mystery is an advantage, for it allows affirmation of far more than we will ever fully know. It offers the opportunity for lifelong learning and discovery, which in turn opens us up to accepting knowledge as a spiraling evolution of information and insight. The implications for pedagogy and composition theory are infinite. Just by looking at a few definitions we can see this point.

William James says the "idea of universal evolution lends itself to a doctrine of general meliorism and progress which fits the religious needs of the healthy-minded so well that it seems almost as if it might have been created for their use" (1961, 88). I think it safe to assume that people want to be healthy-minded and that teachers are in the profession of guiding other people to healthy-mindedness. It seems clear also that health must embody spirit. Spirituality, for James, is a personal connection with what he calls "God" and all that flows out of the divine (1961, 95). The flow is circular and comes in degrees so that we might distinguish the evolutionary process of knowing spirit. He doesn't care by what term people name God, whether they use "Kindly Light, Providence, the Over-Soul, Omnipotence, or whatever . . ."

(1961, 95). This openness creates a space for the nonreligious also to be spiritual, and it can open our view of writing as a spiritual event.

People can also choose to be spiritual without placing themselves within an organized religion; they can find spirituality almost anywhere, including classrooms. Statistics indicate a growing population who, while still spiritual, do not attend church or consider themselves affiliated with any organized religion.[1] According to a *Newsweek* poll in November 1994, "fifty-eight percent feel the need to experience spiritual growth, thirty-three percent have had a religious or mystical experience, twenty percent of Americans have had a revelation from God in the last year, and thirteen percent have seen or sensed the presence of an angel" (54). People are seeking spirituality.

As global interests challenge nationalistic tendencies, people are also accepting diversity with regard to faith commitments. Such diversity is a healthy signal that a shift in reality is happening. We can see it in education, too. Every time we ask a student to expand and stretch his or her abilities, we are asking for a spiritual act, even if we do not name it as such. Every time we ask students to develop language and rhetorical skills, we are asking that they reshape their world, that they recast their reality. This may be considered a tiny shift, but shift after shift accrues until people are changed, until dreams are realized. Multiple definitions, as acts of language, empower us because they dissolve boundaries and inspire our imaginations to envision even more.

Joseph Campbell, who spent a lifetime studying comparative religion, believed we accept either a personal or an impersonal entity when we define *spirit*. For instance, naming the source of spirit "God" indicates a personalized vision of spirit. In contrast, spirit seen as an infinite energy with varying degrees embodied in the physical and metaphysical world indicates an impersonal source. He says we can choose to experience the ultimate mystery— spirit—without form or with form. We can name it *God*, thereby reducing it to a concept and giving it form, or we can resist concepts in order to welcome *experience* rather than *idea*. Campbell, who chooses the impersonal, says, "God is the vehicle of the energy [Brahman, the energy that is the whole universe] not its source" (1988). For Campbell, one's definition of spirit and way of practicing faith becomes an individual decision. Today people are leaving traditional forms found in organized religion and instead are seeking the mystery of spirit in the forms of their professional lives. Hence, we see a proliferation of spirit occurring across medicine, psychology, popular culture, and finally education. It seems clear that people need to *experience* spirit— *even if they do not name it God*. This does not mean that people should do whatever they want and then call it spirit; it means that they are released from dogma associated with traditional forms in order to discover additional ways

1. David Briggs. 1994. "Boomers' Spiritual Quest and Church Integrity Not Necessarily Compatible." *Morning Sun*, 13 May. Briggs, an AP religion writer, offers statistics about the growing trend among baby boomers who are looking for spirituality outside organized religion.

of knowing spirit. It means they can find the natural mystery of spirit in their own efforts to improve the human condition.

Others offer their definitions that are all different but that are all connected. Beth Daniell, educator and compositionist, defines *spirituality* as "seeking a connection with God, the universe, the life-force, humankind, one's own higher 'self'; attempting to give life coherence and purpose beyond professional, economic, or personal goals" (1994, 239). James Moffett, educational reformer, says, "spirit can be thought of as the subtlest frequency, the one that propagates the spectrum of increasingly slower vibrations. To be spiritual is to identify with spirit across these vibrations" (1994, 22). Inayat Khan, a Sufi teacher, offers four ways to understand the word *spirit:*

> One meaning is essence. The second meaning of spirit is what is understood by those who call the soul spirit when it has left the body on earth and has passed to the other side. The third meaning is that of the soul and mind working together. It is used in this sense when one says that a man seems to be in low spirits. And the fourth meaning of spirit is the soul of all souls, the source and goal of all things and all beings, from which all comes and to which all returns. (1982, 38)

Jean Houston, who practices sacred psychology, places spirit in consciousness and psyche. For her, there is a great "no-thing-ness," a vacuum, that is the foundation of all being (1987, 21). This can be likened to the vibrational world of Moffett, the essence Khan refers to, and the universal in Daniell's view. These multiple definitions reach for understanding the oneness demanded by the spiritual. They can help us understand the infinite possibilities for teaching writing as a spiritual act. Spirituality in writing can be self-defined by the student so that it specifically fits his or her own readiness for experience and learning. Teachers have to lead, however, by building flexibility and tolerance into our assignments. We also have to share our spiritual life with our students and be willing to explore the oneness that can be found in learning from them as we teach them.

Spirituality in Pedagogy

After we reach a personal understanding of spirituality, we need to let writers who have allowed spirituality to guide them act as our teachers. By following their example, we can help students develop into more competent writers and into more spiritual people. Successful writers seem to be spiritually motivated in ways that we rarely hear about in composition classes. Their communication of the ways spirit weaves itself into writing can teach us to see the writing process as a spiritual event of the highest order. If they can feel its mystery, can be challenged by the paradox of discovery, and then be enriched by the potential of learning that takes place when they reach inside their creativity and imagination, so too can we. So too can our students.

When writers write about what it means to be a writer, they often refer to the challenges they face in solitude. They say solitude is the writer alone, facing the page, one-on-one, face-to-face, with the angst of the blank page. Some view the challenge with a sense of discovery as their stories' characters emerge and live through decisions and actions. Others view writing as a journey into self or into community—a joyful journey, but not one that is risk free. Alice Walker and Isabel Allende agree that as writers they place themselves into the role of storyteller and witness. They use *witness* in the Christian sense; to witness is to proclaim the lessons they have learned. They witness to others that which their life-lessons have revealed—lessons of mind, body, and spirit. Allende thinks of her characters as "spirits." She says:

> There is a prophetic or clairvoyant quality in writing. It comes from the fact that you are alone for so many hours concentrating on something that you start living the story . . . all my books come from a very deep emotion that has been with me for a very long time. And those emotions are usually painful—abandonment, pain, anger, death, violence. But there are also joyful emotions that go with the writing. . . . So there's a mixture of both things—the love and the pain. (Writer's Life, 1993, 84)

The solitude is necessary, not always easy, not always without pain, but necessary and rewarding because it brings Allende closer to her own spirit life.

Allende's spirit-based approach is similar to Walker's experience. Walker states:

> *The Temple of My Familiar* was amazing for me because I felt that I had really connected with the ancient knowledge that we all have, and that it was really a matter not of trying to learn something, but of remembering. And that propelled me right through that book. And honestly, I just knew some of the things in it. I didn't learn them. I found I knew them. And this was a great delight. (Writer's Life 1993, 85)

Walker relied on cellular knowledge, on that which was stored in her body, which came from personal ancestry and ancient memory. She drew out of her what was deepest inside and she did it through connections to her spirit.

Frederick Buechner, minister and author of twenty-three books, echoes Allende in his essay "Faith and Fiction," in which he connects faith and writing and understands the inseparable bond they share. He says:

> In both faith and fiction [writers] *fashion* out of the raw stuff of [their] experience. If [they] want to remain open to luck and grace, [they] shape that stuff, less to impose a shape on it than to discover what the shape is. And in both, [writers] *feign*. Feigning is imagining—making visible images for invisible things. (1988, 115)

It is obvious that imagining takes faith just as faith takes imagining. Writers have to have faith that they will imaginatively reflect in symbols—that is, in the written word—the essence of an experience. Their symbology must intensify the essence so that it can be completely transmuted from writer to page to reader. The reception of the essence must result in a lived-through experience for the reader if the writer is effective.

David Bradley, novelist and educator, "realized that no matter how good [he] became at manipulating symbols [he] could never hope to move anyone without allowing [himself] to be moved—that [he] would only arrive at slight truths if [he] wasn't willing to reveal truths about [himself]" (1988, 79). Again an inner journey precipitates writing. Writing becomes a solo journey that requires faith, intuition, compassion, and a willingness to open up to solitude and inner knowing. Even more, it requires a commitment to revealing self and to laying bare all the emotions and thoughts that create self.

Allen Ginsberg offers a superb understanding of this process when he states:

> It's the meditative practice of 'letting go of thoughts'—neither pushing them away nor inviting them in, but as you sit meditating, watching the procession of thought forms pass by, rising, flowering and dissolving, and disowning them, so to speak: you're not responsible any more than you're responsible for the weather, because you can't tell in advance what you're going to think next. . . . So it requires cultivation of tolerance towards one's own thoughts and impulses and ideas—the tolerance necessary for the perception of one's own mind, the kindness to the self necessary for acceptance of that process of consciousness and for acceptance of the mind's raw contents. (1988, 150)

Composition isn't taught this way very often. But when it is, people soon understand the joys and rewards of listening to intuition. An ability to watch words appear in a surprising flow arises from a comfortable faith in one's own courage and spirit. The most common composition methods that attempt to draw on this surprising flow—freewriting, brainstorming, clustering, and mapping—value spontaneity, but a vision of the final product can still dominate neophytes by blocking them from the spontaneous knowing that can be played out.

In this sense, professional writers "play" and turn inward to touch their spirit base, but students have not been taught to see the play. If we, as teachers, are to create spiritual sites for writing like those that professional writers describe, we must take faith in the play we see in writing and create pedagogy that motivates not just a paradigm shift but *a whole-system transition.*

A Whole-System Transition

What is a whole-system transition and how is it different from a paradigm shift? According to Thomas Kuhn, a paradigm shift occurs when intellectual systems break down. Old ways of thinking and solving problems do not work; new ways and major changes occur. One conceptual model is replaced with a new one (Hairston 1984, 14). In composition studies, the most talked about paradigm shift has been the shift from teaching writing as product to teaching it as process. Recently, compositionists have based composition pedagogy on theories borrowed from literary criticism and, even more recently, compositionists have argued for a shift from exclusively cognitive models to one that combines cognition with noncognitive approaches like intuition, spirituality, silence, among others (see Brand and Graves 1994). Paradigm shifts, while useful in promoting change, are actually minor when compared to the whole-system transition Jean Houston describes. A whole-system transition is a global shift, whereas a paradigm shift is usually contained in a specific discipline.

In *The Search for the Beloved,* Jean Houston discusses five factors (1987, 13) that are critical to bringing about such a monumental shift.

1. Planetization posits that we all have a responsibility to maintain a healthy planet.

2. The rise of the feminine champions female sensibility, recognizing the feminine as an essential and crucial component in the human mind pool. Interconnectedness of psyche and nature will help to bring about new values for process and cultural differences.

3. The emergence of a new science and new scientists, accompanied by a miniaturization of technology, means that information, rather than industry, will shape our world.

4. The new understanding of the potential for extending both human capacities and the ecology of consciousness will release dormant human abilities.

5. The emergence of a global spiritual sensibility will reveal that consciousness and psyche occupy the vacuum of existence and will suggest that consciousness might be "the fundamental stuff of reality" (1987, 21).

There is now evidence that all five steps are actively changing education. In composition studies, recently published environmental rhetorics are one piece of evidence that planetization is occurring. The emergence of feminine literary criticism indicates that feminine sensibility is manifesting itself. Word processing, e-mail, World-Wide Web, and fax machines have changed the way we process information and, in composition studies, have changed the ways some of us teach. Additionally, current research into learning styles is reshaping our notions of human abilities, and the proliferation of spiritual book titles currently appearing across disciplines encourages us to believe that a global spiritual sensibility is emerging.

While composition pedagogy can find roots in all five of these factors, I want to emphasize the fifth. If consciousness is the fundamental stuff of reality, then through writing we can turn inward, understand our individual process of learning, and create interconnections with each other. Spirit-based pedagogy can thus significantly contribute to profound levels of consciousness and offer opportunities to connect Houston's five factors within holistic education.

Houston's whole-system transition is simply another lap on the evolutionary spiral, but it is a significant lap because this shift, a shift in reality itself, can transcend fundamental and often limiting differences between diverse groups. If we accept the notion that the infinite power of God circulates in *all* people and through *all*, then we also have to value our differences and tensions that cause *us* to create polarities that divide. By accepting God or Spirit in that which we oppose, we can release ourselves from negative relationships that destroy us or confine us. We are, after all, all part of the same whole. Spirit-based pedagogy, whether it is in science, composition, literature, psychology, math, geography, or music and art, offers a holistic attachment to the oneness of which we are a part. It can connect each of us to one another in ways that foster compassion, acceptance, and growth. Through a spiritual connection, we can recognize and honor ourselves in each other as we stand face-to-face, for each of us *is in the other*. That is oneness. Discovery of this connection can naturally occur when we write and share our writing with one another.

It is imperative to understand that a spirit-based life means finding and maintaining connections with oneness. In the academy, such an idea too frequently gets connected to religion, but it can as easily be disconnected from religion since civil law calls for a separation of *church* and state, not of *spirit* and state. If reaching into the oneness, into the no-thing-ness, can bring about acceptance, tolerance, and a willingness to confront conflict and problem solving with a positive attitude, which I believe it can, the academy needs to take a closer look. The academy needs to question, test, speculate, validate, and sift through what is useful in developing intelligent, fearless citizens, especially as we greet the emerging whole-system transition.

Spirit-based pedagogy can assist in bringing about the whole-system transition because it connects body, mind, and spirit. It is experiential and focused in action, and it allows students and teachers to "follow their bliss." Campbell tells us that our bliss is something inside each of us that lets us know we are in the center, on the beam. In his words, "If we get off the beam we lose our life." In a pedagogy that aims at global change, we will stay on the beam if we develop such qualities as love, compassion, patience, generosity, courage, and wisdom. We will learn writing by writing; by doing; and by experimenting with style, word choice, images, symbols, voice, and all the other rhetorical devices available. Competence will develop naturally if we allow "the flow of life to set the rhythm, like the tides, instead of fighting each new wave of experience, [and] harmony [will be] found through subtle adjustments'' (Sams 1993, 199). Since writing competence does not appear overnight or as a result of one experience, we will patiently coax its growth, and we will practice writing, knowing that change is inevitable. As educators, we will have the courage to follow our bliss, to dream, to share our visions, and to transform our world into one that is balanced and harmonious. We will model this lifestyle for our students so that they, too, will learn that writing is essentially a spiritual act.

5

Writing the Spirit
Interviews with John Bradshaw, Larry Dossey, M.D., and Thomas Moore

Regina Paxton Foehr

What can we who teach writing learn from other disciplines about the inner and transcendent forces that influence the act of writing? To explore this topic, I shall focus on three areas: 1. definitions and paradoxes of *spiritual empowerment*, 2. archetypal psychology as a metaphor for the inner and transcendent spiritual forces that influence the act of writing, and 3. an interview with successful writers from medicine and psychology about the inner and transcendent spiritual forces that empower their writing. The interview features three nationally prominent authors who are leaders in the fields of therapeutic psychology and holistic medicine: physician Larry Dossey[1] and psychologists John Bradshaw[2] and Thomas Moore.[3] These writers blend discussions of their disciplines with a consciousness of the spiritual nature of the self. Dossey, a scientist, physician, and former Chief of Staff of Dallas Medical City Hospital, serves as cochair of the National Institutes of Health Panel on Mind/Body Interventions, Office of Alternative Medicine, and Executive Editor of the journal *Alternative Therapies in Health and Medicine*. Bradshaw and Moore

1. Books by Larry Dossey include *Prayer Is Good Medicine*, 1996, San Francisco: Harper; *Healing Words*, 1993, New York: HarperCollins; *Meaning and Medicine*, 1992, Boston: Shambhala; *Recovering the Soul*, 1989, New York: Bantam; *Space, Time, and Medicine*, 1982; and *Beyond Illness*, 1985, New York: Random House.
2. Books by John Bradshaw include *Family Secrets*, 1995, *Creating Love*, 1992, and *Homecoming: Reclaiming and Championing Your Inner Child*, 1992, New York: Bantam; *Bradshaw on the Family*, 1988, Deerfield Beach, FL: Health Communications, and others.
3. Books by Thomas Moore include *The Re-enchantment of Everyday Life*, 1996, HarperCollins; *Soul Mates*, 1994, and *Care of the Soul*, 1992, New York: HarperCollins; *Dark Eros*, 1990, Dallas: Spring Publishing Co.; *The Planets Within*, 1993, Hudson, NY: Lindisfarne, and others.

are practicing psychologists who, like Dossey, have written *New York Times* best-sellers.[4] People, trying to understand the unconscious and transcendent forces that affect their own lives, are buying the books of these three writers literally by the millions and are learning from them. The academy can learn from them too. The interview addresses two main questions: How are these authors tapping spiritual energies in their own writing process? and Is there something that they do that could be useful in the writing classroom?

Spirituality and the Postmodern World

In recent years many areas of mainstream culture, from medicine to psychology, have expanded their disciplines to include concerns for spirituality. Even such conservative bastions as the National Institutes of Health and the American Medical Association acknowledge connections between spirituality and healing. In clinical studies, meditation, creative visualization, and other nontraditional therapies have been found to be effective for lowering blood pressure and for treating cancer and heart disease.[5] In psychology, twelve-step groups acknowledging a "higher power" have become mainstays of group therapy. Yet, despite such expanding perspectives and other doors beginning to open to spirituality in some fields, within the postmodern academy concern for spirituality has not expanded noticeably. In fact, a literal, linear, one-dimensional interpretation of spirituality—one associated with sentimentality, gimmickry, and religion—has been so thoroughly ensconced that the topic of spiritual empowerment in language and in learning has been all but excluded from the conversation.

So strong is this oversimplified definition's hold that we in the academy hesitate to say the word *spiritual*. We may even react physically to it. For many of us (until recently, this writer included), when we hear the word *spiritual* in academic settings (we would never say it, of course), our muscles tighten, our bodies become tense, and we squirm in discomfort; we don't know what to expect or how to respond. In short, we are afraid. Our tension and fear arise from three main sources:

1. our *denial* of the holistic and paradoxical nature and power of spirituality

2. our having *internalized* the academy's oversimplified interpretation

---

4. The following books have all had long stays on the *New York Times* best-seller list: John Bradshaw's 1992 *Creating Love* and 1992 *Homecoming* (fifty-three weeks); Thomas Moore's 1992 *Care of the Soul* and 1994 *Soul Mates* (seventy-eight and twenty-eight weeks, respectively, as of this writing); and Larry Dossey's 1993 *Healing Words*.
5. See Dossey, *Healing Words*, 1993, for a compilation of numerous reports of scientific research studies on the effects of imagery, meditation, biofeedback, and prayer on healing.

3. the *identity conflict* created when these forces (the just-mentioned
   first and second sources) collide with our former, our ongoing, and
   even our rejected personal and internalized interpretations of spirituality

As we struggle to have our voices heard within the academy, we hesitate to acknowledge openly the spiritual nature of learning and language. We
fear being professionally discounted if we stray from accepted conscious and
unconscious definitions and conventions. We fear being misunderstood or
labeled unfairly. We fear the alienation of ourselves and—worse—of our
ideas from serious consideration by other professionals. Therefore, at a conscious level we choose not to be alienated from the academy; we not only
need fair treatment in decisions regarding hiring, tenure, promotion, and
other professional matters, but we also need to be recognized as thinkers and
scholars whose ideas have merit. Choosing to participate seriously in dia-
logues on spirituality and learning, we fear, could associate us instead with
shallowness, religion, or questionable practices we cannot respect. Whether
or not one appreciates religious ideologies, who among us has not felt antag-
onized by shallow religious hucksters or zealots proselytizing their brand of
religion either outside or inside the classroom? Because we do not want to
be associated with either, we often overreact to the topic all together, disas-
sociating ourselves from all conversations on spirituality. In so doing, we
unwittingly contribute to further ensconcing the academy's literal, linear,
one-dimensional interpretation of spirituality.

Paradoxically, in choosing not to be alienated from others in the academy, we have chosen alienation from the self. Aside from legitimate concerns about separation of church and state, our thorough disassociation of our
selves from the spiritual nature of language and learning has created a rup-
ture within the self and the whole of learning. Unable to acknowledge the
wholeness of others and ourselves by including our spiritual nature, we feel
split, individually and collectively, because of this separation of the self, and
we therefore experience tension and anxiety in discussions of spirituality in
the academy. We are experiencing what Dick McCleary refers to as an
alienating behavior disorder (1993, 72), a condition Erik Erikson and other
psychologists labeled during World War II a classic *identity crisis*. Erikson
and others found "identity confusion" in "severely conflicted young people
whose sense of confusion is due . . . to a war within themselves" (1968, 17).
Paradoxically, our alienating behavior disorder or identity crisis derives from
our having internalized two conflicting interpretations of spirituality: our
own deeply personal perceptions of spirituality, and the one-dimensional
sentimentality-based interpretation that permeates the academy.

Spiritual empowerment within the academy should not be confused with
religious or New Age ideologies. In this article, *spiritually empowering forces*
or *energies* refers to those energies having to do with creativity, imagination,

inspiration, intuition, kinesthetic knowledge, felt sense, passion for knowing, the aha experience, archetypal energy, and the collective unconscious. Although people within the academy sense a duality—that is, either deny spirituality or feel alienated from the academy—such feelings are the antithesis of the nature of spiritual empowerment. Spiritual energies are universally available. Their nature is holistic; it is not dualistic. It does not polarize individuals based on binaries of intelligent/inane, subjective/objective, valuable/useless, or substantive/shallow. Rather, spiritual energy is paradoxical; it is simultaneously personal and cosmic, inexplicable and lucid, elusive and present. Ironically, at the personal level, we understand the paradox of spirituality: It is so complex that it is beyond our language to explain it but so simple and intrinsically familiar that it transcends our need to explain it.

Archetypal Psychology, a Metaphor for Spirituality

Even though we may not be able to understand spirituality intellectually, we understand it metaphorically and archetypally. In *A Guided Tour of the Collected Works of C. G. Jung* (1992), Robert H. Hopcke summarizes Jung's views on the powerful influence in our lives of the unconscious, particularly the influence of archetypes. Jung describes the unconscious as having two layers: the *personal* unconscious layer, containing personal memories, and the deeper, far more significant layer, the *collective unconscious*, containing those patterns of psychic perception common to all humanity, the *archetypes*. Archetypes, according to Jung, are the ultimate psychic source of power, wholeness, and inner transformation; distinct from symbols and images themselves, they are like psychic molds into which individual and collective experiences are poured and where they take shape (13–15). "They function autonomously, almost as forces of nature, organizing human experience for the individual in particular ways without regard to the constructive or destructive consequences to the individual life" (16). We can draw upon archetypal power consciously when we open ourselves to it, but even when we don't, archetypes affect and organize our personal and shared experience continuously at the unconscious level.[6] Consequently, in certain kinds of experiences, including writing, we share feelings, emotions, and a similarity of responses at a deep archetypal level. For example, if we were to ask students to write about experiences they have had regarding such archetypal themes as fear, death, mother, water, or mountains, we would notice from one piece to another parallels in students' images, emotional responses, and language, although no two writers would have had the same experience. We too might feel deeply connected to something within their experience. This occurs because all of humanity shares collective responses to, and psychic

6. In my forthcoming edited collection of essays, *The Writer as Hero: Archetypes, Creativity, and the Unconscious,* psychologists, writers, and teachers of writing investigate the power of archetypes and the unconscious upon writing.

perceptions of, different kinds of experience; they are contained within archetypes of the collective unconscious. Spirituality is shared, collective, and archetypal. According to Mihaly Csikszentmihalyi, "Spirituality is a fundamental condition of being human" (Henderson 1994, 40).

Within the academy, however, our collective denial and oversimplification of spirituality have evoked another powerful archetype: our dark side or our collective shadow. Because the shadow of spirituality has so thoroughly permeated the academy, in a sense it has taken ownership of our collective psyche. Shadow energies can give us balance and perspective when we consciously acknowledge them, but when we deny them, they assume a disproportionate, even totalizing, place in our collective psyche. We become consumed, misguided, or drained by them, depriving ourselves of access to the wellspring of power and energies available to us. When, for example, we operate from automatic, knee-jerk impulses to spirituality within the academy, the shadow owns us. But when we look at spirituality from the light of consciousness, we can make conscious choices and we can, therefore, own the shadow and reclaim and activate the disowned part of the self, that is, the power of spiritual energy. As Jung said, "One becomes enlightened . . . by making the darkness conscious" (Zweig and Abrams 1991, 4).

If in the academy we were to transcend limited interpretations and consider the archetypal and metaphorical possibilities for interpreting spirituality, we could discover the many paradoxes of spirituality, including both its shadows *and* its potential. By embracing its paradoxical nature and honoring the whole, we could liberate and activate positive archetypal energies within the institution and within ourselves and our students as learners. Instead of the guarded self-monitoring we now do in response to one-dimensional interpretations of spirituality, we could ignite confidence in our own thoughts, creativity and imagination.

Spiritual energy is as present within the personal and collective unconscious as are all other archetypal energies driving our decisions, including fear, ambition, and the desire for self-expression. Whether we want to name spirituality, honor it, or exclude it, spiritual energies, like all other archetypal energies, can be denied but they cannot be suppressed at either the personal or the (academy's) collective level of the unconscious. These energies demand our attention, and in one way or another, like all archetypal energies, they will have it, if not consciously, then unconsciously.

Spiritually empowering energy should be considered a real force in learning, one that can be activated by practices such as those discussed in the following interview. As Dossey, Bradshaw, and Moore have found, getting in touch with one's spiritually empowering forces enables the writer to reach deeper into the self and, therefore, paradoxically, to reach others. It is time that we consciously acknowledge this wellspring of power available to all and conduct serious research to inform our conversation—research on archetypes and related areas, the unconscious, insight, imagination, kinesthetics, and so forth.[7] In so doing, we may discover for ourselves and for our students answers to some of the questions posed to Bradshaw, Dossey, and Moore on how transcendent spiritual energies can affect how we think, how we write, and how we learn.

The Interview

Spiritual Empowerment in Writing

Foehr: What does the term *spiritual empowerment* mean to you?

Dossey: This question about spiritual empowerment . . . gets to the crux of what writing is all about. For me, it is just communicating with the Absolute. And I want to be deliberately vague about what I mean by *communicating* and what I mean by the *Absolute*. I certainly don't imply that in order to achieve spiritual empowerment we have to *do* anything to get empowered. For me, it's more a process of discarding things and *not doing*. It's really more a way of *being* than it is doing anything . . . a natural state for everybody, so it isn't something to be acquired or developed. . . . Everyone is a creator, whether a writer or a sculptor or a musician. For me it's a sense of being connected with something higher, but this isn't something that's far off. It really has an imminence as well as being something that's transcendent. It gives me a sense of ultimate importance in doing my work, makes it very relevant. It's a calling in a sense. It's inherent in who I am. I know a lot of people think about spirituality as something that's out there. You have to grow into it, or get it, or make it happen, or acquire it; you have to progress to it in some way. I don't feel that. It is innate, inherent, and imminent; it's in-dwelling. And so, that for me is what spirituality is.

Moore: I find the word *spiritual empowerment* difficult for me to use . . . not that the phrase is not a good one. . . . I don't really

---

7. The Assembly for Expanded Perspectives on Learning (AEPL), an official assembly of the National Council of Teachers of English (NCTE), is open to all who are interested in investigating alternative perspectives on composition. The AEPL provides a forum for research and exploration into topics traditionally considered beyond the cognitive. Topics include Archetypes, Dreams, and the Unconscious; Creativity—Imagination, Intuition, Inspiration, Insight; Emotion; Healing; Imagery; Kinesthetics; Meditation and Silence; and Spirituality and Transcendence. AEPL meetings are held three times a year, at the fall NCTE convention, the spring Conference on College Composition and Communication, and the summer AEPL conference. AEPL may be contacted through NCTE, 1111 Kenyon Road, Urbana, Illinois 61801 (1-800-369-NCTE). The premiere issue of the Journal of the Assembly for Expanded Perspectives on Learning appeared in Spring 1995.

understand the phrase *spiritual empowerment* myself, [but] spirituality is something of real importance. . . . We are really a spiritually starved people. . . . I am extremely interested in finding ways to live a spiritual life in our work and in my own work and in everything that we do. I'll just hear [the term] in my own way. I have a background as a quasi monk. I am so interested in not concentrating on or being self-conscious about power . . . [but instead in taking] a humble position and simply getting to work and being receptive to the grace of inspiration and wisdom. . . . I will imagine spiritual empowerment as an appreciation and cultivation of the spiritual element in whatever we're doing.

Bradshaw: Gradually over a period of time, you realize *spiritual empowerment* is when you really trust yourself. You have a relationship with yourself, which is the basis of a relationship with all others, and the world, and God. So that as I've developed a relationship with myself and more confidence in myself, it's sort of like, the two cogwheel each other. I'm finding the more I am inward, the more I am in a place where I'm in touch with my life and my life experience, inner feelings, desires, and experience, then those things appear for me just the way I need them . . . there are pieces of [my life] that will fit perfectly in a writing that I never even thought of [when they happened]. Suddenly, *you know.*

Foehr: Can you give an example?

Bradshaw: For example, I was [writing] a book that I've just finished on secrets. One of the things I'm trying to show is that we carry not only the dark secrets of our family, but we carry the most noble, unexpressed secrets of our family. I was remembering my father. My father just had a high school education, but he was a salesman who married in the Depression. And in a sense he never got very far in terms of this world's evaluation. I think he always felt a lot of shame about it. But he used to buy these correspondence courses and, of course, he was also drinking, but [as I was writing I recalled] this symbol of him with these correspondence courses. . . . I began to realize that in this man, there's a sadness . . . because of his frozen dreams. So [for me] spiritual empowerment when you're writing, really means that you're in touch with your own life experience. And this is sort of all predicated on the Carl Rogers's famous statement that whatever is personal is most general. But, when we really are expressing *our* personal life, *our* human experience, everyone else can tap into that.

Foehr: How or when do you recognize that you or your work is spiritually empowered?

Moore: My work has a spiritual dimension in the following ways or for the following reasons: I trust my own vision. I use nonjargon, non-technical language as much as possible. I study and refer to artists, poets, and religious sources, and not to any quantified studies. I speak to the most potent and meaning-giving aspects of anyone's experience. I don't present myself as one who knows what he's talking about.

Dossey: Well, for one thing, there's the joy factor. It's fun. It's work, but there's a sense of real achievement, satisfaction, and fulfillment that comes along with that. It's the point at which you cease to make a distinction between work and play. The work has a kind of authenticity. It has a ring of *rightness* about it. And it seems to be close to the truth. Also, it tends to be beautiful. And when everything clicks, and it works, there's some sort of aesthetic quality that's there. And the writing doesn't struggle on the page, it really sings. I guess, those are the main ways that I know.

Bradshaw: In comparing myself with myself, suddenly I'm doing something different or I'm stretching. An idea really stretches me. Or I have a new idea that isn't what I thought I had set out to write. . . . The first lights come on when you realize, "Hey, that's something I did," and [at that point] you know spiritual empowerment.

Foehr: At a deep archetypal level, do you have a sense that your work will be empowered?

Bradshaw: I had a *sense* that I was to write this popular book on shame. *Healing the Shame That Binds You* took [only] three and a half months to write, and it has sold a million two-hundred thousand copies. And without any help it hit the *New York Times* best-seller list with a publisher that at that time had one representative around the country.

Foehr: Your work is obviously inspired; can others take steps to achieve inspiration in their writing?

Moore: Trust your own vision . . . become less concerned about technique . . . and perscriptions.

Dossey: Well, I've just about stopped trying to take steps at this point in my life. I don't try to achieve inspiration anymore. For me, it's more like staying on the radar signal . . . being in sync as a writer, for me, is more a matter of *attunement* or *alignment* than *achieving* anything whatsoever. I cannot force writing. It seems to have a life of its own. Sometimes there are good times to write, and other times it would be horrible to try to make it happen.

Bradshaw: You've got to take risks. And in the beginning, the first risk you take is part of your spiritual empowerment, but you don't know it, because you're probably ensconced in too much fear. But [as you] put ideas togetherin your own way, suddenly when you realize that it worked, then the light comes on. . . . [You recognize] that the originality and the creativity is in how you put it together. . . . There are very few ideas that are really brand new and original. And I think that the way you come to new and original ideas is by putting two old ideas together.

Foehr: Some people suggest that anyone who writes is spiritually empowered, that spirituality is inherent in writing. Others suggest that spiritual empowerment is something one can cultivate and develop. What are your views?

Moore: It's a very difficult question. . . . Sylvia Plath, who is a wonderful writer, really had a tormented life. . . . I don't think anyone would say that she was a very spiritual person. . . . She was very difficult to be around, and [demonstrated no] sense of community. People . . . just sort of survived her companionship even if they valued it. And yet . . . there's a sweetness of soul and heart in what she writes. . . . Other writers . . . write with a great deal of sensitivity whose own lives are tormented . . . Dylan Thomas, for example. . . . I think spirituality is much more mysterious [and paradoxical] than we ordinarily think. And these days a lot of people who want to become spiritual . . . see it as going into higher education. You get out of one grade and you go to the next and get a diploma of some kind. I think that real spiritual development . . . may take the form of just being clubbed time after time, of being done in to life. . . . When one gives over to one's fate and you may not go by all the steps of enlightenment and meditation, you may not look like a spiritual teacher, and nobody would want to follow you perhaps, and, yet, at the same time, what you write then may be of more value and ultimately much more full of spirituality than the work of someone who has accomplished a great deal in the usual spiritual approaches and methods.

Bradshaw: "Can you cultivate and develop spirituality in writing?" The only thing that I know you can do is to start writing. And you've got to write realizing that you're going to probably not use a great deal of what you write, but that writing itself engenders the spirit . . . a creative process. . . . You're thinking a different way as your hand touches the paper, the pen, the typewriter, or whatever. And that creativity is the activity, in my belief, that is most spiritual because it's the most God-like. We say in all our creeds, "I believe in God, the *creator* of heaven and earth." And yet we have religions

Sounds very Elbow-en. Boy we should really try to get him to write something for us. Or maybe do an interview.

and churches that try to make people into obedient conformists. Whereas *creators* do new things; they don't conform to old things. [As a creator] I write everything I do by hand. I write all my books by hand. I'm not telling anyone else they need to do that. But there's something that keeps me in contact.

Dossey: I believe that there is some dimension of consciousness that is nonlocal, that is unbounded in space and time and, as such, there is at some dimension of the psyche only one mind. For the writer, there are profound implications for this view. If you believe that there is at some level of the psyche only one mind, and if this mind is infinite in space and time, then the writer doesn't originate, doesn't create ideas. (Citing the views of the Russian writer A.K. Tolstoi that ideas are invisible though ageless and everpresent, Dossey discussed the variety of artists seeing themselves as creators.) I believe ideas are infinite. They are timeless. I think that there are a lot of writers who aren't going to like this idea because it isn't very flattering to the idea of creativity. In other words, it goes beyond the idea that you are a creative writer. *Creative writing* becomes an oxymoron. Furthermore, if you take the idea of nonlocal mind seriously, how do they know whom to award the Pulitzer and the Nobel prizes in literature to? Who is the creator? What's the dynamic? What's the ecology of ideas? So, for me, writing is simply learning to function as a conduit for ideas that are already out there. I think that we have about as much wisdom as the human race has ever had or will have. I think that the job of the writer is to tap into this source . . . there's a tremendous amount of arrogance with this idea that the writer is creator, the writer is originator, and so on. I wouldn't try to argue anybody out of that point of view, but as I try to explain in my work, I think that there's a tremendous amount of empirical evidence that the mind is indeed nonlocal. If people took this seriously, it could give us a whole new idea about the writer's function.

Foehr: Tom, you discuss this concept at some length in an article you wrote for the forthcoming collection I am editing, *The Writer as Hero: Archetypes, Creativity, and the Unconscious.*

Moore: Well, I guess, a few minutes ago I hesitated to use the word *self-expression* because I don't really imagine writing as self-expression. The word *self* is too small for me. . . . Sure, they're there [the ideas]. They're always there. They're in nature for one thing. I love the idea of the Christian monks, that the world is a book. It's really in a sense the first book and all of us who write simply plagiarize from that book. It's all there, we're all reading what we see.

Everyone who writes is reading what you see out there. It's already written. . . . I think in writing I find as I start something, what I am doing is tracing what I am seeing, like figure drawing. You write something that preexists. That's a very platonic way of looking at the thing, that it exists already and it's alive and has a soul and heart and a body. It is alive, like an animal, in that sense. And so what I am doing is bringing that animal into a certain form of existence. I'm letting it show itself, but it has existed already in some way. Plato says that all knowledge is reminiscence, you know, it's a remembering, and in that way what I am doing is that I see myself as a sort of Platonist writer.

Foehr: How do you deal with writer's block?

Moore: If I feel stuck when writing, I'll play Bach or Mozart on the piano, and I find a better attitude.

Dossey: I have no concept of writer's block and I think that that's a terribly destructive idea, as a matter of fact. I think of writer's block, and these problems that writers perennially struggle with and describe, as usually a function of not honoring the life of the writing itself. You cannot force it to happen. It's not the writing's fault. It's not the ideas that are out there. It's that you are trying to impose your own ego, your own will, on something that really should be honored as having a life of its own. D. H. Lawrence once wrote a poem called "Blank" about this very idea. He wrote this poem when he was suffering from an inability to write, and he decided to honor being blank. He said, "Am I Blank? Yes. Very well, I will continue to be blank until something comes along and shows me that I am not blank any longer." That's a paraphrase of Lawrence, but the idea is that we'd best cooperate, not try to tell the universe what to do, whether it's in our own lives or in our writing. So, again, it's a view of writing as a kind of natural state. It's nothing to achieve or make happen or acquire. *Writing* is letting writing happen.

Bradshaw: So, how do you overcome the blocks to writing? The only thing to do is to write and to realize that probably the most dangerous thing about writing is that once you do put it on paper, there's a tendency to want to guard it and protect it. My sense is it's like nonattachment. It's like the Buddhist virtue of nonattachment. You cannot be attached to your own writing. You've got to be willing to give it up, to take that pencil and slash through line after line of it. When my stuff comes back from the editor, there's a struggle, there's a struggle with me wanting to keep pieces of it. And the way you write it down the first time often gets sealed in your mind, and it sort of takes you on a direction. So you have to write because the writing takes you to new portholes. Doors open up as you write. But you have to also be willing to have the ... the spirituality—the nonattachment—the letting go and rewriting, and the giving up of a whole idea and starting over.

Spiritual Empowerment in Teaching

Foehr: Is the topic of spiritual empowerment appropriate in the classroom? At what levels? How would you suggest fostering it in the teaching of writing?

Bradshaw: Well, that would go back to my point about [having students] just start writing and trust their unconscious. You know far more than you know you know. There are really gifts to be gotten from yourself that you don't even know you have. So you just have to dive in, dive into the stream. And sometimes you'll think you're drowning. Sometimes you'll think, you know, you've got to get back to the shore. That's okay too. More than anything it's trust yourself, but get it that there's depth and there's never been anybody like you, and you're unique and unrepeatable. One of the lines I love is from Hopkins, the Jesuit poet Hopkins says, "What I do is me. For that I came." "What I do is me. For that I came." It's like I came here to be me. There's never been anyone like me.

Moore: Never get caught up in the technicalities of writing that become dominant.... When you talk to people in almost any field, [they say that] when they focus on the technique, they lose something. Leonard Bernstein's students ... [said] he never talked about technique ... but always about the music and how to bring out the expression of the music. I think there is a very good lesson in that. We could make all of our art work more spiritual if we could become less concerned about technique.... Really, it blasts away the mystery that is interent in the work.... We want our language to be so clear ... we wind up writing like *USA Today* ... a few choppy sentences and a short paragraph ... and [we] don't say very much. I think that the spirituality of language is lost in that kind of thing because the emphasis there is full of ego: "I have to understand, and I have to explain in order to be successful." The spiritual world is one in which you address mystery all around us and you honor that mystery. You realize the limits of our own human efforts and personal efforts. Therefore, what you do is simply try to evoke the richness and the fullness of the mystery that you are approaching, whatever it is ... and I see no reason why we can't do what people did in Renaissance times, which was to write books on technical matters that were very poetic and full of spirituality.

Foehr: Did any of your teachers affect your sense of inspiration or empowerment as a writer, either positively or negatively?

Bradshaw: I remember the first essay I wrote at a university; it came back with this big red cross across it and the phrase *Wads of hogwash.* And even if the teacher had explained why, [it would have been] a distraction of energy; it was not energy being used well for my creative project. *Wads of hogwash* is just shaming. I remember that I grabbed that paper; I remember turning it over. I didn't want anyone else to see it. And it certainly doesn't give you the permission to keep creating. . . . But that professor certainly did not help or empower me in spiritual empowerment; he curtailed me. . . . After that, I just never said anything that the text wouldn't say and stayed very conservative and very frightened of him and his criticism. And I did okay, but in a sense, not my own stuff; I went to a lot of critics. That . . . throws you back into a very conservative codependence.

Dossey: Oh, yes. A woman who had a great influence on my life was a sixth grade teacher of mine. And, actually, it's a good example because it's full of paradox. . . . Most people, most of the kids hated her because she was so demanding . . . and [being] such a disciplinarian that she was . . . they thought [her] a horrible old woman. But I picked up something different from her. This woman practically never smiled. I don't think I ever remember her smiling, but there was something that came from this woman that was like an arrow to my heart. I knew that this woman had a sense of caring about me and how I performed under her tutelage; it was like a laser . . . like a radar beam. And she never, ever said anything like, "You're a bright kid. I'm going to do everything I can to help you achieve, and I'm proud of what you do," that sort of thing. That's not it. There was something that was ineffable. It was certainly invisible. It wasn't obvious in her behavior. . . . She was intimidating. But that quality was there and that's the quality that I'm talking about, some sort of dignity . . . in spite of her harshness, that she just exuded. There was something beyond that. And it's that something beyond that I'm struggling with in terms of vocabulary. I don't know how to describe it. But I think it is the heart of this nonlocal, transpersonal power that teachers can tap into.

Foehr: Why do you think some students saw her as harsh but you saw something beyond that?

Dossey: Every spiritual teacher worth his or her salt confronts the student with this awfully important question, "Who are you?" I mean who is it that's getting their feelings hurt in this transaction? And so, it's part of the game ... to confront the ego ... that wise teachers of whatever sort play with those that come to learn from them.

Foehr: What do you think the benefits are to the student when the teachers do tap into that nonlocal, transpersonal power?

Dossey: The students themselves are empowered ... learning increases one's sense of self-worth. Self-esteem is enhanced. You know you can do it. Because those expectations that you're on the receiving end of are given out, not with meanness really, but with love. And it's the love that comes through. I knew that this woman cared about me and cared very, very deeply. You know, this is paradoxical stuff. It happens not just in the classroom but, as I say, particularly out in monasteries and spiritual centers and so on.

Bradshaw: The whole goal is, Nietzsche said it, "One repays the teacher badly who remains a student only." And that's a slogan [to live by] ... to empower if I've done my job well.

Moore: I'm not sure that students have a context for their writing that makes sense. . . . [Feeling spiritually connected] helps students have a context for what they are doing ... and gives them a vision that is quite big ... more serious ... and far beyond what they get from American media.

Foehr: Do you think spiritual empowerment is being sufficiently tapped in schools today? If not, why not?

Moore: I don't know what's happening at the grammar and high school levels. From my own children's experience, it appears to me that preschool and kindergarten children in some places are being encouraged to trust their own individual resources and talents. My experience of higher education was just the opposite. The most serious problem we have is our devotion to the scientific method, defined in modern terms, and in its accompanying technology. [Academicians believe they must] give you all these numbers and do tests and count heads and prove that what they are saying is right. But what poets can prove that what they've just said is right? ... the result is that the academic style of life is again full of worry about "Can I prove what I just said?" and "Can I stand in front of my peers and say, 'This is right because I have quoted the right number of authors or I've quoted the right studies'?" So that part of the academic world, I think, is largely defensive ... [and characterized by] battles ... a rather savage environment in some respects. I'm not complaining about science and technology as such, but rather our overestimation of these quantifying, reductive, experimental approaches to human experience.

Dossey: No, I don't. I think teachers could do a good deal more. I think educators, and people who design curricula, could be a good deal more courageous in promoting spirituality. And I certainly want to make a distinction between promoting spirituality versus religiosity. I am much against the conduct of religious rituals in schools. But I am much in favor of doing something ritually to promote a sense of the spiritual. An example would be having a period of silence where kids could be quiet, turn inward, turn outward, turn upside-down, whatever they want to do to honor their sense of the spiritual. But I certainly don't favor using any formal religious invocation or prayer because when you do that, somebody's religion always gets left out, at best, or trampled and put down, at worst.

Moore: In order to include a spiritual element in education, we would have to become more comfortable with mystery, poetry, contemplation, intuition, and a host of other open-ended approaches to experience.

Foehr: How could teachers promote spiritual empowerment?

Bradshaw: By encouraging and always validating what the child has done well, that you can *honestly* give them data on, not just saying "Oh, that was good," but telling them something in their work that you liked. We sometimes don't know when it's good. To have a respected, revered teacher stroking you for what you do well, that is a kind of a higher power. (For Bradshaw, shaming a person is the surest way to stifle creativity. He did not address specifically the problem of careless, disinterested writing among secondary or college students, but believes that "having children write as soon as it's possible and then really focusing on what they did well, even saying, "Here's what I liked about your story. You don't have to say anything else" encourages creativity. He bases this belief upon clinical experiments he and a colleague conducted on behavior modification. "Our premise was that you only point out to them what they do well, and it was unbelievable to watch what would happen to these people in six or eight weeks when all you did was point out what they do well.")

Dossey: I think teachers could be much more effective in promoting spiritual empowerment if they were in touch with their own transpersonal, nonlocal consciousness. There's this overwhelming emphasis, though, that all information has to be delivered through sensory means—speaking, writing, that kind of thing. But if a teacher were really in touch with the nonlocal, transpersonal aspects of one's own consciousness, he or she could realize that there are ways to convey information that go totally beyond the spoken word or any kind of sensory transmission whatsoever. This for me would be a very exciting part of being a teacher. I think that one can transmit to students or to anyone in the world a sense of caring, a sense of empathy, love, and compassion that really have very powerful effects. They certainly are operative in healing and changing the state of the physical body, in my judgment. If a teacher saw a student having trouble, he or she could try, and I'm using this word in a very broad sense, try to heal that student of those troubles by sending compassion, caring, empathy, and so on. In other words, there is a quality, or capacity, I should say, in all people to be distant healers, to try to help those who are in trouble, whether that trouble may be a learning disability, a problem grasping a concept, or an actual physical illness. In order to activate that kind of power, however, one needs really to understand that there are things you can do that go beyond touching, talking, writing, spelling, and all of that kind of stuff. So teachers in order to actualize these talents and abilities really need some sort of spiritual awareness; they need to be in touch with their own spirituality, with who they are as human beings. This presents a requisite of spiritual maturity for the teacher. . . . When they can grow as individuals and human beings and learn how to implement these qualities and abilities in their lives, it's those kinds of teachers that we refer to as the really great teachers we come in contact with. And those are the kinds of teachers who have the ability to change kids' lives.

Role of the Unconscious and of Others in Inspiration

Foehr: What role does the unconscious play in inspiration?

Bradshaw: You must just get started writing and trust that your unconscious knows things that you don't even know you know.

Foehr: What is the role of others in your sense of spiritual empowerment? For example, does collaboration have an effect upon your writing? What about the works you read? Do they affect your own sense of empowerment?

Moore: Writing is a passion. One has to be passionate about something in order to write about it. That passion, of course, has to be coupled with craft and art. I find collaborations enticing but difficult, because the passions may not be moving in the same direction, and the art element is so individual. [Yet, I collaborate] all the time—in different ways. . . . I collaborate with my literary agent . . . getting ideas and feedback. I have this very small number of friends that I can send pieces of a manuscript to, and they send me their writing.

That kind of collaborating is absolutely essential . . . but for me . . . it's not possible to create a work of art with someone else on an equal footing. I find support and direction—guidance, really— from all the arts [e.g., playing Bach or Mozart on the piano]. I think it's important to read good writers and avoid bad ones.

Dossey: Well, when it comes to writing, I really am a lone wolf. I cannot collaborate with cowriters. Frequently, people will approach me and want to "do a book together." I haven't the slightest idea how I would ever manage to do that. Writing is such a solitary activity for me that to cowrite a book is incomprehensible. Plus, I view writing basically as a spiritual activity and a spiritual path. And since spiritual paths probably are different for every human being, it's unclear to me how I could cowrite anything with anyone else. I think we just need to do our spiritual work, in many ways, alone; it is a solitary, personal issue, and, for me, writing is part of that category because, for me, it is a spiritual activity.

Bradshaw: Well, I've never written a book with other people, but in a sense their works have influenced my writing. For example, two manuscripts came to me when I was writing *Creating Love.* One of the manuscripts was called *Trances People Live,* by Steven Wolinski. It gave me a whole new way to look at what Freud called the ego defenses. And I could experience my own dissociation and my own sensory numbing and my own age regressions in my life as an adult. And so that became a way for me to see in a fresh new way. Then I took Ronald Lang's term *mystification* and expanded it, and then did this whole thing on "mystified love." . . . Then from Thomas Moore's manuscript *Care of the Soul,* [I incorporated "soulful love"]. . . . And then came Scott Peck's concept from *The Road Less Traveled,* that love is work. I don't quite like "love as work" because it has a puritanical sort of connotation. So my sense was to write a book titled *Creating Love.* And so the works of those three people [Peck, Moore, and Wolinski] were enormous helps to me.

Foehr: Tom, in your experience, what kinds of writing invite a sense of spiritual empowerment? For example, is there a difference in your writing when you write a magazine article for someone else versus your own writing?

Moore: All writing can have a spiritual dimension—letters, magazine articles, books. The soul is involved more, it seems to me, in the small things than in the larger. I write for a magazine in Leche [Italy]. . . . I [also] write a column for an Episcopal magazine, even though I'm not Episcopalian . . . something like a thousand words . . . and for other magazines . . . with suggested themes . . . and space. I like being given a theme and [a word limit]. Then I don't have to think about them. In fact, when I write my own books, I do that to myself. I usually immediately write out a table of contents, and I immediately give myself a limited number of pages. I find it much easier to write that way than in any sense of free form. That would be the most difficult for me.

Personal Experience: Mystery, Meditation, and Suffering[8]

Foehr: Larry, you have obviously earned the respect of others for leadership in medicine as a prolific scientific writer, journal executive editor, and practicing physician of internal medicine. Yet, as a scholar and scientist you have taken some big risks, particularly in the direction of your latest books *Healing Words,* and *Prayer is Good Medicine* with discussions of numerous scientific studies on the power of prayer and healing. You address the mystery that defies what medicine and the conscious mind can explain. For you, how does writing compare to prayer? Do you see any correlations between the mystery of prayer and the mystery of writing?

Dossey: Actually I do. I think that . . . one of the greatest ways of praying is to step aside, set the ego aside, and try not to tell the universe what to do. You honor its dignity, you honor the fact that there's a tremendous amount of information out there, that the universe is pretty smart, and that you don't need really to give it marching orders every step of the way. Writing for me is the same process. . . . If you want to tap into that, you also need to get out of the way and align and somehow set the stage in your own being for that to manifest through your pen or your word processor.

Foehr: And you Tom?

Moore: I was in a religious order that was half monastic and half very active in the world. I lived that life for a long time. And part of that life was to realize [that] our work—reading, writing, things like that—are a part of the daily spiritual life. So, to me, I don't even think twice that writing is a spiritual activity. . . . It's obvious that writing is a contemplative thing. You can't write unless you can contemplate. You have to reflect. And then . . . if people read your writing, there is . . . community. When I travel, in relation to my books especially, I discover a community and that . . . I'm part of it, and my words are part of it. Community, too, is part of the spiritual life.

8. This section explores writers' personal spiritual practice of Dossey, Moore, and Bradshaw in their own work. It do not believe, however, that it should be interpreted as an endorsement for incorporating prayer or trance states in the classroom.

Foehr: Can you see any implications for teachers or writers?

Dossey: Teaching, like medicine, like almost every other thing we try to learn as human beings, is just smothered with injunctions. The important thing is to learn how to be in the world, how to attune to the universe, and how to set the small self, the *ego*, aside so that you can avail yourself of some of the wisdom that this universe holds and has to offer, regardless of the concrete task you're trying to pursue. I look forward to the time when medical schools teach us to do nothing, to sit down and be quiet. You can call that meditation, or contemplation, or twiddling your thumbs. But it basically is learning to step aside and *not do*, and learning how to align with inner wisdom, and so on. I hope teachers are someday taught to do this. I can't imagine any occupation where this would not be valuable. People growing up in this culture are fighting an uphill battle when it comes to this kind of wisdom, however, because our culture is terribly extroverted. It's aggressive by nature. It is a "go get 'em" type society. It's a society where we say you've got to make it happen. And this robust, cowboy-type attitude, unfortunately, has infected every profession I'm aware of, including teaching.

Foehr: John, you mentioned the trance state in your recent book *Creating Love*. Do you see any application for using trance experiences in writing?

Bradshaw: I think writing itself is a trance experience . . . [as in] classic hypnosis where you stare at the pendulum or the pencil or you stare at the wall. When you're writing, you go into an altered state. The very act of writing focuses your eyes on the paper, on the words that you have written. That narrowing of your ordinary consciousness then opens you up to . . . what all spiritual traditions and many psychological traditions believe, that we have a higher self, that is, a self that is not as limited by space and time as what we would call the "adapted self" or the "ego" or the "surviving self." The ego part of me is like a flashlight; the higher-self part of me is like a floodlight. So if I can take the flashlight and focus it so that it's not distracting me—in other words, I'm not . . . popping from idea to idea, filled with anxiety—as when you're threatened—and my mind is focused, then it opens me up to that larger consciousness, or what I'm calling the unconsciousness, which is really not unconscious. It's stuff you know that at this moment you don't know that you know. And so I think that quietening, any kind of quietening exercise might be a good prelude to writing.

Foehr: In your own writing process, do you spend time in meditation before or during writing?

Moore: Before I write, I [need] . . . reflection . . . [and] quiet . . . to think, to gather thoughts, and to let things happen and to arrive at a place where I'm receptive to ideas and to words. So that in itself makes it a spiritual activity.

Dossey: Meditation has become such an integral part of my life that . . . I don't feel any longer as if I have to concentrate on meditation specifically before I write. I think that it's just sort of gotten into my bone and blood by now.

Foehr: How did that come about?

Dossey: I used to fiddle with meditation as an experiment. I did it for a couple of reasons. . . . It just had the ring of common sense to me. First, I was impressed by the fact that some of the wisest people throughout history have recommended it. That's not for nothing right there. Also, there was some connection with biofeedback. I had terrible migraine headaches, which I no longer have, and I, for my own good, figured that I needed to learn how to turn off my rational mind . . . the evidence [showed] that [it] was a good thing for migraine headaches. I did this for so long, and so many years, that it sort of became a part of my nature.

Foehr: Did you study Zen or transcendental meditation [TM]?

Dossey: I never took anybody's course. I read as much as I could get my hands on, of the literature of the Orient, particularly Zen Buddhism. And I was tremendously impressed by the sanity of the Buddhist point of view, and it's still very precious to me. But, not just Buddhism, the mysticism, the esoteric tradition from Christianity and the religions to the West also are important. I see them forming a kind of seamless whole, really. But, I have just been permeated by this attitude: pondering, stepping aside and doing nothing, and entering what's variously been called "the void," you know, "the greatness," those kinds of things.

Foehr: You mention migraine headaches, and in *Healing Words* you mention your back problems. Can you see any correlations between suffering and effective writing?

Dossey: Yes. Looking back on my own life, I finished some of the most difficult areas of the book *Recovering the Soul* when I was in bed, flat on my back, unable to walk, with horrible pains from a ruptured disc. That for me is a huge paradox and a mystery I don't fully understand. It's as if the suffering somehow opened some flood gates of understanding that were just wonderful. My wife rigged a word processor by a bedside table, which I could swing over my bed. So, suffering is somehow connected with productive writing, although I'm not sure I know how that works. Having said that, however, I certainly don't think it's necessary as a writer to suffer in order to be productive. I'm not much on this suffering writer image. . . . I certainly don't think that suffering is essential to the writing task.

Writing in Clinical Psychology[9]

Foehr: In your work as a clinical psychologist or counselor, can you tell us about ways you have observed the phenomenon of spiritual empowerment through writing with people you are counseling?

Dossey: Writing is clinically proven to be the most effective single thing to help people with the healing process. The reason for that is that the writing focuses the work, serves as a way to clarify a feeling.

Moore: Writing letters carefully—or journals, diaries, and even books— can be a form of spiritual practice. It all depends on the attitude one assumes when writing. I've noticed that when people are going through challenging times, their writing takes on an urgency and importance it doesn't have at other times. A person has to write as though life itself were at stake, as Rilke said in *Letters to a Young Poet.*

Bradshaw: Well, it's the single best way to clarify feelings . . . even years later. For example, with all the work with posttraumatic stress disorder, incest survivors, trauma survivors, people who are severely shame-based, we'll do twenty to thirty weeks of having people come to the group with a written episode, something they remember that happened to them. And we say, "You cannot fail with detail." If individuals write the traumatic scene out, even years later, they can connect with the feelings . . . although when it was happening, the person probably just went into . . . dissociation, just going up on the ceiling and looking at the cobwebs or sensory numbing. Sensory numbing [occurs when] . . . you just numb out so you can't feel the onslaught that's coming at you . . . a kind of trance survival technique. What the person didn't *then* have available to them was the *actual experience*, the *awareness* of having fear, terror, hurt, sadness, and then anger that someone would treat them like this. Writing that down, the very focus of the writing [clarifies feelings].

9. The following discussion demonstrates the power of writing as it is used in other disciplines, specifically in group therapy. I do not believe, however, that it should be interpreted as an endorsement for therapy practices for writing classes or for writing teachers who are not trained therapists.

Foehr: Do you have follow-up activities with this writing?

Bradshaw: Yes, they read that letter or that episode to the group. Not only has the writing helped them to clarify the feeling, sometimes the group—six people—tells them what they were feeling. . . . [For example,] "I was feeling anger when you were reading that." And frequently what that can do is help the person connect with the feeling. . . . And they're saying, "Oh, my God, I can't believe I was feeling all of that." But they were. See, they were feeling all of that while it was happening, although they don't remember it. The writing can focus it.

Foehr: You seem to be affirming not just their writing but their feelings about what they are writing.

Bradshaw: We call it "validation." The other thing we have them do is to . . . write [about the experience] and then read it to me, and I just say, "Well, I can hear how sad you are." This is more my face looking at your face, but what the writing has done is helped to clarify the feelings. It's helped to pinpoint what the feelings were because when they were in the experience, they just had to get out of the feelings.

Foehr: John, in your work, you have written a lot about the importance of one's feelings and dealing with one's feelings. Do you think there is a spiritual dimension to these feelings?

Bradshaw: Yes. I think that our feelings are energy. . . . A feeling is an energy that moves us. If, for example, you were trying to describe . . . , let's say, you believed in the inspiration of the Holy Spirit somehow. How would that inspiration work? How would it move you? Well, there are people who think we are directly encountered by God in our dreams. But I think also . . . that there are body memories that are just feelings that come up in the person's body that actually in some way embody the trauma that was done to them. And I believe that feelings have energy. They pick up on the energy of our life, and they pick up on the energies around us. . . . They are nonlogical ways of knowing, but they are ways of knowing. They are more right-brained ways of knowing . . . that is metric, the rhythm the sound communicates the meaning. The same is true of music . . . the vibrations, the energy vibrations of the sound. Poetry . . . needs to be listened to because the sound communicates the meaning. And how does it do that? It does it through energy. So feelings are also energy. And I think we ought to go with our feelings . . . allow yourself to go with a strong feeling and try to express it, and let the feeling take you wherever it's going to take you. Sometimes when people say, "I have a premonition of something," it's both cognitive and affective. There's some kind of energy that's moving you over toward it. And so I think feelings are very important in writing. Writing our feelings is very important. It helps clarify things for ourselves and others.

Foehr: Many people have difficulty expressing feelings although they feel comfortable working on impersonal topics. How do you think writing teachers can help students to understand the spirituality of their feelings?

Bradshaw: Well, it might be that you could just . . . have a desire for something greater than yourself? How could you have a desire for a higher power if there was no energy there? If there was no emotion, if you were emotionless, if you were just numbed out. In a sense, how could you have desire for anything? One of the vehicles of desire is emotion, and emotion is an inner state. So the spirituality of it is that it is an inner condition. Codependent people can't go inside. Toxicly shamed people have had all their feelings shaped. So if you feel a feeling, you feel shame. So what happens is that you become other-centered to such an obsessive degree that you don't know what's going on inside of you. Well, how can you write anything *that's you* if you can't go inside of you? So your feelings, getting in touch with your feelings are the way that you connect with the inside of you, in your own inner condition, your own inner space. And that's where spirituality is. It's something that's much more about our inner life than it is about our outer life. It can be manifested in our outer life, but "I've got to be in touch with an inner life, where I can be quiet and feel what I'm feeling, and get to that still, quiet place and know what I want and what I desire."

Concluding Thoughts

Foehr: What are the consequences of feeling spiritually empowered in writing? If you were not spiritually empowered in your writing, how would your life and world be different?

Dossey: Well, I've tried it both ways. And I much prefer this one. It's a heck of a lot easier. The mind seems to flow and it's a lot more fun. There's a sense of, once again, going with something and not trying to push [against] the river. And I'm much more productive as well from this perspective. Things happen in a joyful, bountiful way. Life seems to work.

Bradshaw: Well, it's given me a great deal of confidence in trusting my inner experience. Writing about my experience when I wrote *Bradshaw on the Family*, and having people [identify personally with] this very bad experience—addiction, codependency, shame, and getting well—gave me a lot of confidence to talk about *other* parts of my experience. It's as if it opened up so much more to believe and trust—that my *positive* experience was also okay. And maybe a lot of people who haven't gone through victimization or had a lot of pain in their life don't have to go through any of that. Telling your story and having people say, "Oh, that's wonderful," when you thought it was terrible, gives *you* the experience. And that's why I think that it's very important for people to write and have it validated.

Moore: I would have to find some way to manifest my own soul and my submission of the world that I see. . . . Writing and making music do that in a way that is very important. I need to be involved in music everyday. I got here to this office this morning in a snowstorm; the first thing I did was play Francis Poulenc on the piano, before I did anything. And sometimes when I am under a terrific deadline, I'll still stop to play the piano. I have friends who find that in sports.

Foehr: With what thoughts concerning spiritual empowerment would you want to leave your audience?

Moore: Whatever they imagine spiritual empowerment to be . . . they are going to have to discover . . . something that is about the opposite of probably what they expect. Their expectations might be turned around and reversed. And that's natural to any spiritual activity. I think it's almost the role of the spiritual traditions to turn everything on its head—all of our expectations. Certainly the Zen teacher does that, the Sufi stories and poetry do, the Buddhist stories and teachings do. In a sense it is like the monks say, you have to have a contempt of the world. They didn't mean that you didn't love the world or that you don't love your life, but there is a way in which you do not accept the expectations and the standards of the world around you. And I think that's a very, very important part of this, because as I look around these days, whenever I see spirituality being discussed, its very rare that I find very real humility in it. I find a huge amount of ambition . . . to find the best teacher . . . to know the truth and to tell other people the truth. . . . [But] it's only when you are filled with paradox about it that you discover what power is. If you read the *Tao te Ching,* all that I am saying will be spelled out, that it's exactly in the lowly place that you find the sense of power. It's when you have failed that you discover the meaning of success, or what it means to succeed—that ambitions are met when you have finally reached a point where all your ambitions have been exploded, and they don't mean anything anymore. When the answers to your questions show that your questions are the wrong questions in the first place. It's that kind of taking apart—the deconstruction of one's own spirituality, spiritual expectations, I think—that . . . happens when you're really

Power / Powerless
12·5 hp
paradox.

being spiritually empowered, and it's a lifelong process, so that you never get to the point where you can say, "I'm now empowered," and that's fine. Because that's where the power is, in knowing that you don't have it.

Dossey: I would suggest that people stop looking for formulas on how to become "spiritually empowered." We have become bewitched with *doing* and not *being*. And until we see through the folly of that, then we will forever be divorced from our innate, inherent spiritual power. The formula really is more of a doing less, not more. It's getting back to knowing who you really are. It's discarding all the things that keep you from understanding your innate spiritual power that's there already. Rather than devising clever ways of acquiring power, spiritual power that you [think you] don't have, . . . you've already got more than you could use. The task is to allow it to manifest. That's basically what I would suggest.

Bradshaw: "To your own self be true." I've learned this after thirty years of being a counselor. The more we can trust ourselves, the more we can go deeper into ourselves. But be docile, I mean be open to soul, and know that we don't know anything really. We don't know the final line on anything. So I'm open to every teacher that comes along. Every viewpoint has something to say to me. I'm open to that, but I must be true to myself. That's what I'd say.

Part Two

Eastern and Navajo Spirituality

Non-Western approaches to spirituality can open new vistas for the creation of meaning and for understanding perspectives that differ from those traditionally defining Western culture and learners. As the essays in this section reveal, these cultures can offer knowledge, wisdom, and value systems not only affecting teaching and learning but also leading to harmony within the individual and in the world.

Combining perspectives of Eastern philosophy and quantum physics, William S. Haney offers a philosophy of the self that informs the art of reading. He postulates that the gaps between conflicting theories cannot be theorized; that they "comprise a nontheoretical, nonlogical, or spiritual dimension that is basic to literature but rarely fathomed by students on the level of a direct experience of the self"; that the self cannot be fashioned through intellectual activity because it depends on the direct experience of the fundamental unity of consciousness—the "unity [that] characterizes the silence of the gaps between contending theories."

Herbert Benally explains the Navajo way of knowing and why Western education does not make the same sense to the Navajo as it does to the Western mind. For the Navajo, all knowledge, learning, and life itself are spiritual; all are interconnected parts of a sacred whole. Discussing their implications for Western educational practices, Benally presents the source of Navajo knowledge; the nature of Navajo identity; the spiritual, mental, and emotional endowments of human beings and their relationship to the universal order; and the process of internalizing principles implicit in the universal order to achieve the Blessing Way, a state of "much good, peaceful, beautiful, and harmonious life."

The last writer in this section, Donald R. Gallehr, invites the reader along on the spiritual journey that took him from personal meditation practices, through Eastern meditation philosophies, to using meditation practices in his writing classes; his students solve Zen koans—puzzling questions to bring about enlightenment in their writing. He offers a prolific and informative annotated bibliography for those interested in learning more about Eastern philosophies.

But spiritual traditions are only partly about the discovery of self. They're also about "self" as an illusion. About transcending ego, becoming one with the universe.

6

The Role of Eastern Philosophy and Quantum Physics in Literary Criticism

William S. Haney II

Gerald Graff argues that we should teach students the conflicts between contending theories rather than present our particular perspective as the final truth: "In teaching any text, one necessarily teaches an interpretation of it . . . what literature teachers teach is not literature but criticism, or literature as it has been filtered through a grid of analysis, interpretation, and theory" (1994, 42). As the rhetorical power of language replaces the correspondence theory of truth, universal wisdom gives way to conflicting theories and the indeterminacy of meaning. What each of these conflicting theories has in common are the gaps between them that cannot be theorized. These gaps comprise a nontheoretical, nonlogical, or spiritual dimension that is basic to literature but rarely fathomed by students on the level of a direct experience of the self. In the postmodern era, indeterminacy and the decentered subject replace the classical certainties of truth and self. As a result, the spiritual empowerment of students through a development of the self in the classroom is conspicuous only by its absence. Because spiritual empowerment through a realization of the self is not in the same category as the contending theories that Graff would have us teach, it cannot be developed through intellectual analysis. While indispensable to literary studies, theoretical understanding cannot replace the spiritual empowerment that accrues through the direct experience of the fundamental unity of consciousness. This unity characterizes the silence of the gaps between contending theories.

Spiritual empowerment, which depends on the realization of the self as unbounded consciousness, is a process of developing the observer and increasing the integration between the observer, the observed, and the process of observation. Despite the claims by deconstructive postmodernists regarding the finitude and fragmentation of the self, truth, and language,

71

without a pedagogical method for the development and integration of the observer as unbounded consciousness, the current focus in the classroom on the text as an object of observation will remain incomplete and increasingly frustrating for the student.

Although deconstructive postmodernism has pointed out the limits of language and consciousness, it has been unable to go beyond these limits, except to argue, as Lyotard does, that "demystification is an endless task," a "permanent revolution" (quoted in Gablik 1991, 26). This endless revolution claims to subvert the intuitive experience of unity with the notion of difference. As an alternative to deconstruction, a reconstructive postmodernism has emerged in the work of Suzi Gablik, David Michael Levin, Harold Coward, Dana Zohar, and others. The reconstructive approach emphasizes what Gablik calls an "aesthetics of interconnectedness, social responsibility and ecological attunement" (Gablic 1991, 22). This holistic paradigm defines consciousness and language, subject and object in terms derived from both quantum physics and Eastern philosophy. From the viewpoint of quantum unified field theory and nondual Vedanta,[1] subject and object comprise a unified whole. The observer, process of observation, and observed are integrated in such a way that the observer is "a codetermining factor in the reality producing process," not just a spectator (Gablik 1991, 22). As Nobel Laureate Ilya Prigogine states, "Whatever we call reality, it is revealed to us only through an active construction in which we participate" (quoted in Zohar 1991, 29).

Constructing the world from our beliefs and intentions draws upon our creative intelligence, which like any form of energy is more powerful at its source. The source of creativity can be understood in terms of the source of thought, or the gap between thoughts, found in what Dana Zohar calls the quantum self, the unified field of consciousness. As Zohar emphasizes, the quantum unified field, being a state of perfect coherence, is also found in biological tissues and, indeed, "*is what distinguishes the conscious from the non-conscious*" (1991, 67–68, Zohar's italics). By experiencing the inner coherence of the quantum self, one gains a greater capacity to create order out of the world's chaos and confusion and "to pluck reality from multiple possibility . . . to make experimental worlds, some of which will be improvements on the last" (1991, 183). If this level of the observer were developed more in our schools and colleges, not only would students gain in spiritual

---

1. Vedanta is one of the six systems of Indian philosophy, which include Nyaya, Vaisheshika, Yoga, Samkhya, and Mimamsa. As Dasgupta notes, "Vedanta means 'end of the Veda,' i.e., the Upanishads, and *Vedanta Sutras* are so called as they are but a summarized statement of the general views of the Upanishads" (Dasgupta 1988, 70). Whereas the other systems investigate "the objective truth of things or our attitude in practical life towards them . . . Vedanta sought to reach beneath the surface of appearances, and inquired after the final and ultimate truth underlying the microcosm and macrocosm, the subject and object" (Dasgupta 1988, 439).

empowerment, but the world they create would gain in "aesthetic interconnectedness, social responsibility, and ecological attunement" (Gablick 1991, 22). Keith Wallace, one of the early researchers on the physiology of consciousness, finds that by developing the quantum self or higher states of consciousness, we become aware of "pure consciousness as the field underlying everything we encounter through our senses in the world around us. Our nervous system then constructs for us a reality far richer, more delightful and fulfilling than the one we were accustomed to when the classical viewpoint dominated our sensory experience" (Wallace 1993, 11).

The endless task of demystification from the classical, ordinary states of consciousness continues because it seems effective and is fairly easy to implement. All you need is an object of observation, such as a text, either from high art or popular culture, and a particular theory—both of which are in plentiful supply in an economy of supply and demand. As far as the observer is concerned, it is easier to decenter the subject and subvert transcendentality than to investigate the self beyond its illusory fragments and logical misconceptions. That is, since the self as transcendental consciousness has not been readily available to direct experience, its very existence has been put in question by an approach to knowledge that dwells on the contextual, interpretive, and metaphorical dimension of language. This epistemological stance derives largely from the tradition of Western philosophy, which has never discovered an effective means of integrating the two faculties of rationality and intuition. Western metaphysics itself depends on intellectual analysis or blind faith. It lacks the systematic and practical means of investigating the self both subjectively and objectively that are found in Eastern Philosophies.

As a tradition that highlights the self and its role in constructing the world we live in, Eastern philosophy as a whole and Vedanta in particular have much to offer the West in terms of developing a pedagogy of spiritual empowerment. If the implementation of this philosophy in Asian society leaves something to be desired, its basic principles are upheld by recent discoveries in modern science, particularly by quantum physics. In this paper I propose a methodology of spiritual empowerment based on Vedanta and supported by quantum mechanics. This proposal models itself not on the subjectivist views of writers on quantum physics such as Fritjof Capra (1982, 77), who holds that the individual self is the only source of "value" and that the sole "truth" in the world is based on one's perspective, but rather on the notion of the coexistence of subject and object found in the nondual Vedanta[2] of Sri Shankara, one of India's most popular philosophers. In pro-

2. Nondual or advaita Vedanta refers to the earliest commentary of the Vedanta, that of Shankara. It is nondual because it holds that the subject and object are united, that unity is the ultimate reality. As Dasgupta explains, the main idea of Shankara's nondual Vedanta is "that the ultimate and absolute truth is the self, which is one, though appearing as many in different individuals. The world also as apart from us the individuals has no other truth to show than this self.

viding a theoretical framework for spiritual empowerment in terms of consciousness, I will interpret spiritual empowerment as being synonymous with self-empowerment, with the self being understood as pure, unbounded consciousness. In so doing I will point out some of the many ways in which spiritual empowerment relates to literary studies and the project of reconstructive postmodernism and suggest how it complements the underlying tenets of deconstructive postmodernism.

Philosophy and the Self

Beyond the three ordinary states of waking, sleep, and dream, the existence of the self as the fourth state of transcendental consciousness (*savikalpa samadhi*) and its corresponding physiological state is so well documented by Eastern philosophy and modern scientific research that it hardly bears reviewing in the present limited space. Shankara, reputed to have lived five thousand years ago, has written a popular version of his nondual Vedanta (end of the Veda) in *Vivekacudamani*, which the contemporary Indian philosopher Surendranath Dasgupta provides a thorough commentary on in *A History of Indian Philosophy*, volumes One and Two. Harold Coward contrasts Shankara to Derrida in a book that warrants reading by anyone interested in literary theory, *Derrida and Indian Philosophy*. Over the past twenty years, Shankara's principles of self-development have been implemented at an experimental university in Fairfield, Iowa: Maharishi International University of Management (MUM), which integrates a conventional academic curriculum with research into consciousness through the Transcendental Meditation (TM) technique and the TM-Sidhi program.[3] In a significant way, MUM provides a model for spiritual empowerment in pedagogy by providing students with a practical means for directly experiencing the self as transcendental consciousness and then relating this experience of the self to academic knowledge in such a way that all knowledge becomes a living reality and thus provides the basis for success in action. Although the self and spirituality can be approached in different ways, the basic principles of consciousness and language found in Indian philosophy and corroborated by quantum physics are essential for any method of spiritual empowerment.

All other events, mental or physical, are but passing appearances, while the only absolute and unchangeable truth underlying them all is the self" (Shankara 1988, 439).

3. This university was founded in Santa Barbara, California, in 1971 by Marharishi Mahesh Yogi, originally called Maharishi International University, and relocated to Fairfield, Iowa, in 1974. By integrating objective and subjective epistemologies, the university curriculum attempts to maximize students' development of the self in the study of all traditional disciplines. MUM offers a wide range of B.A., M.A., and Ph.D. programs, including an M.A. in English and an M.A. in Professional Writing. For more information, contact MUM, FB 1147, Fairfield, IA 52557, tel. (515) 472–5031.

While the issue of self-empowerment has already been taken up by reception theorists and reader-response critics in reaction to the overemphasis on the text in Russian formalism and new criticism, these approaches do not account for the self in all its aspects. Even phenomenology, as a science of subjectivity underlying reader-response theories, fails to restore the transcendental subject by making it accessible to direct experience or by defending it against charges of subjectivism by deconstruction. The "linguistic revolution" made it seem as if meaning for phenomenological criticism was something that predated language when, in fact, as Saussure and Wittgenstein had demonstrated, meaning is not reflected in language but produced by it. From the perspective of a reconstructive postmodernism based on Vedanta and quantum physics as proposed here, Husserlian phenomenology was on the right track. It lacked only a systematic understanding of the levels of consciousness and their corresponding levels of language, as found in the ancient tradition of Indian philosophy.

On the one hand, for deconstructive postmodernism, the subject—caught within the boundaries of space and time and causality described by classical physics—consists only of the ordinary waking state of consciousness and is, therefore, never able to generate meaning from the depths of transcendental consciousness, which deconstruction, of course, regards as an illusion. On the other hand, for reconstructive postmodernism, the subject, while forming part of a network of social relations, consists also of an unbounded level of consciousness in which knower and known, subject and object are united. At this level meaning does not predate language; rather, meaning and language are coterminous in their most unbounded states. The first requirement for spiritual empowerment in pedagogy, then, is the incipient understanding that the subject is not a product of materialism but an unbounded reservoir of creativity capable of operating from a level within itself where matter and spirit, body and mind are integrated and where language consists of a unity of sound and meaning, sign and referent. The second requirement is a practical means to realize the fullest potential of the self through direct experience.

If the spirit-based pedagogy introduced here in terms of Vedanta seems overly subjective or lacking in theoretical rigor, this is due partly to the bias among Western academics in favor of intellectual analysis over the intuitive sense of a unity-amidst-diversity associated with spirituality and the arts in general. Yet a brief look at Indian literary criticism and philosophy of language, which extends for thousands of years from the Vedas to Panini, Shankara, Bharata, and Bhartrhari, will indicate that this tradition is highly sophisticated and complete (Charkrabarti 1971), combining theoretical understanding and direct practical experience. As we have seen, in addition to the three ordinary states of waking, sleep, and dream, consciousness in Indian philosophy consists of a fourth, transcendental state (*savikalpa samadhi* or *turiya*), with each of these states corresponding to its own physiological condition.

Transcendental consciousness is not a mere abstraction for Indian philosophy as it is for postmodernism. Its reality is depicted in Indian epics such as *The Ramayana* and *The Mahabharata,* which includes *The Bhagavad-Gita.* For instance, *The Bhagavad-Gita* advises one to be "freed from duality, ever / firm in purity, independent of possessions, / possessed of the Self" (Maharishi 1969, 126). Similarly, the *Mandukya Upanishad* defines the ordinary three states plus a fourth state of consciousness, "turiya which is a state of spiritual consciousness" (Radhakrishnan 1989, 695). In describing the self (*atman*) in terms of the highest reality (Brahman), Shankara states that "It is devoid of the trinity of the knower, knowledge and object of knowledge. That is because It is limitless. It is *nirvikalpa,* that is, not admitting varying conceptions. It is pure intelligence only.... The wise know It as the supreme truth. As It is one's own atman [self or soul], It can neither be discarded nor taken up" (Shankara 1988, 255). As Dasgupta explains, the main idea of Shankara's nondual Vedanta philosophy is "that the ultimate and absolute truth is the self, which is one, though appearing as many in different individuals" (1988, 439). In realizing the truth of "That art thou," one "becomes the truth itself, which is at once identical with pure bliss and pure intelligence" (Dasgupta 1988, 439). The practical aspect of these philosophical assertions is the actual experience of transcendental consciousness made available through yogic meditation.[4] Thus while the literature describes the fourth state of consciousness, its ultimate reality is a matter of self-confirmation through the actual experience of transcending. In this way, spiritual empowerment begins with the experience of the self as a field of unity.

The Self from a Scientific Perspective

In addition to its confirmation in ancient texts, the experience of transcending also finds confirmation in objective science. In an analogy increasingly legitimized by modern physicists, transcendental consciousness has been likened to the unified field in quantum mechanics. The field theorist John Hagelin notes that "the proposed identity between pure consciousness and the unified field is consistent with all known physical principles, but requires an expanded physical framework for the understanding of consciousness which leads to a more integrated picture of the physical world and the full range of human experience" (1987, 56). This picture involves a paradigm shift from the classical, mechanistic worldview of Newtonian physics to the quantum mechanical worldview. The quantum paradigm holds that the four fundamental forces of nature—electromagnetism, strong and weak interactions,

4. Yoga (union) is identified with *samadhi,* the "state of consciousness with no subject-object distinction" (Coward, *Sphota* 1980, 151). As Dasgupta writes, "The purpose of yogic meditation is to steady the mind on the gradually advancing stages of thoughts toward liberation" (1988, 270) or *samadhi,* where the self enjoys its eternal and free status as unbounded, pure consciousness.

and gravitation—are united in the unified field at the so-called Planck scale beyond the boundaries of space, time, and causality. As Hagelin states, "If, as particle theorists are inclined to believe, all the laws of nature have their ultimate origin in the dynamics of the unified field, then the unified field must itself embody the total intelligence of nature's functioning" (1987, 58). He also points out that, "according to the Vedic tradition, consciousness is not an emergent property of matter that comes into existence through the functioning of the human nervous system, but is considered fundamental in nature. It is the essential core of life—a vast, unbounded, unified field which gives rise to and pervades all manifest phenomena" (Hagelin 1987, 57). Consciousness is thus equated with the unified field of all the laws of nature.

Pure consciousness as manifested in the unified field of the laws of nature and in human awareness is said to have a three-in-one structure in which the subject and object and the linkage between them are united. This coexistence of opposites in terms of the knower, the known, and the process of knowing at the ground state of both consciousness and objective reality is what Shankara's Vedanta, as mentioned earlier, refers to as the state "devoid of the trinity [difference] of the knower, knowledge and the object of knowledge" (1988, 255). Following in the tradition of Shankara, Maharishi describes this wholeness as "the state of pure knowledge, where knower, known, and knowledge are in the self-referral state ... that all-powerful, immortal, infinite dynamism at the unmanifest basis of creation" (1969, 27). Hagelin, who proposes that an attribute of "self-awareness" can be found in the self-interaction present in the unified field, suggests that "one interpretation of these observations is that the distinction between 'subjectivity' and 'objectivity' becomes less meaningful at microscopic scales" (1987, 59).

An understanding of the inherent power of the self is an important first step for the development of spiritual empowerment through the study of literature. Not only is the self associated with the silence of the gaps between conflicting theories of interpretation, but the metaphorical, suggestive nature of language itself has the effect of alternating the reader's attention between the concrete word and an abstract, some would say, indeterminate meaning. This swing of awareness from the sensible to the intelligible, from the concrete vehicle of a metaphor to its abstract tenor, in effect, takes the reader's awareness from the limitations of the ordinary waking state of consciousness toward the unboundedness of the fourth state of transcendental consciousness (please see Orme-Johnson 1987). The move in literature, therefore, beyond appearances to an unseen, even if undecidable, field of all possibilities is a move toward the quantum self and the benefits of self-empowerment. These benefits include greater richness in one's perception of the world, greater "aesthetic interconnectedness, social responsibility, and ecological attunement" (Gablick 1991, 22). Yet because literature and multiculturalism deal with the imagination and fantasy, postmodernists are tempted to indulge in localized and relativistic theories of truth and meaning. These theories

attempt to subvert the unseen—and politically incorrect—sources of meaning in the "oneness of Being," the universal structures of the self and nature
posited by Vedanta and quantum physics.

In *The Quantum Self,* Zohar develops an extensive and convincing argument for a state of transcendental consciousness on the basis of the new paradigm of quantum physics. She observes that the nonlocal quantum-level
correlations of photons and other elementary particles through which "two
events can be related across time in a way that ensures they will always act
'in tune' [beyond causal relationships] . . . is the basis of all quantum
mechanical relationships, lending a very modern note of support to the pre-
Socratic Greek notion of the 'oneness of Being'" (Zohar 1991, 21). Zohar
argues that the Cartesian worldview is now "barren" and that consciousness
must have a central role in developing an aesthetics of interconnectedness for
a reconstructive postmodernism: "While the soul of modern man cries out for
more, for some sense of being at home in the universe, our reason, too,
demands that we make better sense of our experience. Consciousness is a
fact of that experience, and a philosophy or a science which can't account for
consciousness is a necessarily incomplete philosophy or science" (1991, 35).
As a scientist, Zohar emphasizes that consciousness "has become almost a
home truth to quantum physicists struggling to make some sense of develop-
ments in their own field, but it has yet to percolate into our general intellectual outlook" (1991, 35). A spiritual pedagogy can serve the practical goal of
establishing this intellectual outlook.

Zohar goes on to demonstrate how human consciousness is continuous
with other entities in the universe: "Consciousness and matter arise together
from the same common source—in our terms, from the world of quantum
phenomena" (1991, 73). She does not actually defend a panpsychism, the
notion that conscious beings include inanimate objects like stones or particles, although this notion has been with us since pre-Socratic times in the
One of Parmenides and the divine Flux of Heraclitus (Solomon 1993, 69–
71). She does demonstrate, though, how one kind of basic matter underlies
all things, whether animate or inanimate. On this basis, "at the quantum level
at least there is a creative dialogue between matter and consciousness such
that the observer's conscious mind actually influences the material development of that which he observes" (Zohar 1991, 39-40). Our experience of this
interconnectedness has not been cultivated in the West, which since Plato has
emphasized the rational, analytic side of the brain instead of the intuitive.
Literature is typically associated with intuition, which draws on wisdom,
imagination, and creativity.

Self-Empowerment in the Classroom

Spiritual empowerment can be implemented in the classroom in a practical
way with few modifications in our teaching practices. This facility is due

partly to the fact that students reading literature already experience the expanded states of consciousness and meaning elicited by the text even in a poststructuralist setting. There are two aspects to spiritual empowerment: theoretical and practical, or experiential. In theoretical terms, the coexistence of opposites that characterizes the quantum model, in which "the mental is really a basic property of the material and vice versa" (Zohar 1991, 78), is found in both the deconstructive and the idealist enterprises. Ironically, poststructuralist theories of meaning and subjectivity evince the same unity of opposites found in humanism. In the former case, however, the coexistence of opposites such as mind and body, signifier and signified results in the logical impasse of undecidability or indeterminacy, whereas in the latter it results in an intuitive leap beyond temporal boundaries toward the connectedness of the knower, the known, and the process of knowing. Even if idealist approaches to literature do not adequately heighten awareness of the self, the knowledge that deconstruction does not in fact succeed in undermining the self but rather seems to aver its unbounded nature inadvertently constitutes a form of self-empowerment.

Deconstructive postmodernism subverts the binary opposites in Western culture and metaphysics: speech/writing, history/fiction, reason/emotion. First it calls into question the privileged terms on the left, reverses the hierarchy, and then in a third move makes the two terms equal in the attempt to move beyond binary oppositions, yet still without abandoning the logics of neither either/or, nor both/and, nor neither/nor. Deconstruction wants to have its cake and eat it too, and in a way it gets more than it bargained for. The two terms of the opposition remain in a state of coexistence. This coexistence reflects one of the basic tenets of quantum theory: the Principle of Complementarity. As Zohar says, Complementarity "states that each way of describing being, as a wave or as a particle, complements the other and that a whole picture emerges only from the 'package deal'" (1991, 9). Deconstructive undecidability thus corresponds to the Uncertainty principle of quantum physics, in which only the particle or the wave description of a thing is available at any given time. The resulting uncertainty leads in deconstruction to a logical impasse, a fuzzy duality caused by the freeplay of the signifier. Infinite freeplay, however, inadvertently takes the awareness beyond the boundaries of reason toward a field in which reason and intuition coexist, that is, toward the "package deal" of quantum indeterminacy.

On the one hand, this indeterminacy is a powerful metaphorical way for conceiving reality, while on the other hand it describes the unbounded possibilities of pure consciousness. Both deconstruction and quantum physics, as theories, point toward the silence of transcendental consciousness at the source of thought. The inability of quantum physics to account for particles and waves simultaneously may be due to a deficiency in quantum theory, as Zohar suspects, or it may be due to a deficiency in the perceiver's awareness. One way of overcoming this deficiency seems to be the deconstructive enterprise itself. Although in theory deconstruction undermines the subject, in practice it expands the theorist's attention beyond binary opposites to a logical impasse that borders on the "package deal" of consciousness as a field of all possibilities. With its practical effects undermining its theoretical claims, deconstruction self-deconstructs by undermining its own attempt to subvert the metaphysics of presence. Ironically, then, the practice of deconstruction in itself can be seen as a form of spiritual empowerment.

Indeed, the movement of *différance* that defers meaning *ad infinitum* has the effect of expanding the reader's awareness in a manner similar to yogic meditation. Although yoga (union) is misunderstood by the average Westerner, both yogic meditation and deconstruction rely on a signifier or mantra to expand the awareness beyond the determinate meaning of a word toward the direct experience of being as a field of all possibilities. This expansion of consciousness is the essence of spiritual empowerment. Ostensibly reinforcing a thematics of difference, deconstruction enhances the mind (theory) / body (experience) connection. Like yoga it increases the wholeness of the reader's being and helps to unfold the nonlocal quantum-level correlations of the self.[5] Granted, deconstruction does this through a negative path, but the aims of spiritual empowerment are also served through the play of difference. From the quantum or Vedantic perspective, moreover, difference is nothing less than a manifestation of unity. Spiritual empowerment accrues from any practice that relates the object of knowledge back to the self, thereby increasing the interconnectedness between the knower, the known, and the process of knowing. While this pedagogical method of self-referral can be applied to the study of any discipline, it works especially well in the case of literary studies. There are two reasons for this: first, because the human subject, even though reputedly decentered, plays a key role in literary studies and, second, as mentioned earlier, because the reader's awareness swings from the concrete to the abstract, from rationality to intuition, from boundaries to unboundedness.

Central to a practical program of spiritual empowerment in the humanities, then, is the reader's experience of self-referral consciousness. This experience in theory differs from the poststructuralist idea of self-referral as the infinite freeplay of the signifier and the indeterminacy of meaning. While deconstructive self-referral involves the centrifugal move toward increasing diversity, the taste of self-referral of consciousness involves the centripetal

---

5. The benefits of deconstruction suggested here must be understood as stemming not from deconstruction itself but rather from the self; they are the side effects of curving back onto the self. In the case of yogic meditation (see note 3), the self-reflexive move toward unbounded consciousness has been shown to produce a variety of practical benefits, including increased energy and intelligence, improved cardiovascular performance, enhanced immune functioning, and reversal of the aging process (Wallace 1993, 28, 41, 125, 144).

move toward the unified and eternal self, where the knower, the known, and the process of knowing are united. The former self-referral is rational and the latter intuitive. In practice, as suggested above, the move toward diversity ultimately has the same effect as the move toward unity. That is, figurative language, which on the one hand evokes the self-referral of consciousness through the swing of awareness from the concrete to the abstract, on the other hand produces a self-referential freeplay of the signifier, which in turn constitutes a radically abstract pole for the swing of awareness. A practical program for self-empowerment can begin with the rudimentary sense for how the awareness swings in reading literature from the boundaries of concrete images to the unboundedness of suggested possibilities.

The spiritually empowering effects of self-referral are of course more direct in the idealist model—as represented by quantum physics, Shankara's nondual Vedanta, and other philosophies—than in deconstructive postmodernism. As mentioned earlier, Indian literary theory accounts for different levels of consciousness and their corresponding levels of language. We have already seen that the fourth state of transcendental consciousness or *turiya* (a state of spiritual consciousness) differs from the three ordinary states of consciousness: waking, sleep, and dream. There are four levels of language, which can be separated into two sets: a higher unified level and a lower temporal level. Transcendental consciousness corresponds to the higher level of language, consisting of the unity and absolute unity of language, while ordinary waking consciousness corresponds to the lower level, consisting of outward speech and inward speech or thought (Coward, *Sphota* 1980, 126–33). To oversimplify, the higher level of language consists of a unity of sound and meaning, name and form, while the lower level consists of a temporal gap between sound and meaning. The higher level of language as experienced in the fourth state of consciousness constitutes the "transcendental signified." The transcendental signified allegedly undermined by deconstruction really belongs to the temporal level of language insofar that deconstructionists, having decentered the subject, do not have access to the fourth state of consciousness from which to comprehend, much less deconstruct, the unified level of language. The movement of *différance*, as applied to the transcendental signified and the fourth state of consciousness, is a myth of the ordinary waking state of consciousness, for this state has no access to the higher levels of language and the mind. At least this would be the case in theory. In practice, deconstruction involves a swing of awareness that can be said to expand the dimensions of consciousness and language toward a quantum indeterminacy. Nevertheless, the notion of *différance* quite accurately describes the state of affairs on the temporal level of language and the mind. Although a spiritual pedagogy might reveal how deconstruction could enhance one's self-empowerment, deconstructors themselves are blocked from theorizing beyond temporality by a logical impasse (see Haney 1993, 1–31).

The Art of Reading

The work of a reconstructive postmodernism is thus greatly enhanced through an understanding of the levels of language and consciousness provided by Indian philosophy and quantum physics. Spiritual empowerment stems in large part from a growing awareness of the self, through both the intellectual understanding and direct experience of the swing of awareness induced by a work of literature whose metaphors still have the power to defamiliarize. This move from the concrete to the abstract, the familiar to the unfamiliar, whether through the idealist thematics of universal truth or the play of *différance*, corresponds to the move in yogic meditation from the boundaries of ordinary waking consciousness to the unboundedness of the fourth state of transcendental consciousness. Both literature and yoga function by taking the awareness beyond the temporality of a word to a level where sound and meaning are united. That is, the repeated alternation of the attention between the concrete (sound) and the abstract (suggested import) swings the awareness between the differential field of ordinary waking consciousness and the unified field of transcendental consciousness. In this way the field of difference gradually becomes infused with the value of unity until one is capable of living the fullness of the coexistence of opposites. Readers who become in tune with this all-powerful level of reality where opposites coexist, both through the swing of awareness as a private experience and through the pedagogical understanding of this process, naturally gain in spiritual empowerment. This phenomenon may be illustrated through a reading of Edgar Allan Poe's "The Purloined Letter."

Poe's detective story follows the fate of a letter to the Queen purloined by the Minister and recovered by Dupin, who turns it over to the police, who then returns it to the Queen. In a poststructuralist sense, the letter is like a signifier with no meaning in itself except as an infinitely deferred possibility. Because we never discover its content, the letter allegedly symbolizes the elusive play of the signifier and the unconscious mind. So argues Jacques Lacan, who claims that "the unconscious is structured like a language" (1979, 20). Lacan holds that the self is undermined by the unconscious just as the transcendental signified is displaced by the play of the signifier. If the letter for poststructuralists signifies an openness or absence, that is, an unconscious desire for the unattainable, this is true insofar that its meaning on the temporal dimension of language and consciousness, the only meaning posited by poststructuralism, can never be unified or complete. From the perspective of the reconstructive postmodernism proposed here, the transcendental signified is evinced only by the quantum self, that state in which transcendental consciousness coincides with the unity of language.

Whereas a poststructuralist self-referral sends the reader on a quest for an ever receding signified (letter) and self, a reconstructive self-referral leads through the swing of awareness toward the bliss of pure consciousness, a field of quantum fullness. This self-referral allows the reader to fathom the purloined letter in the way Dupin does. Dupin identifies with his opponent, the Minister, by curving beyond his personal boundaries back toward the quantum self and thereby retrieves the purloined letter. Similarly, the reconstructive interpreter comprehends the text by curving back upon the self, that level of consciousness from which the text was written. Considered in its full range, the self-referral play of consciousness subsumes the play of the signifier. Moreover, as suggested here, this play of language can in practice bestow a taste of unity as the coexistence of opposites, a unity of consciousness that corresponds to a quantum mechanical unity. As the physicist Roger Penrose says,

> might there be any relation between a "state of awareness" and a highly coherent quantum state in the brain? Is the "oneness" of "globality" that seems to be a future of consciousness connected with this? It is somewhat tempting to believe so. (1987, 274)

This wholeness of the self, as evinced through both types of self-referral, is the basis of spiritual empowerment.

Self-empowerment in literary studies, then, hinges on the integration of reason and intuition, conceptuality and direct experience in the process of reading and writing. Through this integration we can better appreciate the coexistent nature of life, its relative changing aspect, and its absolute nonchanging yet dynamic source. This nondual absolute—posited by quantum physics and Vedanta—is not only the source of the relative but also its essential nature. The point here is that the unified field, language, and the quantum self all consist of a coexistence of opposites. Without a spiritual pedagogy for understanding this coexistence, our experience even of the swing of awareness through the rhetorical play of language could be misapprehended as a loss of unity instead of a move toward spiritual wholeness. Self-empowerment depends on an openness to the intellectual possibility of unity and to the intuition that multiplicity means a genuine coexistence of opposites and not merely duality on the temporal plane.

7

The Pollen Path
The Navajo Way of Knowing
Herbert John Benally

Navajos divide the passing on of their sacred knowledge between the winter and summer seasons. It is taboo to discuss winter stories in the summer, and most of their sacred knowledge—for example, the knowledge of the powers that the medicine man uses in conducting a healing or blessing ceremony—is revealed only in winter. In addition, certain ceremonial knowledge is kept within the circle of the ceremony and cannot be shared with the general public. With these restrictions in mind, I begin this essay on Navajo epistemology and the importance of internalizing knowledge. This essay speaks for Navajo epistemology only and not for that of other native Americans.

There are differences in how learning is perceived by Western and Native American traditions. Western tradition separates secular and sacred knowledge and thus fragments knowledge. Consequently, some learning is forgotten soon after academic program requirements are met because it was never grounded or connected to life processes. For this reason, the notion of "true internalization of knowledge" does not make the same sense to the Western mind as it does to the Navajo because this true internalization is not in the Western system of learning. But for the Navajo, knowledge, learning, and life itself are *sacred, inseparable, and interwoven parts of a whole*. The quality of each determines the quality of the other. They are natural parts of a sacred, reciprocal relationship, a mutual participation in the great universal consciousness.

The metaphorical rug weaver illustrates the holistic view of the Navajo toward all of life and learning. To be a rug weaver is to understand the process involved in internalizing knowledge of the universal consciousness and its essential benevolence. The medium of the artist is nature itself. By manipulating the medium, the artist draws forth nature's endowed goodness. According to the creation story, all things that were created were endowed with spiritual intelligence and adorned with *yódí* (materials soft goods) and

[handwritten margin note: It does now, but did it always?]

84

nitł'iz (all precious things that have enduring qualities, such as jewels). As with all arts in Navajo society, weaving is a way through which the artist lays hold of the primal forces that vibrate throughout life. Weaving is a manifesting process of thoughts, plans, and labor that promotes contentment and fulfillment in the artist's life. This process must be balanced within knowledge and moral values, true sustenance, interrelationships, and our place in the order of nature. The process accordingly is a ritualistic act that transcends this world to draw forth the good mind and the fine adornments of Mother Earth and Father Sky.

Weaving, as well as other forms of work or learning, is a spiritual act and, therefore, must be handled with respect, reverence, and gratitude. For instance, adherence to these understandings and teachings keeps the heart pure, the mind clear, and the health strong—all of which promote the good life. All human activities have parameters for good, and with art the parameter is that which brings one happiness (*iłhóshǫ́*). It includes activities that enlighten, uplift, and inspire. When one comes to understand and participate in this consciousness, one becomes the medium for directing nature's power toward all that is good, thereby becoming part of a circle.

The Navajo also speaks of *ák'éé'jiich'ąą'* (upon oneself one places a design). This idea expresses the belief that the artist's creation is one's thought and life. Whatever the artist creates he/she invites into life. Therefore, when an individual takes art beyond the boundaries of the conditions of good, one endangers oneself and others. Two examples of this are the introduction of a snake (representing evil) into a creative work and introducing nuclear weapons into technology. The mind becomes unsafe with this introduction and thereby turns the design upon oneself. Because Navajos have internalized this understanding of the interconnection of all knowledge, the paradigm from which they operate differs from that of the Western mindset.

In this paper I shall discuss four holistic concepts that are integral to Navajo epistemology, theories that I contend inform and have implications for Western educational practices. I have written on this philosophy in part before.[1] But in this essay I shall attempt to expand and include parts I left out in my previous work. Navajos believe that the four holistic concepts, or areas of endowment, must be met to bring about peace of mind, physical health, emotional health, and ecological awareness. When these areas are not met, life is out of balance. I shall describe the source of Navajo knowledge, including the nature of sacred knowledge and its relationship to the universal consciousness. I shall examine the nature of Navajo identity and its divine relation to ancestral holy people. The concept of duality, particularly the dual but complementary male-female nature of the universe, will be central to this

1. Benally, H. 1992. In *Tribal College Journal.* Spring.
1988. "Diné Philosophy of Learning." In *Journal of Navajo Education,* 6(1).
1987. "Diné bo'óhoo'aah Bindii'a'. Navajo Philosophy of Learning." In *Diné Be'iina': Journal of Navajo Life,* 1(1).

discussion. To be in balance, all beings must honor the male and female nature within the self and within all of nature.[2] I shall focus on the spiritual/mental, physical, emotional, and home/environmental endowments of human beings and the relationship of those endowments to the universal order and inherent knowledge. I shall discuss the process of internalizing principles implicit in the universal order and of drawing them into one's life for fuller *hozhǫ́* (a state of much good, a peaceful, beautiful, and harmonious life). Finally, I shall discuss the implications of these theories for Western educational practices.

First Concept: The Sources of Navajo Knowledge

In the beginning the gods took the dust and light that floated like clouds and made the physical earth and organized the celestial bodies. The lights they placed in the four cardinal directions. They placed dawn toward the East. They placed the blue twilight toward the South. They placed the yellow evening twilight toward the West. And they placed the darkness toward the North. They also assigned the wind spirits as guardians to the East, South, West, and North. For this reason, the Navajo people today believe that the four wind spirits exist with the four cardinal directions. When the celestial body (sky) and terrestrial body (earth) were being formed, they were endowed with all conceivable things that would be beneficial to human beings. And when the endowment was completed, the spirits of Father Sky and Mother Earth entered these bodies, and the four wind spirits became their breath, and Sky and Earth each became a living being.

A male deity entered the celestial body, and the union of the two became the Father of the Upper Darkness. A woman deity entered the earth body, and the union of the two became Mother Earth. The quickened Mother Earth then spoke and identified the essence of her being, which she placed within the cardinal directions for the earth's surface people who would come later. She did this as follows:

1. To meet mental needs, she placed *Bik'ehgo Da'iináanii* (that which gives direction to life) with the dawn toward the East.

2. To meet physical needs, she placed *Nihigáál* (sustenance) with the blue twilight toward the South.

---

2. Following this thinking, our elders have explained that we have a malelike protective and aggressive side as well as a femalelike nourishing and gentle side to our nature. The left side of a man's body is associated with the side that bears the shield. The right side is associated with nurturing. The right side of a woman's body is associated with the male or protective side. Her left side is associated with nourishing. On this side she carries her cooking utensils to ward off hunger and disease. When a man and a woman stand side by side facing the east, both of their aggressive sides are on the outside and their female, nurturing, and nourishing sides are on the inside. Children are raised within the protective side of both the male and the female sides. When our aggressive side is checked by our gentle nature, we find balance, harmony, and beauty in life.

3. To meet emotional needs, she placed *Aha'áná'oo'nííł* (the gathering of family) with the yellow evening twilight toward the West.

4. To meet one's need to understand and relate to one's physical home and environment, she placed *Háá'ayííh dóó Hodílzin* (rest, reverence for all creation) with the darkness toward the North.

These are the sources of Navajo knowledge that provide the basis for achieving *Sa'ąh Naagháí Bek'eh Hózhóón* (Blessing Way), a harmonious, peaceful, and happy way of life. Just as the rug weaver draws forth and synthesizes nature's endowed goodness, its soft materials and precious jewels to create happiness, the synthesis of these great branches of knowledge puts one on the path of *Sa'ąh Naagháí Bek'eh Hózhóón*, which is a sacred path of the gods who created this world, as well as a title ascribed to holy people and the way of life of the holy people. It represents life in which one is emotionally happy, physically healthy, morally good, and economically able and secure. Related Navajo terms for this Blessing Way include *The Pollen Path, The Way of Dew,* and *The Protection Way.* Navajos believe that by following these paths, one lives in harmony with the universe. They are integral parts of the cosmic order that address the basic composition of human beings.

Just as nature provides for the rug weaver, for traditional Navajos the natural order and the cyclic nature of creation, like the parts of the day, bring to us these four themes of knowledge. Navajos believe that they must follow the Navajo way of ordering as presented by the day itself. The day, not metaphorically or figuratively, but the day itself literally gives direction for life. The day is divided into four parts, with each giving different kinds of direction: the dawn (spiritual/mental), the day (physical), the evening (emotional), and the darkness (home/environmental). Spiritual knowledge and discipline exist within the *dawn* and give direction for spiritual and mental development. As one takes the dawn's directions for life, those directions become one's thoughts. From that comes one's plan, from that one's life, and finally one's fulfillment. From birth one continually experiences the influence of these four nurturing principles. Unfortunately, even many modern Navajos do not comprehend this and as a result they experience difficulties. But these branches of knowledge are holistic; they are so interdependent and interrelated that the absence or lack of any one of them creates imbalance within the individual or society.

Not sure what this means.

The Nature of Knowledge

The Navajo understand the nature of knowledge within the paradigm of *Sa'ąh Naagháí Bek'eh Hózhóón.* Knowledge is spiritual. This concept recognizes the existence of both harmonizing and opposing principles in the world, as illustrated by the metaphorical rug weaver. The Protection Way teachings deal with *naayéé',* the destructive forces in the world and the universe and inoculates one against vices and evil; Navajos believe that as long as one keeps these teachings, one remains unseen by the destructive forces. These teachings also address the struggle against hunger and illness, and they require an understanding of the rights and protection of those rights as they relate to families' beliefs, land, and freedom. Blessing Way teachings include those teachings that direct, inspire, and enlighten. They may have to do with developing personal discipline, family relationships, or one's relationship to the environment. Protection Way and Blessing Way as ceremonies are performed when needed to assist individuals in remaining on the path of peace and harmony and to clear one's spiritual, mental, physical, and emotional system of any deterrent to physical health, vigor, and vitality. But in Westernized classrooms, failure to recognize the holistic and spiritual nature of values, work, interpersonal relationships, and the environment has left the individual's needs vastly unmet.

Human Beings' Endowments and Their Relation to the Four Branches of Knowledge, the Universal Order

Navajos value learning and knowledge and see them as interrelated to all that they do and all that they are. As the sons and daughters of *Sa'ąh Naaghái Bek'eh Hózhóón*, eternal and indestructible beings that are the cause and director of happiness and peace, Navajos are endowed with minds, physical bodies, and emotions when they are placed on the earth, their home. These endowments subject the person to the natural laws and orders of the physical world. Like the rug weaver, when they follow those natural laws, their lives will be in balance, and they will experience physical, emotional, moral, and economic health.

I am not advocating that classroom teachers attempt to teach Navajo epistemology in the classroom. Only a person whose own life is balanced according to the four areas of knowledge can teach that balance to another. Otherwise, fragmented and distorted views of life continue to be perpetuated. I am, however, suggesting that taking a holistic approach toward education not only in writing classes but across disciplines would result in a better world. It would help individuals see learning and themselves as connected to each other and their worlds, as part of a whole in a mutually beneficial, reciprocal relationship. Assuming their responsibility in this relationship would have advantages not just for themselves personally but for all of society at every level—socially, environmentally, and technologically.

Second Concept: *Sa'ąh Naaghái Bek'eh Hózhóón* as Navajo Identity and Way of Life

The concept of *Sa'ąh Naaghái Bek'eh Hózhóón* is revealed in our ancient tribal stories. In this concept, Navajos believe, is the very element from which the universe is constructed: It is the power by which all things were created, organized, and governed; it is the life force of the universe. In this concept lies the sacred and spiritual identity of the Navajo as mentioned earlier. Our elders have always believed and taught that we are the literal sons and daughters of *Sa'ąh Naagháí Bek'eh Hózhóón*, the gods who created this world. We spiritually call ourselves the holy people on the face of the earth. We believe that we are spiritually and intellectually endowed to find balance, harmony, and peace. This notion is celebrated and affirmed through prayers, ceremonies, and teaching.

Navajos believe we must be taught the Navajo way of life to become fully functional beings. This includes the recognition of *Sa'ąh Naagháí Bek'eh Hózhóón* not only as the sacred way of life of the holy people but also as the natural order of all life, which is inseparable from learning. Learning is the internalization of the principles of *hózhǫǫgo iiná*, the way of happiness. Only by embracing all of these teachings and principles, as the rug weaver embraces all of nature, can we evolve into our true selves. If we do not internalize these principles, we are shut off not just from our heritage but from the quality of life we might live. But in many schools, even in the schools that affect large Navajo populations, Navajo teachings are not being taught. In such schools many Navajos are placed in conflict both with the self and with Western culture, whose educational system does not promote "true internalization of knowledge" but instead fragments knowledge.

From this concept also comes the notion of duality, an essential component of epistemology. In our language, the *k'é* language, this sacred word *Sa'ąh Naagháí Bek'eh Hózhóón* is a combination of separate male and female concepts. Representing constitution, the first concept, *Sa'ąh Naagháí* is defined as "indestructible and eternal being." It is male and exhibits masculinelike qualities. The second concept, *Bek'eh Hózhóón* is defined as "the director and cause of all that is good." It is female and exhibits femininelike qualities. The two concepts do not operate apart, but are complements and halves of each other. Everything in the universe is perceived to exist in male and female pairs. Life as we know it, including knowledge and learning styles, is the interaction of these pairs. The whole of the universe, the whole of every system within the universe, and the whole of the individual contain both of these pairs. If the universe, the system, and the individual are to remain in balance, both of these sides must be honored.

Honoring both male and female nature brings into balance the whole. Within the educational system, reasoning, logic, and analytical processes represent the male parts of the whole and intuitive, creative, instinctive processes represent the female parts of the whole. To honor both counterbalances aggression with gentleness and nurturing, and thinking with feeling. Navajos believe that this awareness of duality and balance also carries over to other systems such as language. Because thoughts and words have the power to honor, heal, degrade, and curse, people, including both students and teachers, should be cautioned to balance their language because what they think and say may happen.

This concept has implications for teachers and their response to Navajo students' learning styles and academic performance. First of all, Navajos and nonnatives are trained differently. We operate from different paradigms. Nonnatives can seem overly analytical or emotional to native students. Moreover, teachers who do not have a grasp of the native mind, when they hear natives' ideas, may expect natives to change their way of thinking to fit the teachers' paradigms. This expectation does not expand teachers' perspectives or foster native students' self-worth or respect for their own ideas. Receiving conflicting signals about one's sense of belonging creates doubt, and this breeds alienation, loneliness, frustration, and anxiety. These conditions can be expressed in rebellion, defensiveness, and suicidal tendencies. To promote students' self-worth as well as their intellectual and personal development, teachers, too, must keep in check a tendency to be *either* analytical *or* emotional. Too much of either could confuse or bewilder the student conditioned to respond to balance. An educational paradigm that fragments learning by favoring either aggressive qualities or nurturing over the other can be like the negative design of the metaphorical rug weaver; it can come back on the self in negative ways whereas a design of balance and harmony brings back on the self harmony and balance.

Third Concept: Spiritual/Mental, Physical, Emotional, Home/Environmental Endowments of Human Beings and Their Relationship to the Universal Order

The Relationship Between Mind/Spirit and the First Area of Knowledge, Bik'ehgo Da'iináanii (That Which Gives Direction to Life)

The first knowledge is associated with the dawn, the beginning of light, awakening and growth, those knowledges that guide. Internalized knowledge comes from creation stories and ceremonies that have been taught to the Navajos from time immemorial. They contain spiritual knowledge that reveals ways of harmonizing with the Universal Order and the process drawing on the beneficial powers that were primordially placed in creation. Elders believe in discipline as a means by which knowledge finds permanence. For example, running is believed to be a sacred act, and individuals who run at dawn are believed to be rewarded by the gods. By getting up and running at dawn, individuals learn to control their physical appetites, desires, and passions. They build a strong mental foundation that allows them to prevail over the adversities of life and achieve the good life. It is the mind that regulates the condition of one's physical health. In the not far distant past this was a regular practice, but as more of the Navajo people embraced Western ways, this practice almost stopped. Today individual families, communities, schools, and some treatment centers are practicing running again. Learning is maturing and part of this maturation is learning to control one's primitive desires and demonstrate maturity. Parents, public leaders, and teachers are the most visible people in Navajo and other communities, and they are the ones who demonstrate and uphold standards that individual community members can point to as examples. Self-discipline of any kind is an important leadership quality.

The Relationship Between the Body and the Second Area of Knowledge, Nihigáál (Sustenance)

As illustrated by the rug weaver, the Navajo tradition views the individual and the world holistically. It does not separate the technical and spiritual dimensions of work, including academic work or study. The teaching *t'áá hó'ájít'éégol* (if things are to be, it's up to you) is the key to obtaining and maintaining life. One is endowed to think for oneself, but with endowments also comes responsibility: for example, the responsibility to derive a living without destroying the system established for living. Each must understand that the world has been created and organized in such a way that it must be beneficial not just to the people but to the grandchildren of the people.

The Relationship Between Emotion and the Third Area of Knowledge, Aha'áná'oo'nííł (The Gathering of Family)

For the Navajo, the Navajo's k'é language itself is spiritual. It is a language of the heart expressed among families, friends, community, and the natural world. It establishes conditions in which the emotional needs of each family member are met and shows the speaker's bond with love for, and respect for, those about whom he or she is speaking. For example, in Navajo tradition, one would say, "This is *my* little sister, *my* brother (or mother or friend)" instead of the more detached "This is John." In relating to community, the individual also utilizes the clanship system to establish relationships that make the Navajo Nation function as one extended family, even in sharing the responsibilities of raising children. Within these circles, children develop a sense of belonging and are checked from wandering from the main fold. In contrast to the Western fear of getting involved, this traditional system makes helping an opportunity and provides a positive atmosphere for counseling. It effectively checks child abuse, broken homes, and homelessness because in this system everyone becomes responsible for everyone else.

Rituals and celebrations are considered part of the whole. As mentioned earlier, ceremonial spiritual rituals empower and heighten positive human spiritual and social development; therefore, Navajos offer spiritual celebrations for important stages of child development. An infant's first laugh is celebrated in a ceremony called "Baby's First Laugh." That precious moment is celebrated with a feast and many prayers of blessing for the permanence of that sound of happiness and joy. Traditionally, the coming of age for manhood and womanhood has also been celebrated in a ceremony, called *kinaaldá* (Puberty ceremony), a branch of Blessing Way. This ceremony includes prayers, songs, teachings, and counsel from the elders of the families about the meaning of manhood and womanhood. Following this initiation ceremony a child is expected to act as a maturing adult. Traditionally, when manhood and womanhood ceremonies were not performed, the elders believed the child would be slow in understanding the nature of maturing. Western educators need to consider the effect that celebrating important events and milestones for the individual has on that individual's development.

What does this mean?

The Relationship Between Home and the Fourth Area of Knowledge, Háá'áyį́įh dóó Hodílzin (Rest, Respect, and Reverence for All Creation)

In Navajo philosophy it is with the fourth principle *háá'áyį́įh dóó hodílzin* that the knowledge for understanding one's relationship to home and environment is found. Establishing an intimate relationship with nature begins with the acceptance that all creation is intelligent and beneficial in and of itself. Consequently, when due respect is shown for nature, that respect is returned with more favors. Likewise, disrespect engenders disrespect. When we begin to understand this reciprocal relationship, we begin to participate in the great universal consciousness: We become related to all creation and our views and language toward this vibrating life change, for we are no longer strangers but family. But it is in our failure to understand this interconnectedness that we become alien to this world. We see the world as hostile and wild and something that must be shaped into our image and into an order that is foreign to the natural order of things. We become like the rug weaver who takes art beyond the boundaries of good, and we endanger ourselves and others. The environment that we create and impose mirrors back our own ignorance.

For Navajos, Father Sky and Mother Earth were blessed with untold wisdom and wealth to be used by man. For instance, the mountains were endowed with strength, wealth, teachings, and processes by which man can acquire strength and resources. But these endowments are lost if the mind becomes inactive and one does not plan. In Navajo tradition, it is believed that there is a fine line between how one interacts with nature and how one treats others. A person's heart becomes hard when he or she loses respect and reverence for nature. For how one treats animals and nature directly relates to how one treats other people. It remains crucial that youth be taught to remain close to nature's softening influence. By observing how animals and birds care for and bring up their young and by seeing how plants grow just like a child, one learns to care and nourish. Teachings about relationships to Mother Earth and Father Sky must continue to be passed on to the next generation if we human beings intend to remain not only in harmony but in existence at all.

Each of these four areas of knowledge converge to create balance and a good life or *bik'eh hózhóón* (a way of happiness). Our tradition presupposes that individuals taught in the four areas of knowledge will act in honorable and admirable ways. Such persons are firm in their beliefs, sufficiently sheltered, and nourished. They understand and respect family and community relationships, as they understand and respect their relationship to their environment. If these relationships were also acknowledged by Western culture, this approach to learning could possibly correct the destruction of our environments and oppression of people, establish economics as a means not as an end, and reestablish morality as the basis for learning.

Fourth Concept: Internalizing Knowledge

For the Navajos, life is a process guided by the areas of knowledge just described, which determine the quality of the process. There is no distinction between the internalization process and the formulation of life. Life and learning are holistic and are the focal point of the four great branches of knowledge, which can be synthesized into the four basic life processes: thinking, planning, living, and fulfillment.

Consequently, internalizing knowledge becomes very important because the knowledge that is internalized becomes one's life. Internalization comes in four stages, and each stage is built upon the other: The first stage of this process is called *shintsékees dooleeł* (the knowledge will become my thoughts). The second stage is called *shinahat'a' dooleeł* (the knowledge will pervade my concept structures and action schemes). The third stage is called *she'iina' dooleeł* (the knowledge will enable me to manage my life affairs in a meaningful and fruitful way). The last stage is called *bee siih dinisdzin dooleeł* (the knowledge, skills, and discipline will culminate in my actualization and contentment and will become my prayers, my songs, and my teachings).

The operation of these areas of knowledge as guiding principles in the life processes of each individual is similar to how elements operate in rug weaving. To ignore them impairs productivity, vitality, and fulfillment. When this happens, life becomes distorted and self-efficacy is no longer possible. Thus it becomes absolutely necessary that individuals be grounded in these principles, which are inherent in the four cardinal directions, so that they may internalize these principles. The internalized knowledge immunizes one from destructive forces in the world. It will shield individuals as long as they remain close to the teachings of *Sa'ąh Naagháí Bek'eh Hózhóón* or *hózhǫ́ǫgo iiná (life of more good)*.

When an individual is not taught in this way, the individual becomes spiritually, emotionally, physically, and environmentally impoverished. One becomes narrow in one's views and loses connection with the universal consciousness and perpetuates that imbalance to the next generation.

The goal of Navajo knowledge is holism in peace and harmony. By internalizing the four cardinal areas of Navajo knowledge, individuals will develop sound beliefs and values and will be prepared to make responsible decisions. They will develop knowledge and skills that will enable them to provide for their families, demonstrate good leadership skills within the family and community, and develop a sense of reverence for all creation. The synthesis of this knowledge is manifest in the expression of appreciation, reverence, and love for harmony and life. But for the student who has not internalized this way of knowing, education can seem meaningless, irrelevant, or unendurable.

Regardless of the names and labels they may choose to attribute to the process, Western educators could enhance not just the education of Navajos in their classrooms but all of society, by recognizing the value of Navajo ways of knowing. When one is firmly grounded in spiritual teachings and traditional wisdom, that person finds strength and stability. He or she develops a consciousness and spiritual awareness that provides a basis for learning and living. With this foundation, an individual will weigh decisions against traditional values whenever a choice is to be made. These decisions permeate every facet of one's life. Without this principle, skills and knowledge become groundless and destructive. A mature mind is one whose learning is tempered with spiritual consciousness. All of society can be improved when we recognize that people are spiritual beings with unlimited potential, with *Sa'ąh Naagháí Bek'eh Hózhóón*. They have the light that illuminates all life and the universal order—they are potential gods in an embryonic state.

8

What Is the Sound of No Hand Writing?
The Use of Secularized Zen Koans in the Teaching of Writing

Donald R. Gallehr

I am flying north from New Orleans to Chicago. The sun is above the horizon, shining between cumulus clouds shaped like willows, making the cirrus clouds above them iridescent. I attach a polarizer to my twenty-millimeter wide-angle lens and take pictures through the window of the 757. The light is searing.

When I finish shooting the clouds, I turn to Joyce Tenneson's *Transformations,* a book of seventy color photographs that includes "Suzanne, 1986," which I have seen on the covers of magazines. Her work combines the physical and spiritual in a way I find haunting. In the David Tannous interview of Tenneson at the back of the book, Tenneson talks about how she prepares for a shooting.

> She begins with relaxation techniques that help her to quiet down; then she waits until she feels her higher self become like a vibrating light. She then asks herself a question about something that is bothering her and waits for the answer. If the question is simple—the answer comes quickly. More complex questions, such as those involving relationships, might involve inner dialogue with the person. These answers take longer and yet, like the answers to simpler questions, also arrive suddenly.[1]

I feel close to Tenneson. She describes the process I use in meditating, writing, and teaching. Like her, I become as quiet as I can, ask a question, and

1. Joyce Tenneson, *Transformations,* Boston: Bulfinch Press, 1992, p. 124.

wait for an answer. Even though it took me a long time to discover this questioning technique, as I experienced its power for resolving issues in my personal life, I also came to understand its resolution power for my writing and teaching.

My journey began in 1973 when my office mate Bob Karlson first introduced me to meditation. Through our discussions I learned that meditation is sitting still, watching thoughts as they come, letting them go, and allowing the mind to become still. Bob used a mantra as a focal point during meditation. In my typical experimental fashion, I made up my own mantras ("Peace," "Let go," "Relax," and so on). From time to time I also focused on my breath—the sensations created in my nostrils as I inhaled and exhaled.[2]

In 1973 I was in my early thirties. I had much to be happy about—wife, family, home, and career—but I also suffered from endless thoughts playing in my mind like tapes in a tape recorder. Some of these tapes were of my early childhood, while others were new thoughts that arrived each day but were repeated over and over and over. According to Bob, meditation was a way of training the mind to let go of these tapes, and to bring some semblance of peace.

I knew about peace. I was raised Roman Catholic and took church seriously until my twenties, when I became disenchanted with sermons that were little more than sales pitches. But in my early teens, each night before going to sleep, I would read books about saints and then say my prayers. Occasionally, I would experience a few moments when I felt genuinely peaceful, when I didn't seem to be thinking about anything. I tried unsuccessfully to extend the length of time my mind was calm by varying the length of time I read and prayed. The peace seemed to have its own timetable. Eventually, part of what drove me away from organized religion was the knowledge that the saints had discovered how to achieve this peace and that, given the right instruction, I too could learn. At that time, I blamed the church for withholding this information.[3]

2. Daniel Goleman's *The Meditative Mind: The Varieties of Meditative Experience,* Los Angeles: Jeremy P. Tarcher, Inc., 1988, is a thorough and detailed description of meditation traditions from around the world, including Hindu, Buddhist, Sufi, Jewish, Christian, Transcendental Meditation, Tantric, Kundalini Yoga, Tibetan Buddhist, Zen, and those developed by Gurdjieff and Krishnamurti. Especially helpful is Goleman's description of the different levels of consciousness that result from the regular practice of meditation over time. It is worth noting that Goleman's book is sold in the philosophy/psychology sections of bookstores. Meditation, as described in this book, is about developing awareness and consciousness.
3. It is somewhat ironic that I had read Thomas Merton's *Seven Story Mountain* as an undergraduate, but had not read the books that resulted from his explorations of the similarities of Western and Asian traditions of meditation. In 1968 Merton traveled to India, where he met the Dalai Lama and then went on to Southeast Asia and Bangkok, where he died as a result of touching an electric fan. Works of interest among the sixty-some books published by Merton are *Mystics and Zen Masters,* New York: Farrar, Straus, and Giroux, 1967; *Zen and the Birds of Appetite,* Philadelphia: New Directions, 1968; *The Way of Chuang Tzu,* New York: New Directions, 1969; and *The Asian Journals of Thomas Merton,* New York: New Directions, 1973.

In 1979 my brother wrote suggesting that I look into Philip Kapleau's *The Three Pillars of Zen*.[4] My recollection of this period is fuzzy. I did read Kapleau, but not until much later. Instead, I read two books by Janwillem van de Wetering, *A Glimpse of Nothingness* and *The Empty Mirror*.[5] Van de Wetering is a Dutchman who went to Japan to find the answers to some of life's most perplexing questions; he ended up in a Rinzai Zen monastery where he meditated for over a year under the guidance of a Zen master. I was enthralled by his account and reread these two books every night for the next eight years. I also meditated more regularly.

During the early 1980s, I learned that for me bringing the mind to rest depended on being able to sit still for long periods of time. When I sat in a chair, I tended to slouch and, when I shifted to get comfortable, I interrupted the meditation. I was intrigued by pictures of meditators sitting with ease on meditation cushions, so I bought a cushion from a company advertising in a yoga magazine. At first my knees stuck almost straight up and I gasped from the pain. My thigh and calf muscles were as tight as a bowstring. To stretch my inner thighs, I lay cross-legged in bed, allowing the weight of my legs to stretch the muscles. After five years, I could sit for over an hour without moving, which is sufficient time for sustained and uninterrupted concentration. Although for me it was energizing, this degree of discipline and structure is obviously not necessary for the average writer to benefit from meditation techniques.[6]

I'm sure I would have benefited from practicing with a Zen master, but I couldn't find one in Northern Virginia, and having a family precluded my

4. Philip Kapleau was an American who served as a court reporter covering the Nuremberg and Tokyo war crimes trials. He returned to Japan to study and practice Zen and stayed for thirteen years. When he returned to the United States, he established a Zen center in Rochester, New York. His book *The Three Pillars of Zen*, first published in 1965, contains gentle and easily understandable instructions on how to begin meditating. I would recommend the revised and expanded edition of 1980, available from Anchor Books, Garden City, New York, as well as the companion volume *Zen: Dawn in the West*, Garden City, New York: Anchor Books, 1980, with its engaging stories and question and answer format. As you might imagine, Kapleau is an excellent writer.

5. Janwillem van de Wetering, *The Empty Mirror: Experiences in a Japanese Zen Monastery*, New York: Washington Square Press, 1973, and *A Glimpse of Nothingness: Experiences in an American Zen Community*, New York: Washington Square Press, 1975. From time to time these have gone out of print, but with a little help you should be able to locate them. Van de Wetering is my favorite writer on meditation because he tells a great story and includes an abundance of information on the origins and practices of meditation. He is also a novelist.

6. I read a book on Christian yoga when I was seventeen, but after a few attempts at the postures, I left it to collect dust on my bookshelf. It wasn't until 1988 that I took a yoga class. As I understand it, the physical postures or stretching exercises were devised around 2,500 BC to enable meditators to sit for extended periods of time. Today, yoga is used primarily to relieve stress and maintain flexibility, but a healthy body, supple and filled with the oxygen-rich blood yoga promotes, enables the writer to concentrate for long periods of time. Yoga classes, books, and videos are now readily available. My favorite yoga book (because of its beautiful photos) is *The Sivananda Companion to Yoga*, New York: Simon and Schuster, 1983.

joining a monastery. Instead, I read one meditation book after another from as many traditions as I could find—Christian, Buddhist, and Hindu—although I read most deeply the Zen authors because they seemed less tied to religion.[7] I learned that in Japan there were two major schools of Zen: Rinzai and Soto.[8] Rinzai Zen used the koan (pronounced "ko-an" to rhyme with "go on") more than Soto Zen. The literal meaning of *koan* is the *public record* of the puzzling questions and sayings Zen masters used to bring about enlightenment. I had heard the koan "What is the sound of one hand clapping," but didn't know how to go about solving it. I tried to use logic and rational thinking and got nowhere. So I merely meditated as I had before—clearing my mind to allow for that wonderful period of peace that came after a half hour or so of sitting still.

Eventually I came upon a red paperback titled *The Sound of the One Hand,* which listed koans and their possible answers.[9] I had read enough about using koans to know that I couldn't "copy" the answers but had to "learn" them on my own. I also knew that an answer was both a correct word or gesture *and* a state of mind. The correct answer with the incorrect state of mind would be

7. A fascinating account of transcending the ego was written by a former Roman Catholic nun and mother of four children, Bernadette Roberts: *The Experience of No-Self,* Boulder: Shambhala, 1984, and *The Path to No-Self,* Boston: Shambhala, 1985. As with other accounts by meditators, her work transcends religion. Two other works on the same subject are Sri Nisargadatta Maharaj, *I Am That,* Durham, North Carolina: The Acorn Press, 1973, and D. E. Harding, *On Having No Head: Zen and the Re-Discovery of the Obvious,* London: Arkana, 1986.

8. I read Janvillem Van de Wetering for my introduction to Rinzai Zen and supplemented it with two works by the Zen scholar D. T. Suzuki: *An Introduction to Zen Buddhism,* New York: Grove Press, 1964, and *Zen Buddhism,* Garden City, New York: Doubleday Anchor Books, 1956. Koans were first used extensively during the Sung dynasty, at about the time of the founder of Rinzai Zen, Lin-chi (d. AD 866). Rinzai Zen was taken to Japan in the twelfth century, where it thrived for several hundred years. The reviver of Rinzai Zen in Japan and the progenitor of modern Rinzai Zen is Hakuin (1686–1769), and the work I found most accessible was *The Zen Master Hakuin: Selected Writings,* translated by Philip B. Yampolsky, New York: Columbia University Press, 1971. My favorite Soto Zen author is Shunryu Suzuki (1905–1971), whose *Zen Mind, Beginner's Mind,* New York: Weatherhill, 1970, I have read more than a dozen times. Shunryu Suzuki founded the San Francisco Zen Center. A more recent favorite of mine is Charlotte Joko Beck's *Everyday Zen: Love and Work,* San Francisco: Harper and Row, 1989, one of the most grounded presentations of Soto Zen I have ever read. The founder of Soto Zen was Dogen (1200–1253), *Introduction with Selected Writings,* New York: Weatherhill, 1976.

9. *The Sound of the One Hand: 281 Zen Koans with Answers,* translated with a commentary by Yoel Hoffman, New York: Basic Books, 1975. I also use two other works: Zenkei Shibayama, *Zen Comments on the Mumonkan,* San Francisco: Harper and Row, 1974, and J. C. Cleary, *Meditating with Koans,* Berkeley, California: Asian Humanities Press, 1992. Famous koan collections that I have not used but would recommend are *The Blue Cliff Record,* translated by Thomas Cleary and J. C. Cleary, and two works translated by Thomas Cleary: *Book of Equanimity* and *Gateless Barrier.* A help in switching to right-brain or holistic thinking are the drawing exercises in Betty Edwards' *Drawing on the Right Side of the Brain,* Los Angeles: J. P. Tarcher, Inc., 1979, and *Drawing on the Artist Within,* New York: Simon and Schuster, 1986.

refused by a Zen master. So I worked on koans, and only when I was convinced I had the right answer did I check the answer in the book.[10]

When I entered a mid-life crisis in 1989, I began forming my own koans, including a question that was a burning issue for me: What was I to do with the rest of my life? My children had left for college, and I was suffering from a bad case of empty nest syndrome. To form the question so that I would get an intuitive answer, I asked myself, "What does *my life* want to become?" Unlike a person, my life did not have volition or desires and, therefore, it made no rational sense to ask it what it wanted to become. It took about four months for the answer to arrive, but once it did, I knew it was right. The answer was, "It wants to be finished." At first I didn't understand what this meant. But after a while I saw that I was not at the end of my life but in the middle, and things I had set in motion—such as marriage, family, and career—were unfinished and I needed to "finish" what I had started.

I now use koans almost daily. I work on the larger Zen koans found in such books as *The Sound of the One Hand* and *Zen Comments on the Mumokan*, often taking months on each one. I also create my own koans, some large, some small. A short while ago, for instance, my daughter moved into an apartment. She was out of town and asked me to take her place inspecting the apartment with the superintendent. I enjoyed the idea of doing something for my daughter, but I wasn't looking forward to the walk-through itself. During the twenty-minute drive from work to her apartment, I asked myself, "What does this walk-through want to become?" After about fifteen minutes the answer came: It wants to be "complete"; in other words, if I were careful in checking everything and asking the right questions, neither my daughter nor I would have to go back a second time. This answer calmed me and focused my attention. As it turned out, some parts of the apartment had been overlooked by the cleaning people, and I spent an hour or so after the walk-through making the place shine. Without the koan, I still would have spent the extra hour, but I would have groused about it.[11]

In addition to using koans in my personal life, since 1989 I have also used them in my writing. Like Joyce Tenneson, I ask questions about my writing and wait for the answer. I'll ask the larger question, "What does my writing want to become?" and the smaller question, "What does this piece want to become?" I ask general questions (as above) and particular questions,

10. Equally famous koans are "A monk asked Master Joshu, 'Does a dog have Buddha-nature?' Joshu said, 'Mu' " [that is, 'no,' 'non-existence,' or 'no-thing']; and "The original face—the face before you were brought into this world by your mother and father—what is it?"

11. "Completeness" is a common answer to my koans. I think the cessation of interrupting allows me to see the work in progress as a whole and, if unfinished, needing to be finished. James Moffett makes a similar observation. Commenting on the sessions he led at Breadloaf School of English, Moffett says, "Many students have reported that fragments of unfinished thought or writing came together during or because of meditation so that they were able and pleased to be able to complete them." James Moffett, "Responses," *College Composition and Communication,* Volume 45, Number 2, May 1994, p. 259.

such as "How much background information needs to be included?" Through trial and error, I've learned that it is best if I begin by quieting the mind, just sitting for a few minutes without thinking. When thoughts arise, I let them go. If they're particularly persistent thoughts, I make an appointment with them for later in the day.

I then repeat the question several times until I can feel a sense of "I don't know." I've learned to appreciate this period of doubt because I know it precedes the answer. I make friends with the doubt. In the beginning the doubt used to bother me a great deal. For years I had taken pride in knowing answers to questions my students asked me, and I did not like having to tell them, "I don't know." It took a while for me to relax my body and become comfortable with not knowing the answer to the koan.

After the doubt comes a period when I wait for the answer by simply not trying to do anything, a period that might take weeks for the larger koans and a half hour for the smaller koans. In the beginning this was like being calm while waiting for an important call. It was hard. I had to learn to be receptive to whatever came to mind, whether it seemed relevant or not. I had to be careful that I didn't judge the answer, or change it if I didn't understand it, or be afraid that I might make a mistake and get the wrong answer. My job was to be aware.

I gained confidence in solving koans by recording in my journal the actions, thoughts, and feelings that accompanied the times I got them right, and the times I didn't. I tried to repeat the former and avoid the latter.[12]

Right answers often came at unexpected times or were puzzling because initially they didn't make sense. It was as if my "right brain" had found the answer and my "left brain" had to figure it out. In other words, when I couldn't initially explain the answer, it probably was right. Right answers also were larger in scope—holistic rather than atomistic—and appeared suddenly, at unexpected times, usually when I was not focusing on the koan.[13]

After about a year of using koans in my own writing, I told my students what I did and, when they showed interest, I included koans in my

12. I have kept a personal journal since 1977, and I include notes on my attempts to solve koans. More than anything else, the journal helps me to see patterns over time. I understand that Zen masters tend to discourage journal writing, perhaps because it encourages rationalistic thinking. Janwillem Van de Wetering writes that the practice of "keeping notes," nevertheless, is frequently carried on by monks in Zen monasteries.

13. I have taken considerable comfort in knowing that teacher-turned-writer Natalie Goldberg was herself a serious student of Zen, studying under Dainin Katagiri, first abbot of Minnesota Zen Meditation Center in Minneapolis and author of *Returning to Silence: Zen Practice in Daily Life,* Boston: Shambhala, 1988. Goldberg's account of her Zen training is the subject of her most recent book *Long Quiet Highway: Waking Up in America,* New York: Bantam Books, 1993. Her two previous books, *Writing Down the Bones: Freeing the Writer Within,* Boston: Shambhala, 1986, and *Wild Mind: Living the Writer's Life,* New York: Bantam Books, 1990, have been an inspiration to many beginning writers.

teaching.[14] I did not mention my background in meditation, and I did not use the word koan.[15] I saw no point in teaching meditation in the classroom. The mind-clearing, concentration, and holistic or intuitive thinking exercises that form the core of my writing classes seem to be essential habits of mind in any field, including, for example, baseball—clearing the mind: "Forget about yesterday's game"; concentration: "Keep your eye on the ball"; and holistic or intuitive thinking: "Steal second when you get the chance." I simply talked with my students about forming the question and waiting for an answer, and I called this kind of thinking both intuition and holistic thinking.[16] My students were more receptive than I expected. After all, they had abundant experience asking themselves questions they couldn't immediately answer. "What can I do with a major in English?" and "Is this relationship really good for me?" seemed to be daily imponderables for them.[17]

During the first week of the course I have them ask the question, "What does society want my writing to become?" I give them class time to answer this question, and I also assign it as homework. Their answers usually run about a page in length, and they typically list comments they've received from teachers and peers, as well as conclusions they have drawn from years of reading books, magazines, and newspapers. Common answers (I've condensed them to save space) are "beneficial," "useful," "interesting," "factual," "humorous," "action packed," "something that breaks the mold," "clear," "concise," "easy to understand," and "productive." Generally the tone of their answers is slightly antagonistic. They see society as wanting them to, as one student put it, "conform to the norm." Another student

14. I will always be indebted to James Moffett for building the bridge between writing and meditation in his essay, "Writing, Inner Speech, and Meditation," in his book *Coming on Center: English Education in the Evolution,* Montclair, New Jersey: Boynton/Cook, 1981, pp. 133–181.

15. For my view of the complementary nature of writing and meditation, see "Wait and the Writing Will Come: Meditation and the Composing Process" in *Presence of Mind: Writing and the Domain Beyond the Cognitive,* edited by Alice Brand and Richard L. Graves, Portsmouth: Boynton/Cook, 1994, pp. 21–29. A number of famous authors have practiced meditation, including Thoreau, Yeats, Eliot, Rilke, Hesse, Hopkins, Emerson, Ginsberg, Salinger, Snyder, Dillard, Matthiessen, Harvey, and Merwin.

16. I use both terms interchangeably so that my students will associate with the positive experiences of thinking intuitively (insight or the direct perception of reality) yet disassociate from the negative connotations of intuition (noninferential or unverifiable knowledge). I like it that the term *holistic thinking* comes under the category of holism—that wholes are other than the sum of their parts. When I asked my students what they thought the difference was between intuition and holistic thinking, one wrote, "I think intuition comes naturally. Holistic thinking is a conscious effort—something that must be practiced." Her answer suggests the commonly held notion that intuition comes naturally and, therefore, cannot be taught.

17. Although there must be others, I know of only one other person who has used koans in the classroom: Raymond Weaver at Columbia, teacher of Allen Ginsberg. Ginsberg wrote, "In a way, I learned the most from Weaver because he already had some knowledge of Zen, and he used koans as part of his teaching method, which, at Columbia, was unknown." Michael Schumacher, *Dharma Lion: A Biography of Allen Ginsberg,* New York: St. Martin's Press, 1992, p. 24.

admits, "Perhaps society wants the best for my writing, be it whatever. Perhaps it is a cop-out to say society does not want the best for my writing." Only a few students do not know what society wants their writing to become.

A few days later, I ask them a second question, "What do you want your writing to become?" These answers too run about a page in length and, when condensed, include "open," "interesting," "creative," "my voice," "organized," "a source of relieving stress," "high quality," "well-educated," "informative," "a legacy to my children," "appreciated," "a pleasure to others," and "to express thoughts and feelings." The tone of these answers is sincere, honest, hopeful, and thoughtful. Some sound almost idealistic, as with the student who writes that she wants her writing to become a "reflection of the good things . . . in life," while others sound down-to-earth: "I want my writing to become something that comes completely natural to me." One student, aware of having suffered at the hands of English professors and their red pens, ends her statement by saying she wants her writing to be "unafraid." All students seem to know what they want their own writing to become.

During the second week of the course, I have them ask themselves the intuitive or holistic question, "What does my writing want to become?" I tell them that they have already answered the questions about what society and they themselves want it to become, and that this is a different question. I talk about holistic or intuitive thinking, about seeding the mind by asking the question and allowing the doubt to arise without panicking, and about the answer coming at unexpected times—while exercising, or showering, or gazing at a stop light.

A few students switch over to intuitive thinking and discover an answer the first time. Their answers are rarely more than a word or a phrase (I have not condensed these answers): "honest," "a point," "a path to freedom," "stronger," and "an independent body." Some students do not understand their answers. One student said her writing wanted to be "complete," but she didn't know what that meant. When I asked her how she came up with the answer, she wrote, "It was the progression of questions—what society wants, what I want . . . I think this question encompasses bits and pieces of those answers and many other facets. It takes all these aspects and incorporates them until they function as a whole." Their experiences of answering this question mirrored my own: They were able to make sense of their answers only after thinking about them for a while. After two weeks, the student who said her writing wanted to become "stronger" wrote, "Stronger, meaning more of an impact on my reader. More powerful, more thought provoking. So powerful that my reader won't be able to leave it alone. The idea or impact will linger."

After a month I ask them what influence their answer has had on their writing. One student wrote, "Because I got the answer through intuition, I've tried to trust it [my intuition] more. Especially since my answer is 'free,' I've tried to give it [my writing] more freedom. I'm not sure yet what result this has had because I'm still letting it develop." The student who wrote that her writing wanted to become "honest" said that her answer helped her to be "open to suggestions. I've tried not to be biased in my writing. I write about the truth without being judgmental, but it is hard." The student who said his writing wanted to become an independent body wrote, "My answer caused me to detach my writing from myself and look at it as an independent body. I saw where improvement was needed."

Some students take a week, a month, or even a semester to get an answer to "What does my writing want to become?" Some end the course without reaching an answer. One student wrote, "I have no idea what my writing wants. I'd rather that it speak for itself and when it tells me I'll let you know." I tell them to be patient. "You have done the job of seeding the question in your mind, and when your mind is ready, it will produce an answer." When students guess, producing a different answer each week, I advise them to relax, to let the mind do the work. I have noticed that when students do get an intuitive answer, they refuse to change it even when challenged, even when they don't know what the answer means. This is the certitude that often accompanies intuition.

About halfway through the course, I teach my students how to use intuitive or holistic thinking to revise individual pieces by posing the question, "What does this piece want to become?" Because the question is more specific, students find it easier to answer. One student wrote, "The horse piece wants to be inspirational and real," then went on to explain, "Real in that it is written by a serious horse person who considers riding to be much more than a hobby. Inspirational in that it was an empowering experience for me and I want this to show through."

I also teach students how to customize the question. For instance, one student was writing about having moved to the United States from Cyprus as a youngster. When she was a junior in college, she returned to Cyprus for a short stay and found that she really liked being with her relatives. For more than a month she wrote about trying to decide where to live after she graduated from college. She agonized over this dilemma, weighing the pros and cons, listing reasons for staying and reasons for leaving. When she reached the point at which she was ready to revise, instead of asking "Where should I live, Cyprus or the United States?" she asked, "Where do I belong?" This question helped her see that she was a North American and that where she lived was less important than who she was.

Anyone interested in using koans in the classroom need not follow my long journey through meditation, but to understand their process and power, I do recommend first practicing koans at home. I also recommend reading books in this field, perhaps starting with those cited in the footnotes. People like me, who can't find a Rinzai Zen Master or koan teacher, may wish to join with others who study koans.[18] Finally, I recommend keeping a journal. Photographer Joyce Tenneson, meditator Janwillem van de Wetering, and many others—including me—have used the personal journal to record experiences, to discover patterns, and to build on what works.

18. Teachers in the National Council of Teachers of English have formed the Assembly on Expanded Perspectives on Learning (AEPL) for discussions of teaching practices beyond the cognitive. AEPL may be contacted through NCTE, 1111 Kenyon Road, Urbana, Illinois 61801 (1-800-369-NCTE). AEPL meetings are held at the fall NCTE convention, the spring Conference on College Composition and Communication, and the summer AEPL conference.

Part Three

Personal Spiritual Journeys

Students' stories and personal issues may so influence their lives that they refuse to be ignored. While English classes, for good reason, should not become therapy sessions propelled by students' stories, the need to decide whether or not to allow students to deal with personally compelling issues in our writing classes does raise questions that English teachers must address. What do we *know* about personal spiritual journeys in the classroom? What do we *do* about them? Do we deny them entry into the curriculum? Do we relegate them to personal journals and hope they do not appear in essays we have to evaluate? Or do we allow them space within our classes and within our conceptions of writing to learn?

The following three contributing authors show how they have allowed students to integrate their personal spiritual journeys effectively within the study of writing and how both the journey and the writing have a powerful complementary effect on each other. Students become better, more confident writers while teachers and students become more humane, considerate, and accepting individuals in their responses to each other and to themselves.

Paul Heilker contends that the remarkable appeal of popular books of meditation "springs from the rhetoric they embody." Basing his work on social construction theory, he invites his students to "analyze the rhetoric—the characteristic *ethos*, subject matters, structures, tropes, diction, and so on—of popular books of meditations," and then "imitate and thus internalize this rhetoric of spirituality as they write their own short books of meditations."

Jacqueline Rinaldi reveals the power of writing to heal, which she discovered in a writing seminar she taught for people diagnosed with multiple sclerosis (MS), a chronic disease of the central nervous system that impairs the body's motor functions. Through writing and sharing their writing, participants were able to connect to others, to nature, and to their inner selves—an endeavor that graced their lives with feelings of transcendence.

Wendy Bishop chronicles the journey of teaching as spiritual, offering moments of opportunity, danger, allure, and confusion. Teaching calls us to inquiry and to civic action. It calls us to question "the ways we make students . . . produce texts we don't value and the way we . . . do this ourselves for academic promotion." And it calls us to incorporate the public and the personal, the creative and the academic as we become more playful in our interaction with students, with colleagues around the country, and with ourselves.

9

The Rhetoric of Spirituality in Popular Meditation Books

Paul Heilker

One way to gauge our recent collective hunger for spirituality in this country is to look at the tremendous growth in the popularity of meditation books. These texts demonstrate a striking degree of uniformity in their rhetoric, which can be attributed to their common genealogy. Since appearing in the early 1980s, many meditation books have been written by—and specifically for—members of various twelve-step recovery programs such as Alcoholics Anonymous. Initially published exclusively by Hazelden, these books included titles such as *Each Day a New Beginning: Daily Meditations for Women* (1982) and *Touchstones: Daily Meditations for Men* (1986). But meditation books soon began to cross-over from this limited audience to a mass market. In 1990, Anne Wilson Schaef's *Meditations for Women Who Do Too Much* found a large and grateful readership and its success prompted a number of imitators.[1]

The mass appeal of these popular meditation books indicates, I believe, more than some urgently indiscriminate need for *any* kind of spiritual help in American culture. Rather, their remarkable appeal springs from the rhetoric they embody and enact, a rhetoric that offers their readers an especially attractive spirituality: one that is easily accessible, distilled, and potent; one they can readily internalize and make their own. This rhetoric is also one we

---

1. Large, mainstream publishing houses such as HarperCollins, Simon and Schuster, Avon, and Bantam Books now regularly publish meditation books, and we now find entire shelves in almost every bookstore full of little books with titles such as *Body, Mind, and Spirit: Daily Inspiration for Wholeness and Healing* (1990), *Believing in Myself: Daily Meditations for Healing and Building Self-Esteem* (1991), *Meditations for Men Who Do Too Much* (1992), *At My Best: 365 Meditations for Physical, Spiritual, and Emotional Well-Being* (1992), *Meditations for Parents Who Do Too Much* (1993), *Healing Hearts: Meditations for Women Living with Divorce* (1993), *Bright Words for Dark Days: Meditations for Women Who Get the Blues* (1994), and *A Man's Book of the Spirit: Daily Meditations for a Mindful Life* (1994).

can offer to our students if we wish to incorporate spiritual empowerment in our pedagogy. Basing my work on social construction theory, which contends that thought is internalized discourse—that we can think only in ways we have learned to talk/write—I will begin this chapter by arguing that if we wish to empower our students to think spiritually and "do" spirituality, we must first help them learn to talk/write about spirituality by offering them good models of such discourse and easy access to the necessary vocabulary. I will then explicate a practical way I have developed to accomplish these goals. By having students analyze the rhetoric—the characteristic *ethos*, subject matters, structures, tropes, diction, and so on—of popular books of meditations, students can imitate and thus internalize this rhetoric of spirituality as they write their own short books of meditations.

Teachers interested in incorporating spiritual empowerment in their pedagogy have special cause to be concerned of late and need to beware of attacks from both the political left and the political right. We need to acknowledge that the debate over the separation of church and state has again captured our national attention (as a result of a recent series of court rulings upholding the exclusion of prayer from schools—but allowing a problematic moment of silence nonetheless—and a series of vituperative responses to these rulings that have received widespread media play). One faction would see no place at all in schools for any kind of spiritually empowering pedagogy, while the other would see no place in schools for any but the "right" (as they define it) kind of spiritually empowering pedagogy. The teaching practice I discuss here thus has much to offer teachers interested in spiritual empowerment. While it encourages students to learn and use a distilled and potent rhetoric of spirituality, it can also be readily assimilated into secular environments because it employs a time-honored writing pedagogy to achieve traditional goals: the rhetorical analysis and imitation of model texts to produce highly focused, concise, well-developed student writing based, in part, on research and outside sources. Furthermore, such teaching can be defended against political attacks from both the left and the right because what it actually requires is for students to scrutinize and critique a nonsectarian text from popular culture. Finally, resistant students who would rather not learn how to think spiritually and "do" spirituality are not coerced to do so: They are always free to write a book that parodies this rhetoric (something on the order, perhaps, of *Meditations for Geeks Who Talk Too Much*).

More important than the benefits this teaching practice offers teachers, however, are the benefits it offers student writers. First, like any good writing pedagogy, it offers students practice in crucial aspects of rhetoric and the writing process. By writing their own short meditation books, students gain essential practice in assessing and addressing a *real* rhetorical situation, in writing to a *real* audience for a *real* purpose; in analyzing model texts to discover, assimilate, and reproduce their conventions; and in prewriting, drafting, revising, and editing a substantial text. Even students who choose to write parodies of meditation books will still learn and practice valuable rhetorical reading and writing skills. After completing this assignment, students will be practiced in a variety of skills they will need to utilize in order to enter into other discourse communities of their own choosing in the future. Second, and more significantly, I think, this teaching practice offers interested students an education in spirituality. There is more to the universe— more to the ways we can think about it, be in it, and respond to it—than just logic and rationality. But logic and rationality are the *only* forms of thinking, being, and responding we are conditioned to value and teach in academia. Spirituality is an alternative, *complementary* way of thinking about, being in, and responding to the universe in which we live. It is a kind of thinking, feeling, and being that is very rarely, if ever, valued, taught, or practiced in academia, but which is nonetheless an essential form of problem solving and thus is an integral part of the liberal education of a well-rounded individual. Students who write short meditation books gain essential practice in (and are given the opportunity to come to value) this alternative, complementary form of problem solving. In completing this assignment, my students typically write themselves toward spiritual solutions to problems in their relationships with their parents, siblings, significant others, friends, and roommates, or write themselves toward spiritual responses to the stresses of student life, such as paralyzing anxieties, perfectionism, failure, disappointment, loneliness, and depression. Writing their own meditation books gives students practice in a neglected but essential set of problem-solving skills, one that complements logic and rationality and that (like logic and rationality) they can (and, we hope, will) carry with them beyond the assignment and beyond their lives as students.

Reflective Thought as Internalized Discourse

While social construction theory is neither new nor limited to a particular discipline, and while it has become widely accepted and utilized in English studies and composition studies over the past decade, it is, nonetheless, challenging (if not deeply troubling) for many of us because its epistemological assumptions run directly counter to those that most of us, however implicitly, consider commonsensical, natural, and, thus, unquestionable. For instance, in "Social Construction, Language, and the Authority of Knowledge," Kenneth A. Bruffee writes that a social constructionist perspective "assumes that entities we normally call reality, knowledge, thought, facts, texts, selves, and so on are ... community-generated and community-maintained linguistic entities ... that define or 'constitute' the communities that generate them" (Bruffee 1986, 774). Moreover, Bruffee continues, "social construction assumes that the matrix of thought is not the individual self but some community of knowledgeable peers and the vernacular language of that community" (Bruffee 1986, 777). Indeed, to adopt a social constructionist point of view, he argues, means that we must reconceive of "entities we normally think of as strictly individual, internal, and mental affairs," such as cognition, memory, imagination, perception, motivation, emotion, and so on, as inherently social affairs (Bruffee 1986, 775).

The social constructionist assumption that the matrix of thought is not the individual but his/her community, that one's spirituality is, therefore, largely a community-created and -maintained language construct, is perhaps especially difficult to accept and so requires more explanation. In another article, "Collaborative Learning and the 'Conversation of Mankind,'" Bruffee explains how this apparently radical assumption can be justified. His explanation begins by citing Michael Oakeshott's argument that

> As civilized human beings, we are the inheritors, neither of an inquiry about ourselves and the world, nor of an accumulating body of information, but of a conversation, begun in the primeval forests and made more articulate in the course of the centuries . . . a conversation which goes on both in public and within each of ourselves. (quoted in Bruffee 1984, 638)

According to Bruffee, Oakeshott is arguing "that the human conversation takes place within us as well as among us, and that conversation as it takes place within us is what we call reflective thought." Such an argument, he says, "assumes what the work of Lev Vygotsky and others has shown, that reflective thought is public or social conversation internalized." Bruffee maintains that after first experiencing and learning "the skill and partnership of conversation" through direct social exchange with other people, we then "learn to displace that 'skill and partnership' by playing silently ourselves, in imagination, the parts of all the participants in the conversation" (Bruffee 1984, 639). Hence, he contends, "since thought is internalized conversation, thought and conversation tend to work largely the same way." Thus he writes:

> According to this concept of mental activity many of the social forms and conventions of conversation, most of the grammatical, syntactical, and rhetorical structures of conversation, and the range, flexibility, impetus, and goals of conversation are the sources of the forms and conventions, structures, impetus, range and flexibility, and the issues of reflective thought. (Bruffee 1984, 639)

In short, Bruffee contends that the community in which we learn to converse is "the source of the quality, depth, terms, character, and issues of thought" (Brufee 1984, 639), that thought is not some sort of given "essential attribute" of the individual human mind, but "instead an artifact created by social interaction" (Bruffee 1984, 640). In sum, he says, "We can think because we can talk, and we think in ways we have learned to talk" (Bruffee 1984, 640). He agrees with Stanley Fish's contention that the thoughts we "can think and the mental operations [we] can perform have their source in some or other interpretive community" (Bruffee 1984, 640) and concludes this section of his essay by paraphrasing Fish's suggestion "that interpretive communities may also be in large measure the source of what we regard as our very selves . . . [since our] feelings and intuitions are as much the product of social relations as our knowledge" (Bruffee 1984, 641).

Specifically applied to the matter of spirituality, then, a social constructionist perspective maintains that spirituality—an entity we normally consider to be a strictly individual, internal, and mental affair, a personal melding of mental operations like imagination, perception, emotion, and the like—is inherently a social affair. Social construction theory holds that the quality, depth, terms, character, issues, range, flexibility, impetus, goals, conventions, and grammatical, syntactical, and rhetorical structures of conversations about spirituality are the sources of the quality, depth, terms, character, issues, range, flexibility, impetus, goals, conventions, and grammatical, syntactical, and rhetorical structures of an individual's reflective, spiritual thought. But how can one engage with such spiritual talk if one does not have physical access to a group of people among whom such talk is commonplace, if one is not a member of a twelve-step program, a prayer group, or similar spiritual community? If we cannot hear such talk, how might we touch the source of our spirituality? The answer is through reading and writing. As Bruffee puts it, "If thought is internalized conversation, then writing is internalized conversation reexternalized. . . . We converse; we internalize conversation as thought; and then by writing, we re-immerse conversation in its external, social medium" (Bruffee 1984, 641). Popular meditation books are thus a concrete embodiment of one kind of spirituality internalized and then reexternalized, a concrete enactment of one kind of spiritual talk that can serve as the source of one's reflective thought and as a basis for empowering the spiritual in our pedagogy.

Teaching a Rhetoric of Spirituality

As a concrete embodiment and enactment of such spiritual talk, meditation books offer us a tremendous advantage over spoken spiritual discourse; while speech is ephemeral, writing is not. Unlike speech, we can study writing closely and repeatedly, carefully comparing and contrasting one instance of such spiritual discourse with other instances. In this way, we can derive a rhetoric of spirituality; that is, we can discern the distinctive commonalities, the characteristic topoi, tropes, and means of persuasion that distinguish this kind of spiritual discourse, this way of thinking spiritually. As I mentioned earlier, popular meditation books employ a strikingly uniform rhetoric, even to considerations such as page size, the use of particular fonts and font sizes, capital letters, italics, boldface, and the use of white space. Examining any one of the titles I listed at the outset would give us a good sense of the rhetoric employed in all those books. For my purposes, however, I choose to have my students examine one of the most popular meditation books to date, Schaef's *Meditations for Women Who Do Too Much*, because it seems to have spoken to a great number of interested people and seems to have met a great spiritual need, which implies that it embodies and enacts a most effective, most empowering spiritual rhetoric. I reproduce here two typical entries from Schaef's book:

January 14
BELIEF

*Why indeed must "God" be a noun? Why not a verb
. . . the most active and dynamic of all?*

—Mary Daly

Some of us have difficulty with the concept of God because we have seen God evolve into something or someone who is static, a mega-controller, and frankly someone who is not that nice to be around. Traditionally, we have tried to make God static so we would feel safe. That is our problem, not God's.

What if we see God as a process—the process of the universe? What if we begin to understand that we are part of the process of the universe? What if we realize that it is only when we live who we are that we have the option of being one with that process? Trying to be someone else, who we *think* we should be, or who *others* think we should be ruptures our oneness with that process.

IF GOD is a process and I am a process, we
have something in common with which to begin.

September 3
IN TOUCH WITH A POWER GREATER THAN ONESELF
Those who lose dreaming are lost.

—Australian Aboriginal proverb

If we are to have any hope of being in touch with the process of the universe or with a power greater than ourselves, we must learn to move beyond our rational, logical minds and to let ourselves "dream."

That does not mean that there is anything wrong with our rational, logical minds, but we can have trouble connecting with a force greater than ourselves when we *lead* with our rational minds.

There are so many things in this universe that affect us and with which we are connected. Sometimes the only way we can be aware of that connection is to let ourselves dream beyond our knowing. We have so much to learn from everything around us, if we just open ourselves to that which may be.

I ADMIT I don't know it all yet. Learning comes in many forms.

To begin moving students toward internalizing the rhetoric of spirituality embodied and enacted in this text, I first present this book to them as a
good example of a popular meditation book and as a normal and representative text of its genre. Their ultimate assignment, I next inform them, is to
write their own small meditation books, using Schaef as a model. As the first
step in this process of imitation and internalization, I then ask my students to
read at least a half year's daily meditations in Schaef in sequence (I do not
specify which date to start with) and to look carefully for twenty things that
these 180 or so entries have in common. We then spend the next several class
periods reporting on our findings, discussing representative examples of the
common features we have found, and analyzing how and why these features
function—separately and collectively—to form a coherent and integrated set
of conventions, that is, a rhetoric of spirituality. Some of the most important
of these conventions include

- Meditations often use simple, single word titles, titles that are often
  repeated and/or joined to other often repeated titles by a virgule to
  offer the reader straightforward names for his/her spiritual pains and
  to indicate the recurrent, fundamental themes of meditation and the
  interconnectedness of these themes.
- Each meditation begins with a quotation, typically from a famous,
  powerful, successful person, which lends power, respectability,
  credibility, and cachet to the entire meditative project; indicates that
  famous, powerful, successful people are dealing with the exact same
  problems; and shows that the author and reader are not the only
  ones seeking spiritual solutions.
- Each meditation deals with a serious issue in an earnest fashion
  (comic relief, when used, is typically heavily ironic or sarcastic) to
  indicate that meditations are not pleasure reading, that spirituality is
  important, and that spirituality is work.
- Meditations continually construe the problem under discussion as
  the result of a disease, addiction, or insanity to highlight the sever-
  ity and reality of these problems, to break through the reader's
  denial and supposed self-sufficiency, and, more important, to underscore and insist upon repeatedly the need for spiritual help to alleviate this disease, addiction, or insanity.
- References to "God" are balanced or offset by an equal number of
  references to "a higher power" or "a power greater than ourselves"
  in order to point readers to something above the human sphere that
  is yet fluid and undefined enough to allow them to reinvent that
  entity in their own ways, to avoid implicitly invoking and favoring
  a Judeo-Christian conception of deity that is exclusionary and dismissive of Islamic, Buddhist, and other conceptions, to alleviate the

debilitating psychic baggage readers may carry with them from their childhood conceptions of "God," and to imply a less threatening conception of deity by not capitalizing his/her/its name.

- Meditations employ a distinctive set of common themes and oft-repeated words that offer the reader the necessary tools—the necessary concepts and vocabulary—for thinking spiritually (like *ownership, honesty, acceptance, control, selfishness, fear, change, pain, awareness, balance, peace, healing, choices, growth, love, expectations, belief, faith, perfectionism, feelings,* and so on).

- Meditations make exclusive use of "I," "we," and "us" as pronouns to make all references inclusive, and imply sympathy, solidarity, and community with the reader.

- Meditations make heavy use of present-tense verbs to emphasize "living in the moment," to stress the immediate, present-tense, ongoing nature and living process of spirituality and meditation.

- Meditations utilize a familiar tone throughout to avoid "preachiness" and sappy, "greeting card" sentimentality, to encourage the reader to see the writer as a trustworthy friend, a co-traveler in their sometimes difficult but nonetheless "doable" communal journey back from their shared disease, addiction, or insanity.

- The text demonstrates the meditative process we are to assimilate; meditations are repeatedly structured in ways that model the kinds of spiritual thinking we are to take away from the book:
  - Meditations frequently begin by asking a question or posing a problem and then allow the reader to follow the writer as he or she works through the sometimes difficult process of developing a spiritual response to the question or problem.
  - Meditations often begin with a stereotype and then unpack the various ways in which the stereotype debilitates us.
  - Meditations often employ bottom-up processing, suggesting, exploring, weighing, and perhaps discarding various options as they build up to their central assertions (rather than declaring them at the outset and then defending them).

- The text employs a variety of techniques to make abstract concepts more understandable and applicable:
  - Meditations make frequent use of similes, metaphors, extended analogies, and images to help make abstract concepts more concrete, accessible, and visualizable.
  - Meditations often personify our emotions to make these abstractions more concrete and accessible and to highlight the reality that emotions have agency and power and presence, that they *do* things to us.

- Meditations frequently employ short, simple sentences to break complex ideas and abstractions into smaller, more easily managed, more easily digestible elements.
- Each meditation ends either with an affirmation or with a resolution of two or three simple and punchy sentences: The affirmations sum up in a small, portable, memorable package the central spiritual message for the day; the resolutions urge the reader to take some simple yet specific action as a way of concretely applying the abstract spiritual insights gained in the meditative process and as a way of turning the perhaps vague theory into actual, understandable practice.
- The text uses a variety of techniques to secure strong emphases and an attentive reading:
  - Meditations occasionally use profanity to shake the reader out of passivity, cut through his or her denial with a blunt instrument, and underscore the gut-level seriousness of spirituality.
  - Meditations never use negating contractions like "can't" or "won't," but rather always use constructions like "can not" and "will not" to avoid glossing over and hiding the deadly serious import of the *not* and of the author's rare but earnest and stern warnings, directives, and declarations.
  - Meditations occasionally employ classical rhetorical tropes like anaphora and epistrophe[2] to hammer the reader with repetitions of the important concepts, themes, phrases, and/or terms of that meditation.
- The title, quotation, meditation, and ending affirmation or resolution are all unified, all focused on the same issue or theme to underscore the focused and integrated (and the focusing and integrating) natures of spiritual meditation.
- Meditations are progressive and cumulative, building on each other in order to demonstrate the unified nature of the whole meditative project and its various strands or themes and, moreover, to emphasize and enact the ongoing, cumulative spiritual thinking process the reader is supposed to internalize.

After having my students discern, articulate, and study this rhetoric of spirituality embodied in this popular meditation book, I then ask them to define an appropriate audience and purpose for the small meditation book I

---

2. *Anaphora* is the repetition of the same word or words at the beginning of successive clauses or verses; *epistrophe* is the repetition of a word or words at the end of successive clauses or verses.

have assigned them to write: their own meditations covering fourteen consecutive days. Whom do they know who could use this kind of help? Almost invariably—since the assignment has sensitized them to their own (lack of) spirituality and since they are already well versed in the dictum to "write from what you know"—students define an audience and a purpose that are self-reflexive: They write meditation books to meet their own spiritual needs. Students in my classes have written themselves toward spiritual responses to their own problems with such titles as *Meditations for Children Whose Parents Want Them to Be Perfect, Meditations for New College Students Far Away from Home, Meditations for Single People with Newly Married Friends, Meditations for Women with Broken Hearts, Meditations for Students Preparing for the GRE, Meditations for Sisters Who Do Not Get Along, Meditations for Mothers Who Work at Home, Meditations for Men Who Don't Understand Women*, and *Meditations for Teenagers Living in Darkness* (which concerned itself with teenage depression and suicidal thoughts). My students' abilities to internalize and reexternalize this rhetoric of spirituality has been consistently good and frequently remarkable, which is demonstrated, for instance, in the following two entries from Christina's *Meditations for Women with Eating Disorders*:

January 1
ONE DAY AT A TIME

We've only just begun.
—The Carpenters

Life is a one-way street, and there's no turning back. Karen Carpenter is a good example for us because she found out a little too late that the road she was traveling by bingeing and purging brought her to a dead end fast. She, like ourselves, thought she had no choice, had no control. But is this true—that we have no choice over our own futures, and at the least, over our own bodies? NO!

We do have the choice to not think about tomorrow. We have the choice of living in the now. And we do have the choice to be who we are, and not what we are not. We have the choice of loving ourselves and doing it one day at a time. We have the choice of taking our lives by the reins and taking hold of our situations with the help of our higher power. We have the choice of who or what our higher powers are and how we use our higher powers to help us down the road to recovery. We can make the right choice, and we can choose a full life of happiness. We have the choice!

EACH DAY is new and has just begun. We have the choice to honor that day and ourselves.

January 6

RELYING/HIGHER POWER

Company on a journey is as good as a carriage.
—Italian Proverb

Life is an uphill journey for the most part. And most of our lives are spent trying to be independent and self-reliant on the trek of life. But, as most of us have found out, we just cannot rely on ourselves for everything. We need support in some way or another, whether it be mental or physical help. If it were all up to us to save ourselves from this heart-wrenching and physically deteriorating disease, we would not make it all the way up the hill. The reality is that we would end up dead a lot sooner than we should or would like. We'd starve to death or have some other health complication like a heart attack. We might even try to take our own lives.

Desperation leads us to needing others and finally leads us to needing a higher power–God, a tree, a support group or whatever it may be to get us up this hill. We cannot do it alone. We do need help and support in order to make it in this world. We are not weak for asking for help.

IF A SEEDLING could grow without sun or water, it would yet be cold and alone.

My work on this project has reminded me that I once asked a trusted and wise friend of mine what the difference is between religion and spirituality. Religion, he said, is everything that happens on the outside, while spirituality is that which happens on the inside. But his simple answer no longer satisfies me. Social construction theory erases the distinction between inside and outside by insisting that my spiritual insides were once words happening outside of me. Spirituality, I now see, is something that I *do* with language, both internally and externally. And so I have had the happy realization, for instance, that my teaching and my thinking about my teaching are important ways in which I can think spiritually and "do" spirituality. Our students, I think, deserve a similar opportunity to see just how empowering a rhetoric of spirituality can be.

10

Journeys Through Illness
Connecting Body and Spirit

Jacqueline Rinaldi

> I sense strongly that the illness itself either unleashed a creature
> within me that had been restrained and let him run at his own hun-
> gry will; or it planted a whole new creature in place of the old.
>
> —Reynolds Price,
> *A Whole New Life*

What is it like to have a progressively debilitating illness, to live inside a lame
body that limits your mobility, makes you dependent on others for basic needs,
and pitches you into the dark regarding the future course of your life? Curious
to discover whether writing about illness could assuage the spirits of people
troubled by such realities, a colleague and I recently organized a writing
seminar for people diagnosed with multiple sclerosis (MS), a chronic disease
of the central nervous system that impairs the body's motor functions.

My colleague, Ann Spector,[1] who had known many persons afflicted
with MS, had a strong sense that patients suffering from this disease would
find it salutary to write about their illness, and we both concluded that the
writing experience could be facilitated through the formation of a collaborative writing group. My desire to connect with such a group was further
stirred by a yearning to reconnect with my mother, who lived with this crip-
pling disease for thirty years. Our goal here was to create an environment
founded on an enabling pedagogy that would encourage those suffering from
the physical and emotional distress of MS to write about illness in ways that

1. I am deeply grateful to my long-time colleague and friend Ann Spector, recently deceased,
for her participation as co-leader of this workshop and for her astute pedagogical insights while
working with this community of people.

118

would bring spiritual renewal. Within this context, we thought of "spirituality" less as the practice of a specific religious belief than as a way for participants to connect to others, to nature, and to their inner selves—in an endeavor to grace life with some feeling of transcendence. To this end, we sought to instruct the group in using language, in the words of Ann Berthoff, as "a speculative instrument" to give "form to feeling, cogency to conflict and shape to memory," in an effort "not only to name but also to formulate and transform" the meaning of illness in their lives (1972, 646–47). People committed to writing about the often painful, sometimes comic aspects of MS, we assumed, would eventually come to see how bodily deficits could be reimagined as spiritual assets. As psychotherapist Thomas Moore reminds us, "a poetic reading of the body as it expresses itself in illness calls for a new appreciation for the laws of imagination, in particular a willingness to let imagination keep moving into ever newer and deeper insights" (1992, 159). In effect, in forming this writing group, it was our aim to bring to the notion of composition an enriched interdisciplinary context that would link the writing process to the cultural, psychological, and spiritual needs of the writers.

The Impact of Illness on the Group

Despite more than twenty years of experience in teaching composition to undergraduate and graduate students, my colleague and I felt challenged in working with this group in ways we had never imagined. As we began to search for an effective pedagogy to help them transform illness into a healing experience, we realized that most MS patients live lives so replete with hardship in the daily care of their bodies that efforts to connect with a spiritual self are often difficult. As one group member put it, "Multiple sclerosis can grind upon the spirit as doggedly as abject poverty." Based on extensive studies of writing about illness, Anne Hawkins's recent work *Reconstructing Illness: Studies in Pathography* confirms that chronic impairment can so disrupt a life, depriving it of meaning and purpose, that illness "often seems arbitrary, cruel, and senseless" (1993, 2). Because MS strikes most individuals during their most productive years—between age twenty and age fifty—its impact can be physically and psychologically devastating for both patient and family. Before MSers become completely crippled, they often feel adrift in time and space. They stumble, limp, lose their grip on things, and need help with simple chores: opening a can of soup, carrying food from stove to table, taking out the garbage. Diagnosed with MS in her late twenties, essayist Nancy Mairs finds that living with this illness is like being "haunted by a capricious and meanspirited ghost . . . which trips you even when you're watching where you're going, knocks glassware out of your hand, [and] squeezes the urine out of your bladder before you reach the bathroom" (1990, 83).

In *A Leg to Stand On,* neurologist Oliver Sachs, describing the aftermath of a severe leg injury, illustrates how profoundly unsettling any experience of body damage can be, especially when one is unable to register feeling in the affected part. Quoting Freud's observation that "the Ego is first and foremost a body Ego" (quoted in Sachs 1984, 81), Sachs argues that our notion of "self" is intrinsically linked with the biological integrity of our body. "One may be said to 'own' or 'possess' one's body—at least its limbs and movable parts—by virtue of a constant flow of information . . . from the muscles, joints and tendons. One is oneself, because the body knows itself, confirms itself, at all times, by this sixth sense" of proprioception (1984, 71). Calling for a "neurology of the soul" to offset today's mechanistic approach to illness, Sachs urges practitioners to focus on "'centering' the patient, finding . . . an 'I,' amid the debris of neurological devastation" (1984, 219). It was our hope that as the group members began to write their stories, they would eventually, through the transforming power of language, recenter the "selves" that had been disoriented through illness.

Beset by worries about the neurological failures awaiting them in the future, MSers are additionally made anxious by changes in their bodily appearance. In *Stigma: Notes on the Management of Spoiled Identity,* sociologist Erving Goffman confirms just how "discrediting" a physical "failing, a shortcoming or a handicap" can be, and how humiliated the impaired are made to feel by the pitying stares or fearful avoidance of others (1963, 3). As one member of our writing group put it, "Having multiple sclerosis makes me feel useless. I feel shame being married to an ugly wheelchair. Maybe it's because I don't see myself anywhere that I feel I don't matter. I'm not in the magazines I read, not in the soap operas I watch, not in the ads I see on TV." Her words reminded us how marginal many of the disabled feel, given the paucity of media images mirroring people with handicaps. Similar feelings of shame at being publicly effaced are shared by Mairs: "Everyone else is 'there,' sucking breath mints and splashing on cologne and swigging wine coolers. You're not there. And if 'not there,' nowhere" (Mairs 1990, 34).

Because physical disability is so in conflict with American cultural ideals, comfort requires that it not be seen for what it is. In fact, anthropologist Robert Murphy contends that our culture's injunction to build the perfect body and pursue the well-muscled physique has escalated so far beyond real health issues into mindless zealotry that a secularized middle class now focuses more on redeeming the body than on redeeming the soul (1987, 114–16). To display the impaired in the everyday events of our lives would be to concede that disability itself is ordinary, that it could happen to you or me. Still, despite the spiritual isolation imposed on the impaired by our culture's construct of disability and its mechanized approach to health care, my colleague and I had a sense that our group would eventually succeed in taking a stand against these marginalizing forces. For Hawkins's work had shown us just how helpful the writing of a narrative about illness could be in encouraging the "imaginative reformulation of experience that reconnects the isolated individual sufferer with his or her world" (1993, 27). We also thought there might be a complementary correlation between increasing confidence in writing and the writer's self-acceptance, which the workshops would bring out.

Workshop Design

Though small, our group was diverse; the three men and four women ranged in age from thirty to sixty-three. Three had college degrees, four had attended college but had not graduated, and three had careers in the corporate world before illness forced them to resign. All struggled with some neurological disability. Our youngest member's condition had progressed so far that he had difficulty shuffling with a walker and would soon be dependent on a motorized vehicle. One woman was comparatively well, but another was in a wheelchair. We met during the summer months, and because hot weather can so exacerbate the symptoms of MS, we planned several breaks during the three-hour sessions so members could rest and stretch their tightening muscles. Yet despite the brutal heat of that summer—which left several who were in remission in May dependent on canes in July—the group's enthusiasm for writing never waned. At their request, we extended the seminar two additional weeks.

Throughout the ten weeks, we conducted the writing process within the guidelines of social epistemic theory, using several "writing to learn" exercises to show the group how meaning can be discovered and "shaped anew" through language. Sensing that members would need to "get close enough to [their] disease to restore the particular religious connection with life at which it hints" (Moore 1992, 168), we began by having them identify what they considered to be the most troubling symptoms of their illness. Among those mentioned were vertigo, incontinence, limping, slurred speech, foot drop, optic neuritis, lack of coordination, numbness, tingling limbs, bone-tiring fatigue. Next, we asked them to tell how it feels to live with these recurring and unpredictable exacerbations of MS. This time responses were more emotionally charged and most were negative: unmanly, marginal, cosmic joke, asexual, wasteland, freakish, gimp, challenge, useless failure. Confronted by a disease that daily mocked these people's efforts to be well, we gained a better understanding of the source of their painful feelings, and we were hopeful that in writing about the way in which illness had changed their lives, the members of the group would, in the words of Gabriele Rico, "harness that change to transform [their] pain into possibility" (Rico 1991, 41).

During the first three weeks, the group used ideas from these exercises to initiate their stories. Some wrote candidly about the losses that followed diagnosis: lost jobs, lost wives, lost friends, lost hope; others wrote angrily about their doctors' seeming indifference to persistent medical problems created by chronic disability; still others wrote of anguished nightmares over what would become of them once they lost total control over their bodies. In our effort to help the group achieve transcendence through writing, we understood that before any real spiritual healing could occur, they would first have to release the negative energy within. As Rico reminds us, "We cannot order our feelings into—or out of—existence. Under such direct assault, our feelings retreat into the furthest recesses of our minds and bodies and continue a life of their own, often finding destructive paths of expression" (Rico 1994, 213). Thus, writing about conflict will become spiritually regenerating only when we feel free to shape dark splintered moments of chaos into coherence, when given "permission to acknowledge, educate, and own our feelings, our stories, our lives" (Rico 1994, 213).

Writing Towards Healing

Our decision to run the seminar as a collaborative workshop, in which members read stories aloud weekly, proved more valuable than we imagined. Members quickly coalesced into a support group, encouraging and encouraged by one another's candor in revealing the impact of illness on their lives. Because most lacked adequate muscle control to take notes, they used recorders to tape the discussions, and this enabled them, at home, to reconsider recommendations for expanding their work. As members read expanded drafts, we offered directive criticism, prompting them toward further amplification of ideas and concrete disclosure of their material through anecdote, dialogue, and example. Three have since published their essays. One member, Jan, diagnosed with MS three months prior to the workshop, wrote poignantly about a dark moment from early in her illness.

> Last night my husband made me a chocolate "instant breakfast" for supper, as I did not feel up to eating anything solid. It was in a very heavy tall glass. I was sitting in my big easy chair watching TV while I drank it. My tingling hand became suddenly nerveless and the three-quarters-full glass fell from my fingers to the floor. My husband leaped out of his chair, yelling "How can you be so clumsy? You can't tell me that dropping that glass has anything to do with MS; you're just being lazy and not paying attention to what you're doing!"

Later in the essay, Jan describes this incident as a "silly little accident" that shook "my whole being to its roots" and confirmed with "complete and pitiless clarity" that "I would never again paint, dance, play racquet ball, or, worst of all, walk in the woods." Still "stiff with shock at the turn [her] life had taken," Jan saw her life as "a devastated crumbling wasteland," a liminal state characterized by impotence and despair through which she first had to pass before connecting to the God within. Having allowed her buried feelings to surface in image clusters that initiated the healing process (the "tingling hand" that made life a "wasteland"), Jan later reformulated her illness experience as a vital spiritual trade-off, valuing a new bond with others as fair compensation for her loss of bodily agility. Involvement in a community food-share program prompted her to reflect: "I think the key to my change in attitude is having a friend to do things with, and doing things for other people."

John, our youngest member, just turned thirty, wrote about his prolonged angst over years of misdiagnosed symptoms, including "progressive incoordination and persistent lack of grace," which resulted in his being "unceremoniously flunked out" of college.

> Continued failure left me uneducated, poor in spirit and in capital. My proud, patient parents continued to send me back to the "academic trenches" rearmed with their love and the fruits of their labor. I quaked at the thoughts of eternal damnation that awaited me beyond, for in spite of this long disillusion, I firmly maintained a belief in God, moral responsibility, and an eternal hereafter. Throughout the heartbreak of this boiling flood, the malignant anesthetic called marijuana became my crutch.

John's persistent perception of himself as a victim acted upon by other agents ("failure left me uneducated"; "parents continued to send me back"; "marijuana became my crutch") reveals his utter sense of confusion and powerlessness in the face of his medical problems. Yet, in voicing these previously inchoate feelings of failure and taking "moral responsibility" for having failed himself, his parents, and his God ("I quaked at the thoughts of eternal damnation"), John slowly channeled himself away from a potentially destructive story toward one that would eventually be curative. Psychologist Aaron Beck reminds us that as writers learn to clarify "the distortions, self-injunctions, and self-reproaches that lead to . . . distress and disability," they reconfigure disabling events in new terms, imagining their lives as healing stories (1972, 239). Once John exorcised the shame that had so paralyzed his spirit during the early phase of his story, he came to appreciate the sacredness of the stumbling body he had earlier spurned as disgraceful, seeing it now as a holy instrument of connection to others. Recalling a blessed event from his past—falling in love with a young woman, also physically impaired—John relived the moment when he met "beautiful blue-eyed Donna" at the local college he attended after his dismissal from Purdue: "Following her out to her car that night was a memorable occasion. An exaggerated curvature in Donna's lower spine was emphasized by her dependence on canes, but her gait was a most enrapturing sight to a slightly inebriated, lonely man." The concluding lines of John's story reveal his joyous feeling of being born anew, in a holy sense, now that he felt deeply connected to another human being. "That moment marked the beginning of the abrupt end of my use of marijuana," he writes, "and for the first time in my life, I didn't feel the need to be overwhelmed by fantasy in order to feel true contentment." Though writing about illness could not mend John's crippled body, it did give him an opportunity to reflect on a hallowed moment from the past, which, in turn, brought solace to his troubled spirit. Having brought to the fore a sacred memory that had once graced him with "true contentment," John ends his story with a true feeling of transcendence—illustrating the truth of James Moffett's insight that as writers "use composition to achieve composure," their lives will likewise reflect the "ascent from chaos to cosmos" (1981, 141).

Like Jan and John, most group members eventually revised initial images of themselves as powerless victims of a baffling illness to images of people more or less in control of their lives. But how did these changes occur? How did our writers transform negative feelings about MS into more positive ones, convert anger into affirmation, and turn disfiguring deficits into spiritual assets? Without discounting the mysterious workings of grace or the effects of other events in the lives of our members, it was clear that the changes in perspective that we observed during the subsequent sessions stemmed largely from the group's willingness to respond to still other pedagogical interventions introduced during the remaining weeks of the workshop. During those weeks, we focused on helping group members tap into their own spirituality, introducing them first to the notion of spiritual autobiography and then to two exercises from Ira Progoff's *Intensive Journal*—"Dialoguing with the Body" and "Inner Wisdom Dialogue."

Venues for Spiritual Healing

To show our members the way in which writing about illness can offer solace to distressed spirits, we had them read excerpts from Reynolds Price's memoir *A Whole New Life*,[2] documenting his long, painful battle with a malignant spinal tumor and ensuing paraplegia. Together, we noted the ways Price makes writing a curative instrument: mythicizing himself as a modern day "Robinson Crusoe," a "ship-wrecked lone man" who survives by ingeniously inventing "tools for his alternate existence" (Price 1994, 34–5); relying on "steady coaching," to "survive a hairpin turn in the midst of [his] life . . . without forgetting the better parts of who [he was]" (Price 1994, 185); reliving an out-of-body experience at the Sea of Galilee where Jesus

---

2. Other recent spiritual autobiographies exploring the transcendence implicit in illness might have been equally inspiring to the group. Oliver Sachs's *A Leg to Stand On* describes his "dark night" passage from the world of health through sickness and back again to the world of health as a true spiritual "revelation," a "mystery of Grace." Nancy Mairs's *Ordinary Time* describes her search for an earthly transcendence in the midst of her husband's cancer and her own MS. It is Mairs's inescapable decrease in physical capacity that most defines her sense of the all-encompassing love of God. It may well be time to include autobiographical writings that cultivate sacredness as a stay against life's vagaries as regular classroom reading in order to prepare students for the unsettling vicissitudes in their own lives.

poured "handfuls of water" over his "head and back till water ran down [his] puckered scar," an experience Price calls "an external gift" from a much needed Companion who showed him the redemptive side of illness (1994, 43-4). We then asked the group to reflect on the ways in which they, too, might find consolation for illness in realities of a more spiritual nature. In *Coping with Failure: The Therapeutic Uses of Rhetoric*, David Payne explains that one way to cope with loss is to "console" or "persuade" our-selves "to a different order of valuations wherein a new perspective on the loss is possible." When one seeks consolation, says Payne, "loss is neither denied nor erased," but minimized, diverting attention away from its painful consequences. Discourse that aims to console thus seeks to replace material loss with spiritual gains (1989, 42-3).

Next, we focused on the two exercises from Ira Progoff's *Intensive Journal* to help the group minimize the pain of living with an incurable but nonfatal illness. Many had earlier expressed their anger at having to live with bodies that had so miserably failed them. "A cosmic joke," wrote one. "An unjust fate," said another. But now with negative emotions spent, we felt they were ready to bring to the fore consoling memories that would open them to the more redemptive side of illness. "We need to feel the teeth of the god within the illness in order to be cured by the disease," says Moore, insisting that "in a very real sense, we do not cure diseases, they cure us, by restoring our religious participation in life" (1992, 168). Following Progoff's guidelines for "Dialoguing with the Body," we asked the group members to recall bodily experiences associated with activities from the past that had given special meaning to their lives. We had a sense that as members spoke and wrote about the parts of their bodies damaged by illness, they would be girded by memories of more idyllic days. Here's what a few recalled: Jan— "Swimming laps at the Y three times a week"; John—"Sitting next to the most wholesome-looking, buxom young lady in the class"; Ginny—"Fingers and toes, wet and cool from the blue cool water where mackerel are swim-ming"; and Glenn remembered playing kickball at school—"Kicking the ball far into the field and running fast to touch the bases with my strong legs." Most later expanded these memories and refocused their initial stories toward more salutary conclusions.

Glenn's empowering memory of having been bodily connected to a vig-orous activity before his illness ("kicking the ball") sparked him into rethink-ing the ways he could still connect to others despite an inability to walk on his own. He had earlier written of the turmoil that befell him shortly after his MS diagnosis, noting in particular a failed marriage, a lost job, a short bout with memory loss when he "felt sure [he] was losing [his] mind," and a long siege of depression: "I was thirty-three years old and I felt that my life was over." Eventually he was able to redirect a potentially destructive story of victimization towards a more profitable conclusion by reimagining a humili-ating past event (leaving his job) in new and challenging terms (returning to work to assume a lower-skilled, lower-paid job).

> Taking control of my life enabled me to get in touch with the person I once was. Once I felt ready to take another step forward, I returned to my old workplace. I was welcomed by my old friends who told me they'd be happy to have me work for them again in any capacity that I could manage. Their show of faith gave me strength to meet my next challenge.

In reconfiguring his narrative as a healing story ("gave me strength to meet my next challenge"), Glenn's new perspective illustrates the truth of Walter Fisher's assumption that "the world is a set of stories which must be chosen among to live the good life in a process of continual recreation" (Fisher 1984, 8). Glenn's story, like those of Jan and John, is indeed a tribute to his dauntless spirit in triumphing over a turbulent life, preyed on by frequent exacerbations of his illness.

The final heuristic device introduced was an exercise based on "Inner Wisdom Dialogue." The goal here was for members to connect with important life-shaping beliefs, identifying persons linked to these mythic forces, who "embody a capacity of deep and direct knowing" (Progoff 1975, 286). Joseph Campbell reminds us that, when led to a mythic reunion with our origins, we relive "encounters of a centering kind, fulfilling, harmonizing, giving [ourselves] new courage" (1972, 208). After a short meditation in which members listened hard for voices long silenced through the years, the group spoke their memories aloud before writing. Our oldest member, Ginny, shared thoughts of Dutch—a man who had passed on to her his deep love for the sea. Ginny, who had just turned sixty-three and who had only recently begun to use a cane to steady herself, was the only member who chose not to write about illness directly. Instead, she focused on a relationship with a dying old man who had taught her how to catch "two, three, sometimes even four-foot-long, glistening blue and black mackerel," a man who "could see good far off, could spot the fish coming in," but needed her good eyes to "untangle his lures." Reconnecting with Dutch and with the regenerative life of the sea, Ginny returned to her past, reenvisioning the way she had been in an "unspoiled" time before her illness:

> We'd wade off shore at about half tide and cast out there for the gentle creatures. When we'd bring them in, Dutch would put two or three of them onto a stringer attached to my waist. I'd spend the rest of the twilight going after a big one and feeling the little ones softly brushing against my ankles.

Layered within images of the "shore," the "tide," and the "gentle creatures," Ginny reconnected with an important mythic ritual that taught patience and resignation in the wake of mysteries beyond her control. Rewriting the past in a way that sparked the memory of that endurance strengthened her resolve to overcome the unsettling vagaries of her present illness. In "Writing Documentary as a Therapeutic Act," Mark Allister argues that when writing about disturbing life events, the "distance of the metaphor" encourages one to "work through the conflict unconsciously without needing to confront in a direct, cognitive way the issues in his real life" (Allister 1989, 98). Hawkins, too, confirms that when writers "convert literal facts of illness and therapy" into stories, they construct "a necessary fiction out of the building blocks of metaphor, image, archetype, and myth" that is essentially curative (Hawkins 1993, 27). Though Ginny chose to write her way to composure through a story about her wisdom figure rather than deal with illness directly, she later affirmed the spiritual gain from this experience: "During alert hours of the day now, I sit at the computer. Encouraged by the group to believe that my writing is good, I feel worthwhile. I'm told I'm sending out better vibes. I know I'm more pleasant to be with."

For most members, the workshop was everything we hoped it would be. Insights gleaned from writing did indeed offer the group spiritual guidance in dealing with the darker issues of illness, enabling them to reimagine themselves through a "speculative" language that deepened their connection between body and spirit. Working intimately with this group, I felt that I too was benefited because the experience enabled me not only to appreciate their true valor but also to resurrect shared moments with my mother, who had a prolonged struggle with MS before she died.

As we have seen, illness makes an ordinary life a more difficult life; yet sometimes a difficult life is mysteriously transformed into a life that resonates with genuine caritas, as it did for one member who offered this reflection at the end of the workshop: "We were all interested in one another's welfare. We were understanding when we saw another walk awkwardly, or fall, or do some miserable thing. We were not jealous of one another's writing prowess and truly wished each other success. We loved each other, in a way."

Implications for Classroom Practice

Though all members of our workshop shared a common disability, making their self-disclosures less painful than they might have been among people with diverse impairments, writing about disability need not be confined to homogeneous groups. It may well be time to explore the potential for therapeutic healing in the reflective prose that we ask our students to write within the traditional classroom setting. Many college texts[3] now include essays by

3. For anthologies dealing with readings related to disability and illness, see, for example, Lynn Z. Bloom and Edward M. White, eds., *Inquiry: A Cross-Curricular Reader* (NJ: Blair, 1993); Carl Klaus, Chris Anderson, and Rebecca Faery, eds., *In Depth: Essayists for Our Time* (NY: Harcourt, 1993); Philip Lopate, ed., *The Art of the Personal Essay* (NY: Doubleday, 1994); Donald McQuade and Robert Atwan, *The Winchester Reader* (New York: Bedford, 1991); Ann Watters and Marjorie Ford, eds., *Writing for Change* (NY: McGraw Hill, 1995). For an anthology of works exclusively by and about women with disabilites, see Marsha Saxton and Florence Howe, eds., *With Wings* (NY: The Feminist Press, 1987); for an anthology of writings by peo-

the physically challenged alongside those of other minority populations, suggesting a common bond among those marginalized by difference—whether
it be the difference of race, gender, culture, sexual preference, or bodily
appearance. Students working collaboratively in classrooms could also be
encouraged to write about feelings of diminishment stemming from their
own disabling life-circumstances, with a goal of imagining alternative lives,
graced with new possibilities.

ple with MS, see Eric Smirnow, *The MS Autobiography Book* (Cedaredge, Colorado: Special-
ized Computer Services, 1992).

11

Teaching Lives
Thoughts on Reweaving Our Spirits

Wendy Bishop

Spirituality is a troubling word to me. I tend to shy away from spirit even as I'm drawn to it. I tend to focus instead on *humanist*, on what it means to be humane, involved, and human—to be a person with a vocation that fills spiritual as well as material needs. As a for-years-but-no-longer-(and-never-very-convinced) Methodist, I would have equated spirituality with religion and would have found disturbing the idea that writing and the work of teaching can be a powerful form of meditation (a concept I would have found too reminiscent of my growing up in California during the cynical 1960s and 1970s).

For a long time, other words, such as *emotion* and *intuition,* seemed equally problematic to me, discredited by my years in the academy where it seemed I *felt* too much. Even when I was learning to suppress emotion and intuition, the idea of knowing still interested me. ("Why did I go with that lesson plan? Well, my guess was that this class would . . .") I was interested in *knowing* in the self-sustaining, getting-connected-with-a-world-bigger-than-I-am sense, in the, well, *spiritual sense.* I now gravitate to this word *spiritual* because it clarifies certain aspects of my life and points to experiences larger than affect and larger than mind. That is, mind combined with affect creates an exciting experiential tapestry. For me, that tapestry represents the university campus, and the university presents one form of real life, where writing is meditation and teaching is a spiritual journey, benefiting both teacher and student.

How long it's taken me to say so!

* * *

I was delighted with the term *felt sense* when I encountered it in research into composing processes and quickly applied the term to my experiences as a creative writer—as in *felt sense*, that moment of equipoise when the hair on the back of my neck rises as I read a poem and it moves me, as it moves molecules; when my teachers would read in a dull class and, despite the dullness, in the emotion of that reading allow the poet's words to touch my spirit in an inexplicable way. In the same way, trying to understand my teaching life includes a tentative tour, a feeling-through of these difficult-to-define words, a feeling-through years of embracing and avoiding, by questioning, by remembering poems—those that were "taught" to me and those that I write as I teach. In *The Peaceable Classroom,* Mary Rose O'Reilley captures this journey-sense for me when she explains:

> But I stay in teaching because all the models we have for spiritual process—religious, mythic, . . .—tell us that it doesn't matter whether we are right or wrong or successful but merely that we remain faithful to a vision. And that when it's easy, it isn't worth much. Let me repeat and rephrase: because teaching is some kind of spiritual inquiry, what we learn is more important than what they learn. It is more important, at least, to our passage; they are going someplace else; they are in a different myth . . . we cannot control their reactions, we can only determine our own inner weather. (O'Reilley 1993, 72)

My own inner weather, after seventeen years of teaching, tells me that teaching is visionary and spiritual for me—it is what matters—and I return faithfully to the classroom year after year, needing that growing space, no doubt, as much or more than the classroom students need me.

Several years ago, I began to argue in teaching essays that writing is necessarily therapeutic—usefully so, unashamedly so—for, whether sanctioned or not, students will write their lives in our writing classes (if we let them), and so we, as teachers, must write ours with them. I've learned that my intuitive understanding of the power of personal writing and my intellectual understanding of the force of discourse and culture need to commune—that heart and brain have to unite in teaching. When they do, I learn that teaching teaches me, heals me, helps me, centers me in my professional and personal life in a way I've seldom seen talked about.

I've learned that students will always write within the complicated matrix of their daily lives. Last term, students' writing process narratives again highlighted their lives' complexities: from a young man whose parents were divorcing at Thanksgiving; to a young woman pregnant and estranged from her abusive husband; to an older woman, a state worker, who had been in two catastrophic car accidents; to another young man who just didn't feel like he wanted to do schoolwork anymore. Students' lives impinge on their writing processes in serious ways that are seldom studied. The cognitive problem-solving model cannot of course provide an equation for how these students might best be helped to write better. Only a well-trained, invested, interested teacher has a hope of navigating the interrelated cognitive and affective territory of the classroom. Perhaps only a teacher who comes to experience the confusions (collusion?) of avocation and vocation, teaching as a way to confirm and reconfirm, to weave and reweave a life's vision, which is an act of faithfulness.

The affective map has been neglected on several levels. There appears to be a fieldwide refusal to deal with the content of student writing and the contexts of students' lives. I am not suggesting here that I become my students' professional counselor, knowing how untrained and unequal I am for that task. But I'm perplexed by the degree of professional horror I raise when I suggest that I am present as a person in the classroom, that one part of the negotiation all writers partake in is that of their own lives. I welcome a book like Robert Brooke's *Writing and Sense of Self*, which looks at the individual within the structure of the workshop, and Lad Tobin's recent book *Writing Relationships*, for the assertions it makes that what we do as teachers is imbedded in relational processes. If relationships in the classroom represent sticky, dangerous territories—the La Brea tarpits of the mind—they are also the glue of writing as I know it and must be addressed. Mary Rose O'Reilley says:

> I would like to meet the concern about turning the classroom into "some kind of therapy group," then, by observing that good teaching is, in the classical sense, therapy: good teaching involves reweaving the spirit. (Bad teaching, by contrast, is soul murder.) . . . In general, I find it more productive to look at how things (like teaching writing and doing therapy) are similar, rather than at how they are, and thus should remain, different. (O'Reilley 1993, 47)

Soul murder? Strong language. Too strong or barely strong enough? The student who mentioned that his parents were divorcing lingers in my mind as a still-needing-to-be-understood teaching moment. On a fairly dull Tuesday before a recent Thanksgiving, I asked my students to complete a sure-fire invention exercise—writing fifteen metaphoric responses about a person about whom they had strong feelings—to be turned, later, into a portrait poem. I started the exercise near the end of class and, after most students had packed up and swept out, I waited impatiently for one young man to finish— I was ready for Thanksgiving break too. I was surprised that he was still writing since he was usually fairly perfunctory about the class. He looked up and said, "This is a neat exercise. I think I found a poem."

My teacher-self preened, and I almost replied before he said, "I don't really want to go home; my parents are getting a divorce and it's going to be strange."

My teacher-words died in my throat.

I myself had had a difficult fall term, personally, and I felt unable to respond, unable to offer either a dismissive or a supportive reply. It bothers me now to think of that pedagogical pause, as I froze for a moment, saying nothing. I hadn't been writing along with my classes, as I often do and feel I always should, and I was distant from the teaching moment, deciding, finally, on a noncommittal "Oh, well, good. Great, I'm glad you found something."

For me, that moment represents the opportunity, the danger, the lure, and the confusion that teaching writing has always had for me, and because of my own busy life context, I willed it out of being. I did not talk about the purposes or results of the activity; I did not talk about how writing leads into and out of living; I did not talk about anything. The longer I teach, the more clearly I realize that my own and my students' lives are really at the center of what I do, however well or poorly I do it. By attending to my teaching and by tracing and understanding my teaching life, I understand my life, period.

I've been thinking back over moments that brought me to this argument —that teachers should be telling about their emotional and spiritual lives as teachers. In 1992, I recall, I was at several sessions of the University of New Hampshire conference on the writing process movement, and I was struck by the number of times that conference speakers recited poems—others' or their own—about what they do. As a teacher of composition and poetry, I've learned that most of my students harbor a hidden "high school" poet inside themselves, and I know, from working with new teachers of writing, that many in English studies came to be where they are through their aspirations to write like author X, Y, or Z , to create texts.

I continue writing in this manner, though, because I have realized that my poems and more recently my literacy autobiographies, self-assigned in the teacher-education classes I teach, offer me valuable new modes of understanding myself and my professional life. Thinking about teaching by writing, informally, in mixed genres helps me solve—or at least to think differently—productively and creatively about—teaching problems. It enriches my life. Literally, it reweaves my experiences into a usable whole. Not a permanent whole, for I often find the need to tear out the stitching, reconsider the pattern, and construct my understandings anew.

To do this, I use poetry in James Britton's sense of exploratory writing: My informal thoughts are shaped into verse because verse shaping comes by now fairly naturally to me as a mode of thinking. Picking up a book of poetry at the public library, I read "Poetry was part of the everyday social life of an educated man in China, and it was customary for friends and acquaintances to exchange poems on various occasions or to get together and compose poems on a particular theme" (Watson 1994, 9); the tenth-century poet referred to, Su Tung-p'o, has titles such as "At Twilight, Fine Rain Was Still Falling" and "Feet Stuck Out, Singing Wildly" and "Letting the Writing

Brush Go." Why, I wonder, is occasional verse anathema in the modern writing classroom? How lucky I was in New Hampshire, I think, to be around on a day when poetic testimony broke through professional decorum.

Jo'al was taking my poetry class while also enrolled in a first-year writing class whose teacher had learned to teach writing from me. Jo'al was "hearing" different writing rules in each class and became confused by the apparent contradictions.

Jo'al

tells me her other teacher
asks for "no metaphors, please,"
in the personal narrative,
tells me her poetry teacher,
me, asks for "images and no clichés
and the five senses, use them concretely"
but weirdly
make lungs ring like brass bells,
make skin feel hot and foolish like caramel,
make eyes track lucid questions in sky blue—
guides to coax the day into formal
shapes she's hesitant to use.
Jo'al asks me, can she put metaphors
in poetry? Can she use her own words
like chitterlings and cornbread?
Pushed back from a heavy desk,
I see blocks of days,
some for creating, some for composing.
Then I say "Yes." Yes.
Southern fried and hamhocks steaming,
naps, and plaits twisting patient hands.
I share my mother's lost Norwegian
farmlands and lilting syllables
flattened, all rules followed.
Jo'al listens between
the messages. Thanks me.
Her next poem, "When I Was
Black," her best. (Bishop 1991, 4)

After reading Su Tung-p'o's life in poems, I might retitle mine "The Day Jo'al Pointed Out Contradictions in Teaching and Learning" or "Letting the Writing Student Go."

I also see teaching and writing about teaching not simply as pedagogical or personal inquiry but also as civic action, a component in my personal and broadest definition of *spiritual*. Perhaps the analogy here is of piecing a quilt together, or of raising a barn if the needle is not comfortable to hand. I need only to think of my own dissertation director, Don McAndrew. When we get together to share a beer and teaching stories, we don't swap academic citations, we talk about our teaching, share what does and doesn't work. We talk about our writing, explore why we do it, what it means to have done it. We participate in a verbal reweaving. We consider our profession and ask tough questions about our places in it. It's love and passion for a profession that can make us consider leaving the classroom sometimes when we feel we may not make a difference.

It's love and passion and concern that sent this professor into his children's local school district to offer fifty free in-service days in whole-language workshops over a two-year period. He knew there were better ways to teach and, because he did, he had to share them. It is this type of committed teacher who grounds the teacher-research, expert-practitioner movement for me. I'm not suggesting that teachers need to go out and volunteer more time. We're overworked as it is, most of us. But I do argue that it is this type of teacher—along with Nancy Sommers and Lynn Bloom and Mike Rose—who should be writing their teaching autobiographies and exploring their teaching histories in print. When they won't, don't, or can't, I believe all of us who are hearing their stories should take note and pass the stories on in a kind of pedagogical potlatch that moves beyond mere lore in order to highlight, value, respect, and draw our attention to other ways of knowing and saying and being in the professional world.

Postmodern anthropology and feminist theory suggest alternative ways of reporting both practice and research—honoring story, testimony, observational anecdote, informal analysis, regularized lore, and so on—and these movements may connect some of us back to our humanistic roots as writers and readers of fictional and factional texts—back to the spirit of what originally drew us to our field(s). These are certainly new ways teachers may choose to share their teaching lives, and such sharing leads to profound questioning of traditional ways of making knowledge, as we ask what is valuable as research and in publication, what is learned in doctoral exams, and what voice(s) should be allowed in dissertations. Many of us realize that the structures of the academy are slowing rather than accelerating learning; if this is so, we have to redefine our terms and change our processes.

Reweaving the spirit doesn't demand new, whole cloth. Reweaving requires attention as we darn, patch, embroider, and look for connections.

Thought A: Many of us in composition/English departments are people who care deeply about reading and writing, and we need to testify and practice more visibly. We need to question seriously the ways we make students (first-year and graduate) produce texts we don't value and the way we agree to do this ourselves for academic promotion. We'll gain power if we resist trends or theoretical movements that don't fit; yet, we'll know that they don't fit, of course, only if we try them on and test them in the crucible of the classroom.

Thought B: Some models and practices are enduring because they allow for the personal and the public to coexist and to communicate. I'm thinking of the way my expressivist heart negotiates daily with my social constructionist brain and how, as a writer and teacher of writers, I wouldn't have it any other way. I've been struggling for years now to take the "creative" out of certain genres of writing and to (re)consider the active, creative wellsprings of all passionately engaged writers and writing.

Thought C: If we accept the job description of writing teacher, then theory and practice, the public and personal must form a web, a network, a circle, an interconnected chain, a dialog, a mutual refrain in our teaching, a tapestry, a quilt, a momentarily well-constructed whole.

Thought D: We need to be more playful and tell more praise stories. There are many reasons I love being a teacher and this essay is too empty of them. I value the way teaching lets me talk about and practice my favorite subject, writing; the ways students change and allow me to participate in that change; and the way my work puts me in touch with like-minded, intelligent, committed colleagues around the country.

Teachers can listen to students to understand their own worlds and can write with and about their classes to construct the spirit-full story of teaching. Writers who in discussing their papers also disclose childhood abuse, perhaps, are not simply "burdening" us with more than we're trained to handle. Rather, they have connected to us, made our day more whole, more human, more important. We can worry over them and marvel at them—at their strength and survivor's skills, at their excitement right now, at the way they have rewoven their spirit through writing.

It's almost that simple.

I believe in teaching,

because I relearn my life as my students explore theirs.

Part Four

Writing to Transform
Our World

Certain life experiences change us, not just our mood, but *us*. A tired body or a troubled mind is suddenly changed by a summer rainstorm, the laugh of a child, or an action based on principle. When change happens, it occurs at a deep prelinguistic or archetypal level of the psyche, a place so deep within the personality that it can be represented only partially by language. Such change causes us to reframe or recontextualize the self, to see life and ourselves differently from before the experience. Though such change does not come from intellectual knowledge but from experiential, kinesthetic, or spiritual knowledge, it profoundly affects how we see ourselves and our relationship to others and to our world.

In recent decades we have watched our world move from holding forth the promise of flourishing for its people to quaking from the concerns among many about whether the planet will survive. Looking at the social, economic, and ecological problems we face, even cynics are beginning to ask, "What can we *do* to change the fate of people and of the world?" The contributing authors in this final section show how they use their writing classrooms to transform their students' worlds and their students' visions of themselves in it. As students tap experientially into the archetypal energy that changes the individual, they take an important step toward transforming the world.

Thomas Dean teaches the spirit of nature by having his students read nature literature. He describes the magic that happens when his students then move out into nature to observe attentively and to sense their own connectedness to a universe beyond their bodies and minds. Students also experience an awareness of a sense of ethics about their own responsibilities to the universe.

Marianthe Karanakis focuses on two meditation techniques to achieve a type of clarity in the technical writing classroom: insight meditation and loving-kindness practice. Writers become aware of those hidden tendencies of the mind that shape our biases and often hinder our understanding of nature, for example, when recording scientific observations. These exercises can help technical writers develop compassionate critical consciousness.

Christopher Ferry explores the spirituality of Paulo Freire's liberation pedagogy, intended to transform unjust and alienating social structures, and its basis in liberation theology. He compares Freire's spirituality-influenced pedagogy to Ira Shor's secular pedagogy and offers ways that spirituality-based pedagogy can be brought into secular classrooms.

Sherry Swain uses the writing of first-grade students to illustrate the power of her approach. She invites her students to enter the place of wonder where insights become illuminated, where the difficult becomes easy, and where complex details melt into wholes. She discusses three writing approaches that tap this place of wonder: sky writing, silence, and reflection.

12

Connected to the Whole
Teaching the Spirit of Nature Through Literature

Thomas Dean

In *Pilgrim at Tinker Creek*, Annie Dillard describes how she was ambling across a hill one day when she noticed a strange speck of white. Moving closer, she recognized a praying mantis laying eggs. Seven pages later, after progressing through a series of memory chambers, she suddenly found herself on the banks of what she calls "Shadow Creek," a primal place that undergirds the horrors, beauties, and beautiful horrors of the natural world (1974, 5).

In the harsh, biting cold of January on the Minnesota prairie, Paul Gruchow in *Journal of a Prairie Year* trudges across a field blanketed by deep snow. His ears become attuned to the crunching of his boots on the white surface beneath them, learning the difference between the sounds of twenty-degree snow and sub-zero snow. With such aural sensitivity, he approaches "the largely unheard and mysterious music of the universe" (1991, 5).

Such moments of transcendence are also possible in the classroom where such nature writing is taught. I have worked with students on nature writing in a variety of contexts: in a freshman research course, in an upper-division contemporary literature course, even in my "Ethnicity in American Literature" and "Studies in Non-Western Literature" courses. No matter at what level or in what context, teaching literature that concerns human relationships with the natural world empowers students to discover their connections with the world outside their selves, the universe of the transcendent. This usually happens in much the same way that nature writing itself is structured.

As I illustrate above, Dillard and Gruchow are simply meandering about, yet their concentrated attention to the details of the natural phenomena about them moves them into a transcendent realm; the veil of the material universe is lifted to reveal a glimpse of the eternal. Similarly, students are mundanely reading their assignments, and if they are paying close enough attention, they are transported with these writers to great spiritual heights and depths. The best magic occurs, however, when these same students move out into nature, observe attentively, and sense their own connectedness to a universe beyond their bodies and minds. Students achieve not only a kind of spiritual awakening, an awareness of their connections to a greater wholeness of existence outside the self, but also a sense of ethics, that is, an awareness of their own responsibilities to that natural universe of which they are a part.

Perhaps the most fundamental tenet of nature writing, as well as ecocritical theory, is the interconnectedness of all things, illustrated as well in "biodiversity," the scientific concept of an interconnected web of diverse beings, each necessary to the wholeness of the whole. It is the disconnection of human experience and thought from the natural world in Western religion and science over the past several hundred years that has led not only to spiritual hollowness in much of contemporary society but to environmental destruction as well. The idea of interconnectedness that nature writing works to foster, and which can become the center of a spiritual pedagogy of nature writing, can help heal this rift between nature and humanity and, ideally, in the process heal both environmental and spiritual wounds. An awareness of the intimacy and reciprocity between nature and humanity can lead to a sense of responsibility for and stewardship toward the world. This awareness of a world connected to self can also restore to some people the meaningfulness in their lives that has been lost because of alienation from others or because of a society that they perceive has wronged them. Connecting to the whole and healing such rifts is in itself a "holy" act. As Sean Kane has pointed out in his book on mythology, the word *whole,* which for him includes "a sense of mystery, a concealed knowledge about relationship that is available only in story," comes from the Germanic *halig,* which is also the root of *holy* (1994, 45).

A number of contemporary spiritual thinkers base their theology on such notions of healing the gaps between humanity and the natural world. Matthew Fox is prominent among them. Rather than abandoning his roots as a Dominican priest, Fox works to reenvision the Roman Catholic view of the universe by using new stories based not on Augustinian dualisms that sunder body and spirit but rather on an organic unity that helps us rediscover the awesomeness of our physical being, which is "revelatory of the divine" (1993, 247). If we rediscover such earth stories, we can "recover the sense of our bodies and our planet as blessings" (1993, 247). More outwardly, the story of the sky tunes us into "the source of our home; we came from 'out there.' Our entire history is reflected, refracted, and rediscovered when we look out to the sky" (1993, 245). The new sky, or creation, story is one of "a continually expanding organism" that began as a cosmic fireball billions of years ago, and every microbe of existence is part of it and its eternal changes.

Such theological formations are played out in a number of texts regarding nature and the human spirit. Spiritual formation and reformation are at the center of the experience of place in Kathleen Norris's *Dakota: A Spiritual Geography,* for example. The bare natural landscape of the Plains has "formed me spiritually," Norris says. "I would even say they have made me a human being.... 'Everything that seems empty is full of the angels of God' [St. Hilary's dictum]. The magnificent sky above the Plains sometimes seems to sing this truth; angels seem possible in the wind-filled expanse" (1993, 11). The transcendent is so immanent in the Great Plains for Norris that she claims her immediate geography as "my monastery, my place set apart, where I thrive and grow" (1993, 17). Virtually her entire spiritual life originates and takes place in the natural landscape of Dakota.

I am not suggesting, however, that teaching the spirit of nature need be theological. In fact, the pedagogy itself need not be explicitly spiritual. Although I teach in a Roman Catholic college, I am not Roman Catholic nor am I theologically inclined generally. I am an English teacher who loves the power of language and who cares for the earth; I work with my students on the language of these writers admittedly with ecological sensitivity, but the spiritual awakenings usually happen by themselves. Once they do, I certainly try to nurture and encourage them, but it has been my experience that such revelatory experiences cannot be forced. The awareness of the interconnectedness of all things, as well as the revelation of the divine (however an individual student conceives it), that results from our analysis and discussion of texts works its own magic, pushing students to perceive and contemplate with new eyes the transcendent as they leave the classroom and observe their backyards, their parks, their nature centers, and their family cabins in the woods. The curtains to the infinite often part not in the classroom but rather in students' own experiences, sometimes when they least expect it.

I have been surprised to discover that the students who experience the greatest spiritual awakenings are often those least disposed to it initially. In the aforementioned contemporary literature class, I remember three students in particular. One was returning to school after a divorce; at the beginning of the term, she made no bones about how dreadful her experiences in previous literature classes had been, how busy she was, and how low this class was on her priority list. The second student was an art major who, as is sometimes the case with fine arts students, was profoundly focused on her artwork to the exclusion of general education classes. The third student was of average abilities with no particular interest in nature writing or environmental issues. Such students need the freedom to come to understand nature and nature writing on their own terms, so the major project for the course was open-ended. I encouraged students to do whatever interested them most, utilizing their own best talents, in creative formats if they wished, including multimedia.

The first student mentioned above, whom I'll call Jean, used this freedom to do something that was simply convenient for her: She took her camcorder out to a nearby nature preserve. The art student, whom I'll call Mary, was interested in developing her photography skills and decided to shoot some pictures at another nearby nature center. The third student, whom I'll call Angela, decided to read and report on Al Gore's *Earth in the Balance*, I suspect, because it was popular at the time and easily available. All students were also to give oral presentations to the class based on their projects. Jean and Mary came back from their photographic visits to their respective nature centers transformed. Both could hardly contain their enthusiasm in sharing their experiences. Jean had, in the end, produced a gorgeous meditative videotape, complete with musical accompaniment, to which she recited brief selections from nature writings. She had clearly become in tune with some spiritual forces that she had not anticipated capturing in her camera eye. Jean especially, in subsequent conversations with me and in her course evaluations, could not find words to express the spiritual transformation she had undergone, which had changed her perspective on the world and had revealed to her a new relationship to a world that had not treated her well in the past. Feeling disconnected from her fellow human beings particularly as a result of her divorce, which had led to an inward focus that manifested itself in hostility to an imposed core curriculum, she felt a connectedness to a world outside herself in the woods, a world of beauty and peace that she had thought not possible for her anymore. Mary, who admitted that she had never visited any place as wild as the local Audubon Center she photographed, presented an amazingly learned discourse on the flora and fauna in her photographs, punctuated by exclamations of amazement at the beauty and peace she experienced while photographing trees and deer. I truly felt that Mary had made a first step outward to a world beyond her intensely focused passion for art.

Angela underwent a somewhat different transformation, a political one—though more broadly I would consider it spiritual as well—for she became committed to new principles regarding the integrity of her world. In planning her project, Angela visited my office for a conference. She expressed her profound amazement at the ideas in Gore's book, saying how she had never realized the extent of the destruction wrought upon the earth and the delicacy of the earth's biodiversity balance. Throughout the semester, Angela became zealous in her political advocacy in our class discussions. My own spiritual and political beliefs regarding nature had grown fairly gradually and steadily, and I was impressed and startled by Angela's almost epiphanic experience.

These were among the most rewarding moments of my career, and I must admit that I did very little to bring about these transformations. The power of the texts we studied, in providing models of mindful, sensitive attention to the details of the physical world around us, was transferred to actual practice in these students, which then led to the transformative experiences.

A teacher can more actively encourage these spiritual connections, however, and such connections can happen fairly quickly. In my freshman composition research class, I use nature writing both as subject matter and as research model. One of the principles of research that nature writing illustrates is attentiveness to detail and perception of deeper implications. As an exercise, I send my students to the library (usually it's about zero degrees Fahrenheit when we do this assignment, so I hesitate to require students to go outdoors) to sit for fifteen minutes, sensing and recording on paper the ambient sounds, sights, and smells of what is happening about them, and to write down some implications of what they are sensing. Invariably, students are astonished at how novel this experience is for them: the intensity with which they are able to perceive the fullness of the ambient world and the implications regarding behavior and education that they derive therefrom— all in only fifteen minutes. The students' first formal paper, then, is to be a lengthier and more intense observation of the natural world and an exploration of the implications of their experience. Recently, one of my students stopped by after class to tell me how she had spent a great deal of time the previous weekend dwelling within the enveloping boughs of a large pine tree in her backyard. She was amazed at perceiving the multiplicity of life within those branches; it was a small universe itself.

This I would say is the primary pedagogical value in nature writing as well as the primary pedagogical tool: mindful attention to detail. In the details, the writers we study, and often the students themselves, find the keys to the infinite. The primary spiritual concept that I attempt to communicate to my students is that of a realm of transcendence continuous with the world of material detail that we know. In many respects, this is the same way I teach such concepts as literary theme and figurative language in general. While the theme of a short story or the meaning of a metaphor may not be immediately apparent in the specific details of the text's surface, they are not "hidden" behind a wall of language nor are they remote from the language that contains them. Through sensitivity to textual nuance and detail, theme and meaning—which are immanent in the language of the text—resolve themselves in the student's understanding. Likewise, the universe in all its dimensions lies immanently in the details of material fact, and a patient communion with those natural details will often be rewarded with a revelation of a spiritual plane.

In understanding this process of attention to detail as revealer of the divine and in observing it at work in literary texts, students learn to analyze the structure of the literature we read, to become sensitive to the representational nature of language, and to adapt the literary model to their own experience. By way of illustration, let me return to the section of Annie Dillard's *Pilgrim at Tinker Creek* mentioned at the outset.

Recently, I was talking with a student who was reading another Dillard text in another class, and he lamented how he would be reading along just fine, and then Dillard would throw in something "from left field." This is a common complaint among students who have yet to trust Dillard enough to follow her thinking into the infinite. Part of the problem, I believe, is in many students' conceptions of what "nature writing" is, that it is simply a description of the natural world. Dillard is disarming because she starts her cycles of perception in ways that conform to such a definition. The section under question in *Pilgrim at Tinker Creek* starts with a precise description of the upside-down praying mantis, "clinging to a horizontal stem of wild rose by her feet which pointed to heaven. Her head was deep in dried grass. Her abdomen was swollen like a smashed finger," and so on (1974, 57). The heaven metaphor in these early lines is the transport device that students should be encouraged to board. The naturalist's saga of the sex life of the praying mantis continues for two or three pages, and students "get it" with no problem. This extraordinarily detailed account of natural phenomena, however, is only the vehicle that Dillard constructs to carry her readers to more profound depths.

Another example is Dillard's description of a Polyphemus moth she remembers from her grade school days. Emerging from a cocoon that Dillard's class had put in a jar, the moth was unable to spread its wings, and the wonder of birth turned to horror as the wings solidified into useless, twisted appendages. We are left with the image of this monstrously crippled creature ambling down the sidewalk to an unknown yet certainly terrible fate. Perhaps too complacent with an Aristotelian notion of completeness in a logical ending, students will often break off their thematic reading at a seeming point of closure such as the "end" of the moth story. Yet Dillard is not finished peeling back the layers of the spiritual world of nature for her reader, and it is here, often, where students see what follows as "coming out of left field." Such strange and horrible sights as the praying mantis and the deformed moth transport the students into Dillard's world of "shadows," a transcendent realm she calls "Shadow Creek."

> This is the blue strip running through creation, the icy roadside stream on whose banks the mantis mates, in whose unweighed water the giant water bug sips frogs. Shadow Creek is the blue subterranean stream that chills Carvin's Creek and Tinker Creek; it cuts like ice under the ribs of the mountains, Tinker and Dead Man. Shadow Creek storms through limestone vaults under forests, or surfaces anywhere, damp, on the underside of a leaf. I wring it from rocks; it seeps into my cup. Chasms open at the glance of an eye; the ground parts like a wind-rent cloud over stars. Shadow Creek: on my least walk to the mailbox I may find myself knee-deep in its sucking, frigid pools. (1974, 63)

Students tend to gloss over such abstract ruminations, but it is in the teacher's best interest to make sure they hold on to that praying mantis or that crippled moth in class discussion to ride into the depths of Shadow Creek. And then it is important to follow up that discussion by asking students to connect the process and concept that Dillard exemplifies to their own experience. What horrors have they seen in nature, for example, that have made them perceive the dark, shadow world of spirit as well as the light? Such a journey into shadow can still lead to enlightenment.

Once when I asked students to recount such a journey into "Shadow Creek," one student, whom I'll call Sarah, revealed a recent dramatic experience for her. After undergoing breast cancer surgery, she and her family took a vacation at a lake in the north woods. Concealing herself in the loneliness of the forest, this woman let the floodgates open, screaming her anger at her doctors, her body, and God for taking part of her away. In her rage, she physically attacked the trees about her, breaking off pieces of bark (and hurting her hand). But in so doing, Sarah also looked more closely at the trees, noticing their misshapen forms, seeing how they had compensated for a life of dead branches and destroyed limbs. Sarah looked at the bark she herself had shed from the trunk and realized that the tree would accommodate itself physically to this injury. It was in this moment, in this connection to injury in the natural world through attentive gaze and intense thought, that Sarah received comfort, knowing that she could accommodate herself—physically, emotionally, and spiritually—to her loss.

Native peoples may say that the types of places of transcendence I have been talking about are in the "dreamtime," which also contains horrors as well as beauties that are spiritually awesome. I have found that using such texts as Leslie Marmon Silko's "Landscape, History, and the Pueblo Imagination" provides my students, who are predominantly white and middle class, not only with some multicultural education but also with some new cultural perspectives on access to the transcendent through nature.

Silko, in discussing her Laguna Pueblo heritage of storytelling and devotion to place, illustrates the same concepts of humanity's relationship to transcendent nature: interconnectedness, continuousness, and access to the infinite through nature and language. While this particular essay is more discursive than narrative, Silko employs some of the same text moves as Dillard. She begins with necessary concrete detail.

> All summer the people watch the west horizon, scanning the sky from south
> to north for rain clouds. Corn must have moisture at the time the tassels
> form. Otherwise pollination will be incomplete, and the ears will be stunted
> and shriveled. (1981, 86)

From there, Silko expands our vision from these specific details of her home landscape to the "ancient continuous story" of her culture. The continuous interplay between natural object and myth that Silko goes on to describe in her essay reveals to students how utterly entwined culture and spiritual belief can become with the landscape. For example, Silko explains how a road between the villages of Paguate and Laguna is the same route followed by the Pueblo ancients in their Migration after the Emergence (the appearance of the people on this plane of existence). In traveling that road, an individual moves along the same path as the ancestors in one of the greatest spiritual journeys, and everyday experience becomes heavy with meaning. "Continued use of that route creates a unique relationship between the ritual-mythic world and the actual, everyday world" (1981, 90–91).

Silko does not stop there, however. This traversing of the road is not simply a formal ritual but also a mechanism by which human beings can enter into, through imagination, a more direct awareness of the great web of life that connects all.

> The eight miles ... are actually a ritual circuit or path which marks the interior journey the Laguna people made: a journey of awareness and imagination in which they emerged from being within the earth and from everything included in earth to the culture and people they became. (1981, 91))

Such awareness communicates values as well, nourishing the spiritual and physical health of both the earth and the community. This interconnection leads to one's awareness of a relationship to culture as well as to world spirit: "Not until they [human beings] could find a viable relationship to the terrain, the landscape they found themselves in, could they emerge. Only at the moment the requisite balance between human and other was realized could the Pueblo people become a culture" (Silko 1981, 92).

Using Silko as a model, I also ask my students to use story as a vehicle to understanding their connections to the greater world about them, connections that are cultural, natural, and spiritual. In essence, this is a mythical understanding of the world. As Sean Kane has said, "This verbal power makes mythtelling a sacred art, in which the listener [as well as the teller, I would add] is transported by language into the invisible world. . . . Myths [are] flights of the spirit, with the narrative acting as the conduit of supernatural energies summoned and made present by story, and the mythteller acting as the conductor of the souls of the listeners to the Otherworld and back again" (1994, 104).

In my contemporary literature class, we studied Silko's *Storyteller* as well as her essay and modeled our own stories on them. One memorable student essay was written by a seminarian, whom I'll call Bob, who told me of a personal story that he and his family have never forgotten—the story of the death and burial of his cat and of his subsequent curious exhumation of his dearly departed pet. The experience of viewing the decayed body—the natural result of its return to the earth—combined with his family's insensitive scolding and mockery, led Bob to seek out an answer to his question of where "Whiskers" went and then to seek to "save" his family from their lack of awareness of the holiness of the soul of his beloved cat. This story, or personal myth, originating in a curiosity about the natural processes of bodily decay, led Bob ultimately to the priesthood, informing the basis for his spiritual quest. Just as Silko's stories intertwined with the processes of her culture coming into being, Bob's story intertwined with the processes of finding a spiritual home and mission.

In all of these activities that prod my students to connect with nature and thus to connect with the wholeness, or spirituality, of the world, I hope to foster, at the very least, a reverence for the natural world and an awareness of the interconnectedness of all life that sensitizes them to their responsibilities to live softly upon the earth. Such reverence can come about through personalizing the landscape as Silko does; if students realize that the meanings of their lives are invested in such special places, they will be more inclined to care for those places. Even a slight increase of the kind of mindfulness suggested in Dillard or Silko can foster a sensitivity to students' relationships with and responsibilities for keeping our natural home clean and healthy.

Continued mindfulness of the meaning of nature will, I hope, lead to even greater spiritual transcendence. Perhaps, as with Kathleen Norris in *Dakota*, students' personal landscapes can become their monasteries, their centers of spiritual life. Although there can be dramatic flashes of enlightenment, as with my contemporary literature students mentioned earlier, a relationship like Norris's certainly cannot be built in the fifteen weeks of a semester. But I hope that my students will continue their mindfulness beyond the confines of our classroom and our term, for the universe will reveal itself to those who will open their eyes and minds to it.

13

Liberation Theology and Liberatory Pedagogy
Spiritual Teaching in the Real World

Christopher Ferry

The mind motivated by compassion reaches out to know as the
heart reaches out to love. Here, the act of knowing is an act of
love, the act of entering and embracing the reality of the other, of
allowing the other to enter and embrace our own.
—Parker J. Palmer (1983)

The work of Brazilian educator Paulo Freire has become something of a
template for politically progressive and leftist teachers in North America. His
influence has been particularly important in composition studies, and he is
regularly cited in major journals. Freire's philosophy of education informs
the thinking of Ann E. Berthoff, Patricia Bizzell, Henry Giroux, and Jane
Tompkins, among others. These theorists and practitioners refer mostly to
Freire's political aspects, especially to his Marxist sensibilities, and to his
calls for education to be an instrument of social and political liberation. But
the "education for critical consciousness" that Freire describes in his various
texts (*Pedagogy of the Oppressed*; *Education as Cultural Action for Freedom*; and *Pedagogy of the City,* for example) is also profoundly spiritual.
Liberatory pedagogy and liberation theology evolved from the same social
and historical source: a growing sense among Latin American social and
religious activists during the late 1950s and early '60s that oppression and
injustice experienced by "Third World" (especially Latin American) people

resulted from economic dependence on more fully developed "First World" countries. These activists, Paulo Freire and the liberation theologians among them, sought to devise social and religious options (and, not coincidentally, political ones); these options were based on "Latin American reality"—their experience of the world—rather than on experience imposed from without by the First World. I'll explore the spiritual aspect of Freire's pedagogy in this essay and pose some questions about its application when stripped of its spiritual underpinnings: Is Freire's spirituality necessarily religious, necessarily Christian? If so, should only the "mechanics" of education for critical consciousness be used in secular, pluralistic cultures? Finally, I will address these questions with some suggestions for rendering a more spiritual interpretation of education for critical consciousness in our own classrooms.

Liberation Theology, Spirituality, and Teaching

Liberation theology defies easy summary. Nevertheless, a quick review of some key concepts seems in order as a theoretical ground for understanding liberation spirituality. Theology is human reflection on a faith, on the story of faith and salvation that the faithful tell themselves and the world. In the Roman Catholic religious tradition, the storytellers have typically been clergy—priests, brothers, and nuns—writing for an audience of other clergy. Theology has been the domain of the elite. Liberation theology, on the other hand, proclaims a "preferential option for the poor"; the power of storytelling rests with all people and especially with the oppressed. The "product" of liberation theology is not, therefore, another scholarly volume. Instead, people work together to understand and free themselves from injustice and alienation. In this process, they earn salvation. To put it more formally, liberation theology is more than intellectual reflection on the faith. It is, first, Christian action upon the world—Christian praxis to transform unjust and alienating social structures—followed by intellectual, theological reflection upon that action.

Perhaps the most important concept to understand, though, is liberation theology's assertion that human and salvation histories are unified. According to theologian Gustavo Gutierrez, "[T]here are not two histories, one profane and one sacred, 'juxtaposed' or 'closely linked.' Rather, there is only one human destiny, irreversibly assumed by Christ, the Lord of history" (1973, 86). In liberation theology, then, the sacred—God, Christ, the Holy Spirit—enters human history, and all history moves inevitably toward God and salvation. This idea is especially important for understanding liberation spirituality. Technically speaking, spirituality is the dominion of the spirit. Popular consciousness tends to link spirituality with the "other world," an unseen that may or may not interact with the everyday world. Liberation theology places the beginnings of spirituality squarely in the existential world. Gutierrez writes: "A spirituality is a concrete manner, inspired by the spirit,

of living the Gospel; it is a definite way of living 'before the Lord,' in solidarity with all human beings, 'with the Lord,' and before all human beings"
(1988, 117). In addition, liberation spirituality requires what Gutierrez calls
a "radical transformation of the self," a "conversion" to the neighbor that is
implied in one's conversion to the Lord (1988, 118). Liberation theology
links social justice and salvation. The same theme runs through Paulo
Freire's work and informs his liberatory pedagogy. Human beings are
"uncompleted," according to Freire, conscious of their "incompletion" (*Pedagogy* 1990, 27). God is a transcendent "Absolute," a presence in history
who calls people, "limited, unfinished, and incompleted as they are," to share
in His creation ("Third World", 13). Freire argues that human beings are in
relationships with the world, with each other, and with God. Human beings
are "bound" to God in a way that models all relationships with the world and
with other people. God is transcendent over humanity. God is infinite; people are finite. God is Absolute; people are incomplete. God is the source;
people are indigent searchers for the source. Despite this position of apparent eminence, however, God "limits Himself by seeing some value in
men . . . as beings that choose, as sharers in His creative work" ("Third
World" 13). God gives people self-consciousness and essentially makes our
nature human rather than animal. Humanity's task, its "ontological and historical vocation," is to be "more fully human," to develop critical consciousness as beings who separate from and objectify reality, then act upon and
transform it. People can't fulfill this vocation if they are dominated, however;
oppression is "violence" that "interferes" with the task (*Pedagogy* 1990, 40).
While God stands "over" us, then, the relationship neither dominates nor
domesticates; instead, "by its very nature," our relationship with God "liber-
ates" us. Just so, our relationships with other people should neither domesti-
cate nor dominate; the liberating relationship with God "incarnates" human
relationships so that they, "by their very nature," liberate us as well (Educa-
cao como practica de liberdade 15, quoted in Elias 1976, 25).

It is difficult to underestimate the importance Freire places on human
relationships. Freire writes: "[H]umans free themselves only in concert, only
in communion, collaborating on something wrong that they want to correct. . . . [N]o one saves another, no one saves himself all alone, because only
in communion can we save ourselves—or not save ourselves" ("Conscientizing" 1990, 12). Recall the unity of sacred and secular histories in liberation
theology and liberatory pedagogy. When people turn to each other, they turn
to God; when they turn to God, they turn to each other. Either way, they
forgo themselves, enter communion, and earn salvation.

Education for critical consciousness, the process Freire calls conscientization, constitutes a liberatory praxis in that people work together to understand that and how they are oppressed, and then work to free themselves. It
constitutes Christian liberatory praxis in that it demands an "Easter," that
people die to be born again. Freire writes:

This Easter [conscientization], which results in the changing of consciousness, must be existentially experienced. The real Easter is not commemora-
tive rhetoric. It is praxis; it is historical involvement. The old Easter of
rhetoric is dead—with no hope of resurrection. It is only in the authenticity of historical praxis that Easter becomes the death which makes life possible. ("Education" 1972, 35)

This statement binds education for critical consciousness to liberation
theology. The "real Easter," a concrete historical fact for Freire, marks the
"radical liberation" of humanity from sin and death. Like all liberation, it is
praxis. Conscientization marks the freedom of humanity from oppression and
enslavement. Together, these "Easters" comprise the totality of "Christian
liberation." Humanity fulfills its vocation to be more and so returns—
inevitably, for Freire—to its source: God.

Spiritual Teaching in a Secular World

Liberation theology and education for critical consciousness declare the unity
of sacred and human histories; the spiritual informs the secular and vice
versa. Many of Freire's North American followers, however, silence or
ignore the spiritual aspects of his work in favor of the more political ones. A
case in point is the "critical" pedagogy of Ira Shor, perhaps Freire's leading
advocate in the United States. In this section, I will investigate some of the
problems that arise when Shor tries to enact a Freirean pedagogy without
accounting for or incorporating the spiritual. Specifically, I'll consider how
America's "cult" of the individual influences Shor's construction of the
teacher's role in critical classrooms. Shor envisions liberatory classrooms
that model authentically democratic life and a society that values the community's needs over an individual's. A vein of individualism lies deeply
embedded in Shor's thinking, however, and hinders the community's development of collective social action.

In *Critical Teaching and Everyday Life*, Shor describes a liberatory pedagogy derived directly from Freire but cautions that the nuts and bolts, so to
speak, of Freire's pedagogy cannot simply be transferred from the Third
World to the First (1987, 269; 127). Shor circumvents this difficulty, however, by pointing out that conscientization is a "learning process larger than
literacy" (1987, 95). He posits his pedagogy to reflect the larger process of
consciousness raising, reading the world, rather than the particulars of textual
literacy, reading the word. In fact, Shor directs his pedagogy not toward the
textually illiterate but toward the "contextually illiterate," students dominated
and alienated by modern life. According to Shor, worker-students gain
authority over their lives only by claiming responsibility for their own learning: "Overall, liberatory education can be thought of as a social practice out-

of-sync with mass experience, yet rooted critically in the reality of daily life. Its form and content is transcendence of the given" (1987, 82–83).

Both Shor and Freire indict individualism, and both acknowledge the importance of banishing it as a way to promote trust, class solidarity, and an emerging consciousness of political power for social change. The way in which each conceives of individualism, however, illustrates the dichotomy between Shor's secular pedagogy and Freire's spiritually influenced one. According to Shor, individualism leads to mistrust and paranoia and causes "widespread noncooperation of worker-students with even the best-meaning teachers" (1987, 35). Overcoming this profound social isolation in the critical classroom is the first, necessary step in encouraging collective social action. Freire's vision of collective social action, on the other hand, occurs in the larger context of conscientization-as-Christian-liberatory-praxis. Human relationships are significant in and of themselves and, more important, because they are modeled after and "incarnated" by the "liberating relationship" with God. Individualism thus impedes communion and liberation and paralyzes us in our incompleteness: We stop seeking God by turning away from others.

Shor's take on individualism appears to be much more secular, rooted in America's capitalist history as a "cult" of the individual. America's dynamic economy creates opportunities for "clever individuals" to succeed and has led to an "infatuation with the lone entrepreneur." This false consciousness— the economy is directed by giant corporations, not by particular persons— permeates mass culture to such an extent that Americans grant more credibility to individual effort than to "ideas of social intelligence and political empowerment." Further, the American tendency to enshrine the individual at the expense of social effort leads to self-absorption, helps the system "divide and conquer common people" and creates a "conformist culture" (Shor and Freire 1987, 24). America's passion for independent accomplishment and action might seem to be the incarnation of democracy; as Shor points out, these notions are essential to the American Dream (1987, 9–17).

Individualism's infiltration of mass culture also affects education and contributes significantly to what Shor calls the culture of silence among worker-students. Education lulls students into believing that they can and will transform their lives by their personal, individual efforts from the elementary grades onward. This belief, however, ultimately conflates independence and liberation. The false consciousness of independent effort causes people to forgo their potential for "collective life" and social—that is, group—action. At its most sinister, Shor argues, this attitude destroys "class solidarity," trust, and leads to "routine paranoia" in everyday life that isolates people socially and "atomizes" or fragments their perceptions of reality. Shor writes, "Knowledge of reality is as divided as humanity, into confused and conflicting parts instead of a meaningful whole" (1987, 35). A fragmented perception of reality stymies attempts at critical analysis and emergence from oppression, but Shor's liberatory education provides an alternative. In such a class, students and teachers distance themselves from or objectify mass culture and so come to know it critically.

For Shor, then, curbing students' tendencies toward individualism creates a "bridge to consciousness," an "antidote to mass culture," and a "democratic prefiguration of future life and learning" (1987, 180). Freire's opposition to individualism, however, comprises more than a technique to enable critical thinking and effect, perhaps some sort of transformative social action beyond school. It is a lesson in how to live and how to liberate. When Freire asserts that we must accept education's directiveness and ask, instead, toward what and with whom it is directive (Shor and Freire 1987, 22–23), he draws on his Christian roots and contemporary Christian definitions of socialization: people's joint effort to attain goals that surpass them individually, as Pope John XXIII writes in the encyclical "Mater et Magistra." Freire's argument also echoes liberation theology's social critique, here paraphrased by Ricardo Planas: "What is needed is an altruistic ethic that permeates not only the individual but the entire culture, and places the needs of the entire social family (including the individual's) ahead of one's own" (1986, 134). In denouncing individualism, Freire simultaneously announces Christian sister- and brotherhood in service of the ontological vocation to be more fully human. The stakes are high for Freire: Individualism means turning away from others and hence from God, which is a sinful situation. People thereby risk dominating and alienating other people and condemn rather than save themselves.

Shor writes of his own pedagogy in language strikingly similar to Freire's Christian rhetoric: "Liberatory teaching . . . leads a symbolic exodus from oppression." He writes of his role as teacher in similar terms: "In joining my students' exodus from alienation, I became one more pilgrim soul, in an inquiry that pushed beyond confusion for a break with the past" (1987, 98; 268). Liberation theology reads the Biblical Exodus not just symbolically; it is, Gustavo Gutierrez writes, a "historical-salvific fact . . . a political liberation through which Yahweh expresses his love for his people." Liberation in the modern world enacts a "new Exodus," literally a re-creation of the Biblical Exodus. To participate in this event is to participate in the ongoing work of God's creation and, since creation and salvation histories are one, to participate in human salvation (Gutierrez 1988, 156–159). But Shor does not simply "join" his students' exodus; he precipitates it:

> The person responsible for provoking separation and critical re-entry is the teacher. By identifying, abstracting, and problematizing the most important themes of student experience, the teacher detaches students from their reality and then re-presents the material for their systematic scrutiny. (1987, 100)

Freire's work assumes a "transcendent given," the Absolute in which (or whom) human beings find completion. Shor, on the other hand, intends to transcend the given student experience of received social conditions. The question arises, though—just how and by what authority does Shor (or any teacher) identify the *most important themes of student experience?* Shor analyzes student reality in terms of a "network of cultural instruments," among them vocational culture, various forms of false consciousness, and a lack of democratic experience (1987, 49 ff.). Despite the democratic claims, however, no student voices appear in his examination. Shor thus poses himself not so much as Moses, answering God's call to forgo himself, liberate the people, and so transform the world according to God's creative plan, but as a hegemonic provocateur, directing worker-students to transform the world according to his own Utopian vision, predicated on his analysis—although "depiction" might be a better word—of their reality.

Teaching (in the) Here and Now

Is it possible to enact a Freirean education for critical consciousness—including its spiritual aspects—in our own classrooms? North Americans live in a more secular (and, I think, a far less spiritual) culture than do Latin Americans. Further, although liberation theology has been adapted to religious traditions other than Roman Catholicism and Protestantism, it remains largely a Christian movement. North Americans are not only more secular, we're also ostensibly more pluralistic than our neighbors to the south. How might a Buddhist in San Francisco or a Muslim in Detroit react to pedagogy based on overtly Christian beliefs and values? Given even these modest difficulties, Shor's omission of liberation spirituality (or any spirituality, for that matter) seems easier to understand. But the problem remains: Freire's pedagogy emerged and continues to evolve from a historical consciousness that unites sacred and human. Freirean pedagogy must be both spiritual and earthly or it simply isn't Freirean.

How can North American teachers enact an authentic, ethical education for critical consciousness, informed and nourished by liberation spirituality? The crucial feature of liberation spirituality—and the one that powers education for critical consciousness—is conversion to the neighbor, that is, the creation of communion and community. Through this process people surrender themselves to God and to the greater social good, the good that exceeds them individually. In terms of education, teachers should "convert" to their students, take the students' existential reality as the starting point for any class. This idea raises serious questions about the nature of student reality and how teachers come to know it. For example, how can teachers understand something as complex as a single student's lived experience, let alone that of an entire class? While teachers work to curb individualism among students, how do they resist their own culturally constructed tendency toward individualism, especially given the unique authority they wield? (In a related matter, how can teachers learn to be "directive" without being "authoritative"?) Further, if a critical class is a community, what about "teacher reality"? Can the dialogue in a critical classroom be authentic if teachers do not discuss their reality?

I suggest that critical teachers, like Dorothy in the *Wizard of Oz,* should seek their hearts' desires right in the "backyard," in the existential reality teachers and students already share: the classroom, the class itself, the institution. Here are some recommendations. I have an English class in mind as I write these, but they can no doubt be adapted to any discipline.

- One way to begin a semester is to examine with students the classroom's topography and geography. Try to figure out together why the room is arranged the way it is, why it looks the way it does, the types of behaviors it elicits from teachers and students, and how it helps (or hinders) learning. Teachers should talk honestly about how they perceive their positions in the learning community.

- Discuss the mechanics of the class with the students. For example, why were particular texts chosen? What rationale informs evaluation? In this way, the class will no longer be something "done to" the students without their consent or understanding.

- Try a new lesson, or a new approach to a lesson, in class. Involve the students in the experiment by telling them it's new, that you don't know how it will turn out, but that you'll find out together.

- Rather than "performing" knowledge for students (see Tompkins 1990), work with them to create what I call a "learning collective." Certainly, a teacher "knows" a given subject. Nevertheless, he or she should be open to learning and knowing more about the subject, especially from a student's perspective. When students take responsibility for teaching—and I mean full responsibility—everyone learns from each other.

Perhaps the most important thing to remember is that teachers must be converted to their students, that teachers and students must work in communion to transform reality. Parker J. Palmer calls this experience a "community of troth."

> To know something or someone in truth is to enter troth with the known . . . .
> To know in truth is to become betrothed, to engage the known with one's
> whole self. . . . To know in truth is to allow one's self to be known as well,
> to be vulnerable to the challenges and changes any true relationship
> brings. . . . Truthful knowing weds the knower and the known; even in
> separation, the two become part of each other's life and fate. (1983, 31)

For Paulo Freire, a transcendent Absolute—God—exists. God is an active force in human history, mandating human behavior and the just conduct of society. Reality isn't oppressive simply because Freire declares it to be so; God intends that people live justly—that is, in freedom, communion, and community—and that they work to make the world more just. When people deny God's mandate, they exploit and enslave each other and do not save each other. This is no mere rhetorical stance for Freire. Instead, this is Freire's fundamental statement of belief, his perception of existential reality. To make authentic use of Freire's pedagogy, then, we must do what Freire tells us: We must start with his reality, study it with him, and come to a rigorous understanding. We owe Freire, the students with whom we would engage in education for critical consciousness, and ourselves nothing less.

14

Spiritual Empowerment in the Technical Writing Class

Marianthe Karanikas

The adjectives *spiritual* and *technical* appear to be contradictory. To be "spiritual" implies religious belief; to be "technical" implies objectivity. For some who view religious belief to be blind, fervent, and unquestioning faith in dogma, the adjective "spiritual" appears contradictory to the rigor, caution, and skepticism characteristic of scientific objectivity. In these terms, the notion of "spiritual empowerment" thus seems inappropriate to the technical writing class. However, if we view "spirit" as a form of clarity not necessarily related to religion and "spiritual empowerment" as a means of achieving this clarity, then spiritual empowerment may well be of vital importance to the technical writing class. In this chapter, I focus on two meditative techniques: insight meditation and loving-kindness practice (Meadow 1994; Khema 1987; Johnson 1982; Goldstein 1987). While these meditative techniques are from the Buddhist tradition, they can be used to teach writing in secular situations just as James Moffett (1988) and George Kalamaras (1994) have used other meditative techniques to teach composition.

Technical writers often adapt expert discourse for nonspecialist audiences. In the case of scientific writing, the technical writer must communicate with both experts and nonspecialists to facilitate the dissemination of scientific knowledge. Insight exercises can help the writer become aware of what the biologist Barbara McClintock calls "tacit assumptions," those hidden tendencies of the mind that shape our biases and often hinder our understanding of nature (Keller 1983, 178). McClintock herself used meditative means to achieve a clarity that allowed her to observe natural phenomena most of her colleagues could not. In this essay, I briefly discuss McClintock's meditative means of discovering. Then I discuss how Kalamaras uses meditative means to collaborate with biologists in a writing across the curriculum project (1994, 13). Since technical writers must often convince scientists to improve their writing, they may well find Kalamaras's nonintrusive negotiation techniques applicable in a wide variety of situations. Technical writers may begin to develop clarity and nonintrusive negotiation techniques through exercises adapted from insight and loving-kindness practice. I rely here primarily on the works of Joseph Goldstein, one of the leading teachers of insight meditation, and Mary Jo Meadow, one of Goldstein's students who is an insight meditation teacher, a clinical psychologist, and a professor at Mankato State University.[1] Meadow has adapted exercises from these practices to fit the classroom situation.[2] Insight practice develops "mindfulness" or "being aware of what is happening in the present moment" (Goldstein 1987, 13). I describe a mindfulness exercise used by writing teacher Renee Gatsis.[3] Insight and loving-kindness can also be used to help develop compassionate critical consciousness. Insight exercises allow students to become aware of the mind states that give rise to bias so that students can then choose how to act in different situations. Loving-kindness exercises incline the mind to choose action that does not harm other beings. Here I turn to the Vietnamese poet, activist, and meditation teacher Thich Nhat Hanh, who encourages action that springs neither from rage nor from terror but from loving-kindness.

Barbara McClintock: Meditative Clarity in Scientific Discovery

Barbara McClintock, a Nobel Prize–winning geneticist, discovered the phenomenon of genetic transposition almost thirty years before most biologists accepted its existence. "Transposition is a two-part process, involving the [regulated] release of a chromosomal element from its original position and its insertion into a new position" (Keller 1983, 127). McClintock's biographer Evelyn Fox Keller speaks of the meditative clarity that enabled McClintock to observe natural phenomena that eluded her colleagues. According to Keller, this clarity arose from McClintock's focused concentration as well as from her ability to observe clearly. Although scientific concepts precluded the possibility of transposition, McClintock observed and characterized transposition through years of rigorous experimentation. When the evidence from nature contradicted scientific opinion, McClintock followed nature.[4] She did not allow scientific concepts to blind her experience.

1. Meadow is a Roman Catholic sister who is also vowed to the precepts of Buddhist nuns. She teaches insight meditation and offers retreats for special groups like twelve-step programs and Christians of every denomination throughout the United States and abroad.
2. I learned these exercises from Meadow in a workshop in Bolivar, Missouri.
3. Gatsis teaches at Prospect High School in Mt. Prospect, Ill. She told me about her mindfulness exercises in a conversation.
4. McClintock's notion of nature is not objectivist. That is, she does not view nature as a separate object to be studied. Instead, she views everything in nature as interconnected (Keller 204).

Eventually, genetic transposition was rediscovered, McClintock's work vindicated, and the scientific concepts changed.[5]

McClintock's focused concentration allowed her to be so totally absorbed in the material she studied that she moved into "nonconceptual" awareness. According to Kalamaras, "nonconceptual" refers to "those perceptions that are not bound by the categorizing capacity of intellect or thought," perceptions that are still considered to be rational (1994, 8). An incident from McClintock's experience as a master experimentalist illustrates nonconceptual awareness. In 1944, geneticist George Beadle invited McClintock to visit his laboratory at Stanford to identify the minute chromosomes of *Neurospora*, a red bread mold. Beadle had previously shown through genetic mapping of *Neurospora* that one gene led to one enzyme.[6] But Beadle wanted also to identify *Neurospora* chromosomes "so small that they had eluded all previous attempts at identification. It seemed to Beadle that if there was anyone in the world who could crack this problem, it was McClintock" (Keller 1983, 113). After three days of arduous analysis, McClintock made no progress. She told Keller, "I got very discouraged, and realized that there was . . . something quite seriously wrong. I wasn't seeing things, I wasn't integrating, I wasn't getting things right at all" (Keller 1983, 115). McClintock then left the laboratory to sit and meditate under the eucalyptus trees.

For half an hour, McClintock sat and then, in her own words, "Suddenly I jumped up, I couldn't wait to get back to the laboratory. I knew I was going to solve it" (Keller 1983, 115). McClintock did not remember exactly what happened. She told Keller, "I must have done this very intense, subconscious thinking. And suddenly I knew everything was going to be just fine" (Keller 1983, 115). Five days later, McClintock identified the *Neurospora* chromosomes and tracked them through the entire meiotic cycle.[7] According to Beadle, "Barbara, in two months in Stanford, did more to clean up the cytology of *Neurospora* than all other cytological geneticists had done in all previous times on all forms of mold" (quoted in Keller 1983, 114).

This discipline and clarity allowed McClintock to move beyond the scientific concepts of her time and to discover genetic transposition.[8] As biologist Lewis Wolpert notes, in 1944 McClintock made an unusual observation on maize that led to her discovery. She saw "patches of cells in maize with different colors" and dropped everything else to investigate them (1992, 90).[9]

5. In the late 1970s molecular biologists discovered transposition in bacteria.
6. For the discovery that genes act by regulating specific chemical processes, Beadle and Edward L. Tatum were awarded part of the 1958 Nobel Prize for physiology and medicine.
7. In plants meiosis is the par of cell divisions that leads to the production of mold spores.
8. The existence of transposable elements contradicted two important scientific concepts: the notion of the gene as a fixed unit of heredity and the central dogma that states information goes from the genetic material to protein and not in the other direction. These two concepts have subsequently been revised.
9. In his book *The Unnatural Nature of Science,* Wolpert indicates that he would be opposed to the suggestion that meditation can be used to enhance clarity (89).

Six years later, McClintock's "talk at a symposium was met with . . . incomprehension. Her ideas were premature . . . Only in the late 1960s did scientists discover transposition in bacteria," a system that was "much more amenable to analysis" than maize and "could be used to demonstrate the validity of McClintock's theory" (1992, 91). McClintock could see phenomena most of her colleagues missed because she was open to the possibility that things might exist in nature even if science says they don't. According to McClintock, "the challenge for investigators in every field is to break free of their tacit assumptions, so that they can allow the results of their experiments to speak for themselves" (Keller 1983, 179). McClintock described her ability to break free of tacit assumptions as a sort of "mysticism," akin to the meditative traditions of Tibetan Buddhists (Keller 1983, 202). Many scientists think the term "mysticism" refers to woolly thinking uncharacteristic of science. Breaking free of tacit assumptions, however, is good science. Thus scientist James Shapiro characterizes McClintock's "so-called mysticism" as "the product of an unusual marriage of a mind open to any possibility, to one that insists on cogent tests of hypotheses. . . . She does not speculate loosely" (quoted in Lewin 1983, 402). I offer the example of McClintock here not to equate scientific discovery with meditation, but rather to show that meditation can be used to enhance clarity and rigorous thinking—traits that are important to scientific and technical writing. McClintock's focused concentration required great discipline as did her flexibility of mind. She could be open to multiple possibilities at the same time that she insisted on careful testing of hypotheses. Similarly, meditative techniques merge discipline with flexibility.

George Kalamaras:
Nonintrusive Negotiation Techniques

When technical writers serve as consultants, they must be flexible. They must often negotiate with experts who may be unwilling to accept their suggestions. In *Reclaiming the Tacit Dimension,* writing specialist George Kalamaras describes the nonintrusive negotiation techniques he implemented with biology instructors in a writing across the curriculum (WAC) project. These techniques arose from his meditative understanding of reciprocity. Reciprocity is a "condition of psychic fluidity between subject and object," in this case, between self and other (Kalamaras 1994, 8). At first, "psychic fluidity" may seem like a vague term. However, it simply indicates that our thoughts about other people affect the way we act towards them. Our actions, in turn, affect the way other people think about and act towards us.

As a consultant in a WAC program, Kalamaras "sought to reempower students by granting them access to their own language and meaning-making capabilities"; by "relocating students as the locus of knowledge," Kalamaras "sought institutional change . . . through dissolving hierarchical concepts of the making of knowledge" (1994, 29). However, the biology instructors, most of whom were overworked graduate teaching assistants, were resistant to these goals. Earlier attempts to implement the WAC program had failed. The TAs greeted Kalamaras with "apathy," "skepticism," and "in some cases, hostility" (1994, 31). The faculty coordinator told Kalamaras that student writing "'lacked clarity' and 'was generally murky,'" but she rejected his offer to conduct instructional workshops on teaching writing-to-learn because she did not want to burden her "already overworked TAs" (1994, 33). Kalamaras enrolled in an undergraduate biology class and completed its writing assignments. He interviewed teachers and students to "discover the specific ways biology constructs knowledge" (1994, 34). He visited each TA, showed his goodwill, and explained his services. These dialogical approaches prepared the stage for change.

Moments after a weekly staff meeting began, Kalamaras offered his assistance to the TAs. Rather than combat the opposition and hostile remarks, Kalamaras "problematized each objection and recorded the TAs' responses" (1994, 33). At that, the TAs "openly revealed their animosity toward the responsibility of writing instruction" (1994, 33). Kalamaras had won their trust. Soon afterwards, the TAs invited him to conduct writing workshops in their labs. The biologists and Kalamaras began to work together. There was still tenuousness, but as Kalamaras notes in his detailed analysis, this became an opportunity for negotiation. The biologists learned about the teaching of writing and Kalamaras learned about the teaching of biology. Both experts and consultant came to understand each other's ideological positions and could therefore work together to improve student writing.

These nonintrusive negotiation techniques are clearly applicable to many consulting situations. Technical writing students can practice working with experts by assisting science or engineering students with their major reports, theses, or prospective publications. Meanwhile, in business, the importance of establishing goodwill is well known (Beard 1990, 101). The notions of flexibility and reciprocity can help consultants as they work together with their clients to effect change.

Insight Meditation and Loving-Kindness

The reader may ask, Why do McClintock and Kalamaras characterize their clarity and flexibility as meditative? Certainly many people think clearly and negotiate well without any reliance on formal meditative techniques. Indeed, one need never practice formal meditation and still lead a fulfilling, compassionate, and meaningful life. However, many other people find meditation helpful in the cultivation of clarity and flexibility. Meditative exercises can help students uncover their tacit assumptions, become aware of their biases, and begin to act mindfully in any number of situations (aware of what is happening in the present moment). The exercises I discuss here are modified from insight meditation and loving-kindness practice. Before I present the exercises, let me give some background on the meditations themselves.

According to clinical psychologist Mary Jo Meadow, insight meditation is "rigorously empirical. Its profound psychology is based on practitioners' introspective accounts of their meditation experiences" (1994, 37). Practitioners have recounted experiences to teachers who, in turn, have assessed students' progress in terms of what was already known. "The result is a very precise and elaborate developmental psychology that has remained valid, accurate, and helpful over many centuries" (1994, 38). According to Meadow, meditation helps lower blood pressure and resting pulse rate; it also helps to calm and clarify emotions. In addition, "mental benefits include better concentration, the ability to focus and stay focused, and freedom from . . . worrying and other mental wanderings that cause distress" (1994, 38).[10] Meadow then summarizes the four basic points that comprise insight meditation:

1. Become aware of the "dominant" event occurring in the whole body-mind process.

2. Acknowledge and anchor this awareness by "naming" the process at the very first awareness of it. Make a soft whisper in the mind called "mental noting."

3. Observe, resting full attention in it, all that happens within the process until it ends.

4. Maintain a soft, gentle, persistent willingness. Do not try to make any experience come, stay, or be a particular way; do not try to prevent or push away any experience (1994, 61).

In insight practice, one begins by noting the breath. One notes the inhalation and the exhalation, the "in" and "out." One rests full attention in the process of breathing. If an experience draws one's attention away from the breath, one follows the four steps above. Take, for example, an itch on the cheek. One becomes aware of the itch. One acknowledges and anchors this awareness by naming the process at the first awareness of it. Make a soft whisper in the mind: "itching." If possible, use a gerund since it indicates more clearly the sense of a transient process than does a noun. *Itching* is a more fluid word than is *itch*. Observe, resting full attention in the itching, all that happens within the itching until it ends. Maintain a soft, gentle, persistent willingness. Do not try to make the itching come, stay, or be a particular way; do not try to prevent it or push it away.

10. For a readable introduction to the physiological benefits of meditation, see Dr. Herbert Benson's *The Relaxation Response* and *Beyond the Relaxation Response*. Benson, a medical doctor specializing in behavioral medicine and hypertension, is interested in the integration of body and mind. He teaches at Harvard Medical School.

A similar procedure holds for thinking. At the first awareness of thinking, one notes "thinking." Often the thought drops away at the first awareness of it. If the thought does not drop away, one should not try to push it away. Instead, one might note the type of thinking being done, such as "analyzing" or "judging." The mental noting helps one be clear and aware so that one does not become lost in thought. Often, when the thinking drops away, an emotion will emerge. Again, one notes the emotion: "feeling anger." One rests full attention in the anger, in all that happens within the process of anger until it ends. One does not try to make anger come, stay, or be a particular way. One does not try to prevent the feeling of anger or push it away. If another emotion, physical sensation, or thought arises, the same process applies. One notes in a gentle and soft way the physical, mental, and emotional experiences of each moment.

In *Purifying the Heart,* Meadow gives more explicit directions for insight practice. In *The Experience of Insight: A Simple and Direct Guide to Buddhist Meditation,* Meadow's teacher Joseph Goldstein describes the practice in great detail. (Both Meadow and Goldstein also provide excellent bibliographies.) It is not advisable to practice insight meditation intensively without a qualified teacher, because insight meditation itself can uncover emotional and physical issues that may require professional attention. One should practice with a qualified teacher who will refer you to a psychotherapist or physician if necessary. Daily practices of an hour or so are safe to do, though you want to ensure that you understand the method properly. The classroom exercises presented here are modified from insight meditation and are safe to do and to teach.[11]

Meadow has modified two exercises from insight meditation that can be used in the classroom. The first is awareness of the breath, which can help students focus and keep their minds from wandering. Instruct students to sit in a comfortable position and to become aware of their breathing. They may wish to become aware of the inhalation and exhalation. They may wish to count their breaths. Counting the breath (five to ten breaths) is a good way to begin calming the mind. I have used this exercise in classes with success. I do not call the practice a "meditation." I call it a "concentration or focusing exercise." Usually, I have a fair share of skeptical students who think the exercise sounds silly. I don't force anyone to participate. Afterwards, students find that they can

---

11. To find qualified teachers, write to the Insight Meditation Society, Barre, MA 01005. Buddhist meditation is not my major meditative practice. However, I have studied it with Mary Jo Meadow, whose sponsoring organization is RES, P.O. Box 65, Mankato, MN 56002. I choose to write about insight meditation and loving-kindness here because there are many clear texts that describe the practices and many opportunities for readers to learn the practices with a qualified teacher. The practices are also easily modified for use in classroom situations. Meditation teachers in this tradition do not charge for their services; they accept whatever donation the student feels is appropriate. When retreats are offered, the costs cover room and board. If someone cannot afford to pay, many insight groups allow for payment by installment and may provide scholarships.

concentrate better when listening to lectures and when reading and writing. The second exercise involves watching the mind. Meadow instructs her psychology students to watch their minds for an hour. I recommend five minutes for freshmen and sophomores, ten minutes for juniors, and for seniors and graduate students a take-home exercise instructing them to watch their minds for twenty minutes to an hour. They are to have no distractions, no music, no television, no conversation, no eating, and no drinking. For one hour, they are to sit in silence and watch their minds. Just watch and note what happens. An hour works best with small groups of advanced students. When a group of five such students related their experiences in class, one student said that she couldn't sit for an hour because she was too worried about finishing her homework. Another discovered that fear and anger influenced her reactions in certain situations. A third couldn't sit at all; he found the exercise frightening. A fourth couldn't believe how much she thought about all at once. A fifth had to take a bath in order to find a safe and quiet place where she could concentrate; however, Meadow would characterize such an activity as a distraction. Some students often find distractions that hinder their creativity, productivity, and even their health; nonetheless, many other students do become aware of what's going on in their minds.

Writing teacher Renee Gatsis has adapted an exercise on mindful eating from the meditation teacher Thich Nhat Hanh. (See *Present Moment, Wonderful Moment* 1990, 48.) Students bring their favorite foods to class. There they eat the food mindfully, one mouthful at a time. They must chew slowly and taste the food carefully and precisely. They must be aware of the experience of biting, tasting, chewing, and swallowing in the moment it happens. Gatsis found that many students don't like the taste of their favorite foods when they eat mindfully. Others begin to savor them. One of my students felt sick after eating a favorite snack. Others tasted delicious flavors they hadn't noticed before. Most students wrote excellent descriptive essays after mindfully eating their food. Technical writing classes can eat the food mindfully and then describe it for consumers in two ways. First, they write advertisements for the food. Second, they evaluate the food for a publication such as *Consumer Reports*. The exercise often raises interesting ethical issues. Most students become more focused in their observing, and this focus carries into their writing. As James Moffett notes, "writing and meditation are naturally allied activities. Both are important for their own sake, and through each people can practice the other" (90).

Insight meditation has many benefits. According to Goldstein, as we clear away clouds of "greed, hatred, and delusion" through the "unfolding of insight," the "qualities of lovingkindness begin to shine forth naturally" (1987, 126). Goldstein describes its simplicity.

> Sit in a comfortable position. As a way of freeing the mind from any tensions or grudges, begin by asking for and extending forgiveness: "If I have

hurt or offended anyone in thought or word or deed, I ask forgiveness. And I freely forgive anyone who may have hurt or offended me." . . . Then for a few minutes direct phrases of loving thought towards yourself: "May I be happy and peaceful, may I be free of suffering, . . ." concentrating on the meaning of the words. It's difficult to have a genuine love for others until we can be accepting and loving of ourselves. The particular words do not matter. . . . Continue the practice beginning to extend these thoughts and feelings towards others: "As I want to be happy, so may all beings be happy. As I want to be peaceful, so may all beings be peaceful. As I want to be free of suffering, so may all beings be free of suffering." Repeating this in the mind a few times, begin to radiate the lovingkindness outward towards all beings. . . . "May all beings be happy, peaceful, free of suffering" (1987, 127).

Both Goldstein and Meadow provide directions for loving-kindness with respect to particular situations. Meadow's *Gentling the Heart* presents detailed loving-kindness practice for family, friends, neutral people (for whom we feel no strong emotion), and for difficult relationships. The loving-kindness exercise presented here can be practiced and taught.

Insight, Critical Consciousness, and Loving-Kindness

Insight can help writers become not only clear and more focused but also more critically conscious. "To be human," Freire tells us, "is to engage in relationships with others and with the world" (*Education* 1973, 3). Freire, Aronowitz, and Giroux argue for the liberation of human beings through their critical consciousness. They teach students to question, to become aware of oppression, and to transform it. Insight exercises allow students to become aware of the mind states that give rise to bias so that the students can then choose how to act in different situations. By watching the mind, we become aware of the fear, mistrust, and anger that block our capacity to love. Loving-kindness exercises incline the mind to choose action that does not harm other beings. As Freire says, the "oppressor is solidary with the oppressed only when he stops regarding the oppressed as an abstract category and sees them as persons who have been unjustly dealt with, deprived of their voice, cheated in the sale of their labor—when he . . . risks an act of love" (*Education* 1973, 34–35).

In *Love in Action*, Thich Nhat Hanh writes that "to love is to understand" (1993, 66). He suggests there is already a reciprocal relationship between the oppressed and the oppressor, between the violent and the nonviolent. "In each of us, there is a certain amount of violence and a certain amount of nonviolence" (1993, 65). We cannot completely avoid being violent. Even if one is vegetarian, eating necessitates the killing of living things. Soldiers, meanwhile, practice a kind of nonviolence when they avoid killing innocent people. "If we work for peace out of anger," Thich Nhat Hanh says, "we will never succeed" (1993, 66). Instead we must understand each other's perspective and work together. In 1967, Martin Luther King, Jr., nominated Thich Nhat Hanh for the Nobel Peace Prize. Since that time, Thich Nhat Hanh has been teaching mindfulness and the cultivation of loving-kindness. In *Love in Action*, Thich Nhat Hanh applies insight and loving-kindness practice to nonviolent social change, suggesting ways we might cultivate a compassionate critical consciousness. Like Kalamaras, Thich Nhat Hanh emphasizes the notion of reciprocity. His approach applies to a wide variety of public and private situations, from political action to corporate management. Technical writers are uniquely placed to negotiate what Thich Nhat Hanh emphasizes.

The practice of insight and loving-kindness is not sectarian. Insight can help both scientists and writers to be clearer, more creative, and more focused. McClintock's meditative clarity enabled her to see phenomena that contradicted the then-prevailing scientific concepts. Kalamaras's meditative flexibility enabled him to negotiate more compassionately as a consultant. Through insight, students can become aware of the mind states that give rise to bias. Through loving-kindness, students can learn how to negotiate more compassionately. For the specific context of the technical writing class, insight and loving-kindness exercises can help students not only to be better negotiators but also to think and write more clearly.

15

Entering Wonder

Sherry Swain

Recently, while waltzing to the music of a five-piece orchestra, I was overcome by a feeling of surrealism. Conscious thought dissipated; a sense of wonder filled my being. Following my partner's lead required no effort; I had but to focus on his face, and somehow my feet knew the steps and turns of the dance. Lights whirled and blended into a fluid pallet. Faces of the other dancers and patrons melted into a universal smile. Life's complexities spun themselves into perfect harmony during those moments. In this trancelike dream, joy and dance became one, each equal to the other.

Describing that dance experience to a friend, I commented that other patrons of the restaurant as well as the musicians had applauded and asked for more. Unaware of the presence of others during the dance itself, I surprised myself by enjoying the attention it generated. "Is it okay to enjoy the applause?" I asked my partner.

"You can thrive on it!" he assured me. The music began for the next dance; I slipped easily and naturally back into the surrealistic space. And so it went for the remainder of the evening. During the hiatus between dances, I sipped wine and chitchatted with friends. But with the first step of each new dance, I entered the sacred space once again. It was as if the dancing itself were a crystal pool of magic. The music surrounded me like gentle waves, and when it paused, I floated to the edges and remained suspended, waiting for the music's invitation to reenter the mystical pool.

"You were in 'the zone,'" my friend explained, "the magical place that athletes strive to enter—the state in which they can do no wrong." Suzanne Langer writes that dance is "an apparition of active powers, a dynamic image." It is not so much the music or flowing garb or rhythm or steps themselves, but rather the display of interacting forces that creates the aura. "Two people . . . seem to magnetize each other; . . . to be animated by one single spirit, one Power" (Langer 1957, 10). It was this Power, this sense of wonder, that consumed me that evening on the dance floor. And it was this Power that brought forth insights for my classroom.

A few years ago I heard Donald Murray say, "Writing that is easily written is easily read." Similar thoughts rushed through my mind during the dance that evening and continue even now as I reflect on the experience.

Easy dancing is beautiful dancing.
What is easily danced is easily, joyously observed.

Is this true of all art? Are paintings easily painted the artists' masterpieces? Is music easily composed joyously received? Is teaching that comes through wonder, naturally and spontaneously, the best teaching?

I had entered the place of wonder once before on a mountainside in North Carolina. I was writing, not dancing, on that day. The following excerpt is from my journal.

10/19/91

I am perched on a large flat gray stone that emerges from the mountainside. Below me a tiny gurgle of water flows over stones and sticks and under the ivy-covered footbridge I crossed to get here. I can hear the voices of tennis players and the few cars moving around the hotel parking lot, but I am ignoring them. Behind me, I imagine the family of squirrels I disturbed with my noisy scramble up the hillside is watching me, wishing I'd go away.

Now the wind rises, pushing leaves to the ground as it moves through the painted forest. The cool gray stone feels hard; the honest smell of the earth permeates the air; a King cab pickup truck chugs across a rustic one-lane bridge. Small trees, hugging the forest floor appear half lemon, half lime. The dark red leaves are missing this year, replaced by brilliant rose-colored leaves that move with the wind like Spanish dancers. Far above my head, the giants' tufts of dark green, gold, and brown are framed by the china blue sky.

Before me a graceful dogwood spreads a salmon canopy that reaches over the stream in one direction and back this way almost to my rock. Behind me, further up the mountain, its twin displays slightly darker foliage. And I marvel at the idiosyncrasies with which God has blessed us—that two of the same species growing on the same mountainside can be so nearly alike, yet distinctly different.

If man had created the world, every dogwood would look exactly the same. Not only does God alone have the power to create life, he has infinite appreciation for the diversity of life. With the exception of a few people of spirit, mankind spends lifetime after lifetime trying to standardize the diversity God created. Is it not blasphemy to paint and saw and bend and tie one dogwood so that it is outwardly identical to the other?

Oh, God, what are we doing to our children? Must they all master the same body of knowledge to be loved by fellow humans? Must they all read the same books, spell the same words, and write on the same topics to be valuable?

A few days later, taking part in reading workshop with my first-grade students, I reflected in my journal on the need for a classroom environment in which students can enter a place of wonder.

10/22/91

Saturday I spent several hours sitting on a rock on the side of a mountain writing. It was wonderful being still, being aware of the smell of earth, the play of squirrels, the colors of leaves, the sound of bubbling water. I value silent time in the classroom also, time for turning inward and reflecting. In *Living Between the Lines*, Calkins writes of a teacher who attempted to capture true writing silence for her classroom. She had wondered if it were really possible. I, too, wonder. I have no trouble filling these pages during our special journal writing time, but is the depth of reflection and thinking that was with me on the mountainside with me here?

Is it possible to bring children close enough to the mountainside in the classroom so that they will search out their own cool gray stones when they leave here?

How do we bring the mountainside and the apparition of dance into our classrooms? How do we invite our students to enter the zone, the place of wonder where insights become illuminated, where the difficult becomes easy, where complex details melt into wholes? I've heard Richard L. Graves talk about "educating the deep place," but he advises that we must teach to it indirectly, obliquely, and that unless a student decides to share an insight or experience with us, we may never know for sure that we have been success-ful. Sometimes my colleagues in secondary and college education share anecdotes of times their students have tapped into that place of wonder. As a teacher of first-grade children, and as a teacher of teachers in graduate courses, I am sometimes asked by those colleagues whether or not it is pos-sible to reach that deep place in little children or, indeed, whether or not such a place exists in children.

My response to their query is an emphatic "Yes!" My students are whole, complete people—still growing and developing as we all are—but whole and complete nevertheless. And they possess that deep spiritual core that defines all humanity. To the extent that it is nurtured, it will grow. Suzanne Langer describes this feeling core as a sense of life that exists, like a waterfall, only if it continues its motion (1957, 48). Like my colleagues who teach older students, I must offer my students mountainsides and music, allowing personal connections to take hold obliquely and indirectly and then move along. Graves' theory speaks to my teaching of graduate students as well as primary students. It's not the age of the student that invites wonder; it's the process that allows students to enter the illuminated zone. Three possibilities for classroom experiences rooted in academics, yet filled with openings for students to enter their own spiritual spaces, include silence, sky journaling, and reflection.

Silence

Silence in my classroom is a part of the daily routine of reading workshop. First the children and I (and sometimes guests) read for twenty or so minutes. I, of course, read silently, but the children, while engaged personally, can often be heard inventing voices for the characters in their books. "Mama, I've come for your youngun," Victoria reads from Molly Bang's *Wiley and the Hairy Man.* Her voice is deep and raspy; her head nods emphasis on every word. Then a high-pitched voice in reply, "You can't have him, Hairy Man!" Across the room Ben rests his chin in his palm, pushing his gold-rimmed glasses a little higher as he reads yet another book about the human body. Gerilynn and Greta read Ogden Nash's poetry. Jackson and his friend Christopher read *The Boxcar Children* together on the small porch outside the classroom. Occasionally they confer, giggle, and reread a passage together before going on. So silence in this case doesn't mean physical silence but metaphorical silence, an exclusive time for swimming around in text, a time for shutting out all that is not reading.

Physical silence does, however, permeate the twenty or so minutes of time set aside for journal writing. On a videotape depicting the whole process in my classroom, viewers see and hear children reading aloud from their books; yet after the children begin writing in their journals, viewers usually ask me to turn up the volume. "I haven't changed the volume," I reply. "There is total silence in the classroom." The children write; I write; any visitors present also write. When the timer signals an end to the writing time, a few children stop writing; some ask for more time; most just continue writing. They have found their deep places and are reluctant to leave. Just as adults can write into their places of wonder through doors of silence, children can come to know their reflective inner selves through silence and writing.

The following entries from Jerry, one of my first-grade students, show that young children can indeed use moments of silent writing to explore the wonder of the inner self.

In this entry Jerry unconsciously uses the rhetorical device of contrast, exploring antithetical elements such as winning and losing and then culminating with his real question of wonder: Why do parents cry? Jerry, an only child who lives with his grandparents rather than his parents, enters the silence with surface issues, first addressing winning and losing, overcoming a fear of darkness, and learning to swim. Then after writing five sentences about family members, Jerry allows his real question to flow onto the page. It is as if Jerry descends a stairway into a deep well, and when he touches its depths with his question, he quickly ascends, scrambling to the surface with the argument about how fast or slow he runs.

On one page of his journal, Jerry played with his initials, *J.T.,* arranging them into various shapes that might become his logo.

Figure 15–1
Jerry—"Reflections"

My causn lost the chompusihp.
But he got o crafy. I ust to
be sekrd of drdk. I'm hot
sckrd now I cuodnt swim. I
no .how now. Hong is Thais
sustr. I do not have a sustr. I
have a uckole, and, a unt. Jake
has brutre named frichly. Trey
has a sustr. Why do pinrts cry.
Trey told Tim that Jerry ran
slwoe. But he dont. I am
a swimer.

3/8
My cousin lost the championship.
But he got a trophy. I used to
be scared of the dark. I'm not
scared now. I couldn't swim. I
know how now. Hong is Thai's
sister. I do not have a sister. I
have an uncle and an aunt. Jake
has (a) brother named Frenchy. Trey
has a sister. Why do parents cry?
Trey told Tim that Jerry runs
slow. But he don't. I am
a swimmer.

Figure 15–2
Jerry—Logo

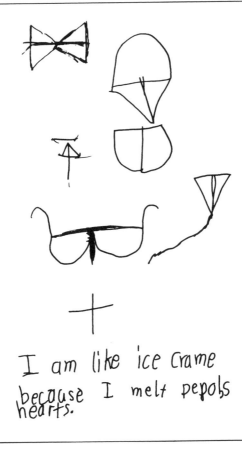

3/28
I am like ice cream
because I melt people's
hearts.

Working in the silence of the classroom and finally deciding on the shape in the upper right-hand corner, one that reminded him of an ice cream cone, he wrote a rationale and in so doing created knowledge of himself. He made himself aware of his connection with other people, with an unseen yet felt spiritual life in which he has the power to affect those around him.

In the following poetic entry, Jerry writes from his own experience and seems to embrace the river as an archetype for his own actions and feelings.

Figure 15–3
Jerry—River

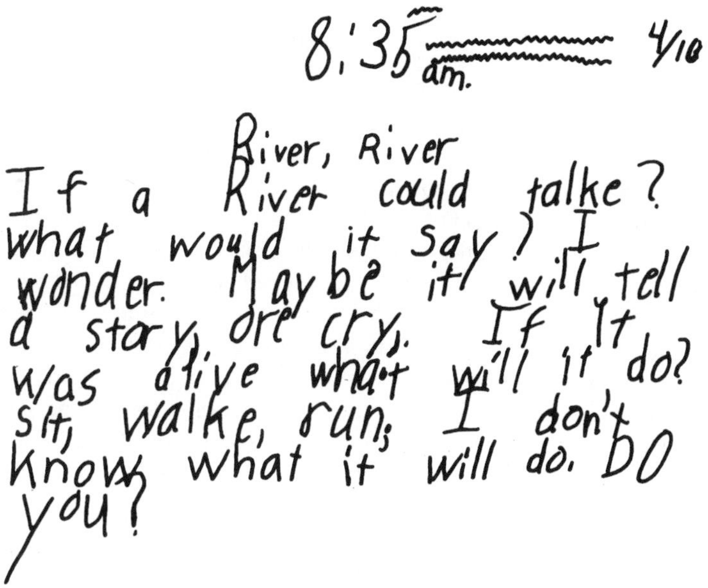

```
8:35 ~~~~~~~~~~ 4/10
   am.

      River, River
If a River could talke?
what would it say? I
wonder. Maybe it will tell
a story, ore cry. If It
was alive what will it do?
Sit, walke, run; I don't
know what it will do. Do
you?
```

4/10
    River, River
If a River could talk?
What would it say? I
wonder. Maybe it will tell
a story, or cry. If it
was alive what will it do?
Sit, walk, run; I don't
know what it will do. Do
you?

Unaware of the history of rivers as sources of spiritual wisdom, Jerry follows his intuition as it leads him to the river as a personal place of wonder. In the daily routine of silent journal writing, Jerry is writing his way into that deep inner well, asking and answering his own questions on his journey.

Journal writing, or *freewriting*, to use Elbow's term for uninterrupted writing in silence, tends to begin with jabber, noise, static, nonsense. Yet somehow this cacophony of internal noise makes room for thought and insight expressed in the true voice of the writer. Graves refers to silence as the "first teacher of writing" (Graves 1994). Students like my student Jerry show us over and over again how silence and writing combine to create insights and windows through which we catch a glimpse of them.

Sky Journaling

Once my students have experienced sky journaling, they clamor for it often. Since it requires a warm day, dry ground, and an absence of pesky insects like fire ants and honey bees, we're lucky to sky journal three times in the spring. We begin in the classroom by connecting to earlier studies of the universe and atmospheric conditions. We discuss the miracle of one sky that covers all people of the world. Children tell about friends and family members living in other parts of the country, and together we marvel that Kelley's father and stepsister in Texas are being warmed by the sun at the same time we are. Finally, each child collects a journal and writing instruments and we walk quietly outside. As we stroll the large playground of our school, the children stop one by one and nestle into private nooks to look at the sky and write. Ethel curls up in the exposed roots of a magnolia tree. Orlicia finds the base of a crepe myrtle. Jereme chooses a square on the sidewalk. Leif sinks into a clover nest. I too find a quiet place where I can appreciate not only the beauty of the sky but also the beauty of twenty-three children connecting with the universe and with themselves.

Although initially observing the physical beauty of the sky, we are free to let our minds dance off in any direction, guided by the images above or the sounds around us. We write and write and write. After about thirty minutes, I catch the eye of one or two children, and we begin to collect ourselves quietly. Often children who have joined the group open their journals again, squat on the ground surrounded by their friends, and continue their writing. Back in the classroom, we sit in a circle on an area rug while volunteers share their journal entries and thrive, as I did after the waltz, on the responses of their classmates. Skywriting allows them to tap into something spiritual, something surreal. Most children have several pages of text, so we respond by helping each other identify the kernel of meaning in each entry. The children recopy these kernels on cloudlike shapes and post them in the hallway. A selection of these kernels follows.

> It seems as there is a king that
> rules the white clouds.
> And it seems as there is a king
> that rules the gray clouds.
> The sky owns the clouds.
> —Bryan

> I see the clouds.
> I see the sun.

I see the color white
up in the sky.
I see the color blue.
I miss my friend Will.
        —Ethel

It feels like the wind is blowing.
It sounds like the birds are singing. They are
up in the sky.
I feel like dancing with the clouds.
        —Orlicia

It makes me happy to see
the sun.
God is in the sky and
Angels are in the sky.
        —Danielle

I want to know
How the sun looked
When it was a baby.
        —Jereme

The sky looks like it
is waving to me.
I see an eye.
It seems to be
Looking at me.
        —Peter

Look again at the last line of each child's poetry. Even as adults, we can leap with them from the reality of the situation to the place of wonder their words reveal. They were not asked to write poetry, just to enjoy the sky and to write whatever came of the experience. They wrote from places of wonder, allowing their inner voices to surface and create what Langer (1957) labels as poetic image or *semblance,* that which need not correspond to actual things or experiences. Poetic creation as Langer describes it is more like a virtual object, a composed apparition of a new human experience (1957, 148). I wish I had thought to ask how the sun looked as a baby.

Reflection

Clarissa Pincola Estes on her tape *The Creative Fire* discusses the phenomenon of artists inspiring each other. The creative energy of the art or the artist at work generates more creative energy. If your creative fire has dimmed, she advises, go where someone is creating something—anything. Just being in the company of an artist who is creating can inspire you to create in your own form (Estes 1991). I've seen her theory at work in my own life. In fact, this article was inspired by the dancing I mentioned at the beginning. I've also seen it at work dramatically in one of my students.

Jackson was a natural poet. His first journal entries, as well as many later ones, consisted of line after line of syllables arranged rhythmically. He wrote with fervor. Naturally reflective, he read quietly, discovering what he had written as he read, almost unaware of his audience of classmates. Often he would pause and giggle at some joke or play on word sounds known only to himself or perhaps to himself and his inner self. Jackson knew about his own deep place before coming to my classroom. I had only to allow him to enter that place and to teach to whatever erupted from it. One of my supreme joys was in discussing Jackson's work with his parents, who understood and valued what they called his "rich inner life."

Jackson was born into a reflective family; his father, an artist, keeps journals in which he connects his own spirituality with his paintings. His mother, a dancer, often uses her talents to celebrate her own spiritual beliefs. In late spring, Jackson's family took him out of school to attend a gallery showing of his father's latest paintings in Memphis, a breathtaking series featuring Jackson and his mother emerging from a primeval forest. Upon the family's return, Jackson's father shared his son's trip journal with me. He had carefully transcribed each of Jackson's entries on index cards, but he also shared the original wire-bound notepad that contained the tiny lettering I'd come to recognize as Jackson's. I was overwhelmed with the volume and variety of writing that Jackson had completed over a single weekend. The experience of the gallery showing, the gala surrounding the event, the public applause of his father's work, and the powerful subject matter of the paintings themselves had combined to inspire the poet in Jackson. The following transcriptions represent a small portion of the writing that flowed from this seven-year-old boy in the span of a few hours after immersing himself in his father's art.

The Party

Tonight I went to Dad's party. We saw Dad's painting of me and Mommie. Many people were there. They looked at Dad's painting. They applauded when Dad gave a speech. He read from his journal and he read poems by [Rainer Maria] Rilke. [Jackson's experience at the party led him to create the following poems.]

Cat Eyes

I can hardly
See them glow—
They turn so slow
I can hardly
See the middle
It's as dark as the

black fiddle—
You can see they're
Wonderfuller
Than me—
I just can't believe!

One Everything

One man
One house
One castle
One horn
One you
One me
I can be most anything!

"16"

2+2 is 4
4+4 is 8
8+8 is 16
That is as far as
I can go—Now it's
Your turn to
Help me.
Count now:
1 2 3 4 5 6 7 8 9
10 11 12 13 14 15
16

Splashing Rain

I told my friend Dustin
I don't know why the
Rain came so suddenly.
Dustin said why don't
You ask your mom and
Dad so I did and my
Dad said, "I don't know."
My mother said the
same old thing—I just
Couldn't figure it out so I
Told Dustin and Dustin
said he heard all about
It. I said, "You did?"
We did and the sun
Came out!

Teachers and students can follow Jackson's example, using reflection to generate creativity. Whether I'm teaching graduate students or first-graders like

Jackson, I ask my students periodically to reflect upon their writing. This means deliberately perusing journal entries or other reflective writings and contemplating them in a metareflective mode. Through this process, they generate reflections on reflections as they look through their journal entries for signs of growth in reading or writing or simply to discover whatever they might about themselves as writers or human beings. The results sometimes suggest something spiritual, like this reflection written by Laura after studying three notebooks of her own journal entries.

Laura is in a state of wonder contemplating having seen her inner self as a person apart from age and time. Her own growth is a personal miracle that leaves her without words. Her expressions "inside to outside," "miracle," and "can't believe" hint at the spiritual wonder this seven-year-old is experiencing as she reflects on her own journal entries.

Another student, Bryan, had struggled with minor depression when his good friend and neighbor moved away early in the school year. Subsequently, Bryan came to love our student teacher very much. On her last day, while his classmates lamented her leaving, he wrote a humorous journal entry chiding her for choosing to attend graduate school at a rival university. During our reflection process, Bryan reread his humorous entry, smiled, and announced, "I've learned that when someone leaves, I don't have to be sad."

I've found that by celebrating some children's reflective self-discoveries in the classroom, others become inspired to take the risk of introspection. After hearing Laura's journal entry and Bryan's announcement, many students pulled out their journals and began active searches for truths about their own inner growth. Our classrooms are fertile ground for becoming reflective communities. As we adult teachers share our own reflective lives, we invite our students to share their discoveries. But we must be honest in our reflections, in our writing, and with our sharing. A first-grade teacher who attempts to write like a first-grader is fooling no one. Students respond to genuine writing, to real spiritual connections with others; they are not people under construction, waiting to participate in life. Students, whatever their ages, are already living their lives, already searching for spiritual connections with others, ready to respond to others' searches for connections with them. In a classroom that is also a reflective community, students like Laura's and Bryan's classmates are nourished spiritually and creatively by the spiritual and creative acts of their friends.

Somehow we must find pools where we, along with our students at any level, can immerse ourselves in the deep place, the zone, the place of wonder that illuminates insight and inspires creation. We must dance the easy dances, not just the technical steps but the divinely inspired apparitions. We must write the easy writing and compose the music of our feelings. We must seek out the silence that will open the doors to our spiritual places of wonder. We must look to the sky and to rivers and to the earth to nurture our wisdom. We must

Figure 15–4
Laura—Journal Evaluation

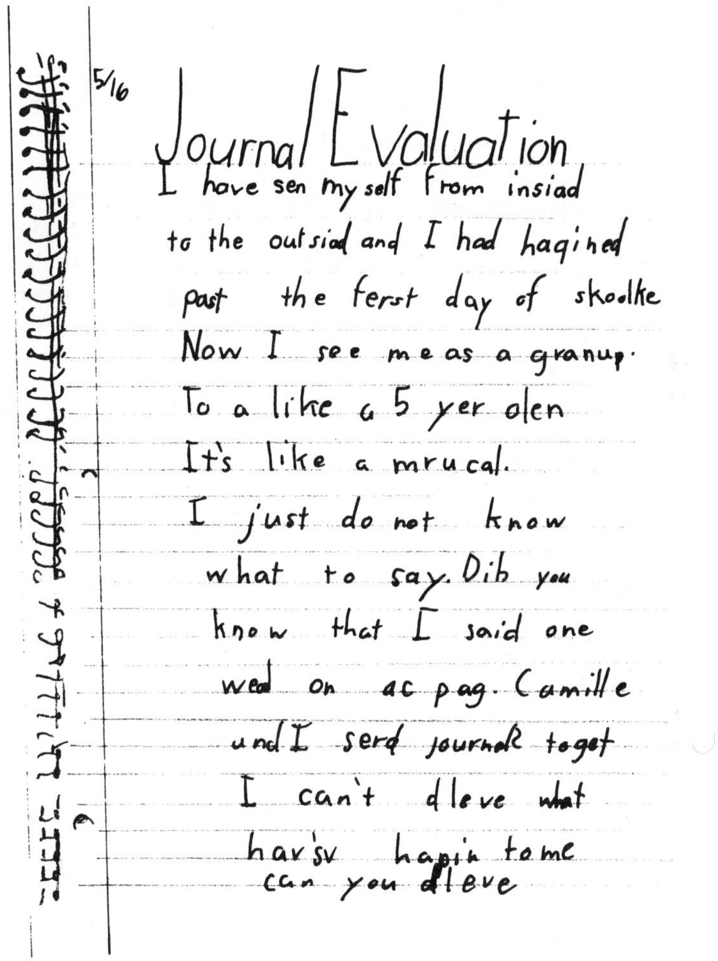

5/16

Journal Evaluation
I have sen my self from insiad
to the outsiad and I had haqined
past the ferst day of skoolke
Now I see me as a granup.
To a like a 5 yer olen
It's like a mrucal.
I just do not know
what to say. Dib you
know that I said one
wed on ac pag. Camille
und I serd journal toget
I can't dleve what
har'sv hapin to me
can you dleve

Journal Evaluation

I have seen myself from inside
to the outside and (all that has) happened
past the first day of school.
Now I see me as a grownup
to like a 5-year-older.
It's like a miracle.
I just do not know what to say. Did you

know that I said one
word on a page. [Laura explained orally that she only one
word in her first journal entry.] Camille
and I shared journals together.
I can't believe what
has happened to me.
Can you believe?

deliberately reflect on our own spiritual insights and wisdom. And when our creative pools run dry, we must learn to seek out and draw from another's pool. We must nurture the Jerrys who wonder, the Lauras who see themselves from the inside, the Jacksons who feast on the creativity of another artist. In our classrooms, we must teach the easy lessons, naturally and obliquely, celebrating easy, natural growth and wonder as the consequence.

Selected Annotated Bibliography

Abrams, M. H. 1993. *A Glossary of Literary Terms.* Orlando, Florida: Harcourt Brace Jovanovich College Publishers. This glossary is an excellent resource for many terms that have recently been adopted by the literary canon.

Alexander, Bill. 1994. *A Man's Book of the Spirit: Daily Meditations for a Mindful Life.* New York: Avon. "The masculine awakening" and movement away from "infantilized, utilitarian masculinity" is driven by "the pain of the dispirited man," a pain that stems from his "lack of ritual, lack of communion, and lack of connection." This book's meditations are designed to help men become "loving, spirit-centered, rowdy, and fiercely determined."

Allister, Mark. 1989. "Writing Documentary as a Therapeutic Act." In *Literary Non-Fiction: Theory, Criticism, Pedagogue,* ed. Mark Allister & Chris Anderson. Illinois: Southern Illinois UP, 1989. Exploring Bill Barich's "Laughing in the Hills" as both a documentary of horse racing and an autobiography of healing, this article stresses the importance of metaphor in therapeutic writing.

Anonymous. 1982. *Each Day a New Beginning: Daily Meditations for Women.* Center City, MN: Hazelden. This book endeavors "to let the wise words of many women, close at hand and far away, some recovering, some still suffering," speak to all women since "much spoken by any one of us is sacred, meaningful, and necessary to the fuller development of at least one person somewhere in time."

Anonymous. 1983. *The Sivananda Companion to Yoga.* New York: Simon and Schuster. This book on yoga includes instructions and photographs.

Anonymous. 1986. *Touchstones: Daily Meditations for Men.* Center City, MN: Hazelden. "The word *touchstone* evokes spiritual images of touching, making contact, having a solid base, and being a tangible reminder of truth. We all have touchstones in our lives—our principles, a word from a friend, a favorite quotation against which we measure our own thoughts and actions."

Anonymous. 1990. *Body, Mind, and Spirit: Daily Inspiration for Wholeness and Healing.* New York: Simon and Schuster. This book is an expression of "the Philosophy of Human Ecology . . . [which] embraces 'the understanding and care of human beings as whole persons in light of their relationships to God, themselves, their families, and the society in which they live.'"

In addition to the authors in this collection, the following scholars have contributed to the bibliography: Margrethe Ahlschwede, Mary Ballinger, Dolores M. Johnson, Mabel M. Khawaja, William Kraemer, Marjorie Maddox, Brad Peters, and Keith Rhodes. We appreciate their contributions.

181

Anonymous. 1992. *At My Best: 365 Meditations for Physical, Spiritual, and Emotional Well-Being.* New York: Bantam. "The physical, emotional, and spiritual components of well-being are not unlike the legs of a tripod. Each contributes to the balance and solidity of the whole. When we fail to attend to any one, the structure of our life soon becomes shaky and insecure."

Aristotle. 1984. *Rhetoric.* Trans. W. Rhys Roberts. New York: Modern Library. Aristotle attempts to establish rhetoric as both a systematic discipline and an ethical one. Departing from Plato, he grounds rhetorical ethics more empirically than spiritually, apparently believing that a method aimed at improving the empirical quality of rhetorical arguments would tend to lead to a greater understanding of real truths. Interestingly, though, Aristotle's method consists in great part of highly "epistemic" techniques for invention and audience analysis. The meaning of this seeming contradiction has no single answer within traditional philosophical analyses.

Avery, Carol. 1993. *And with a Light Touch: Learning About Reading, Writing, and Teaching with First Graders.* Portsmouth, N.H.: Heinemann. The pedagogy of Carol Avery is inclusive, respectful of ideas and persons, and a model not only for elementary teachers and their students but college teachers and students too. Avery builds on the work of Nanci Atwell and Lucy McCormick Calkins and parallels the classroom approaches of Peter Elbow and Donald Murray.

Ayers, William. 1993. *To Teach: The Journey of a Teacher.* New York: Teachers College Press. This work presents the spiritual journey of a teacher.

Aylwin, Susan. 1985. *Structure in Thought and Feeling.* London: Methuen. This book investigates the relationship between thought and feeling, contending that the three main forms of mental representation (enactive, visual, and verbal) involve in various ways cognition, affect, and imagery.

Baldwin, Christina. 1991. *Life's Companion.* New York: Balantine, Doubleday, Dow. Journal writing is seen as a site of mining for spiritual insight and of fuel for living.

Bang, Molly. 1976. *Wiley and the Hairy Man.* New York: MacMillan, 1976. Bang retells this folk tale in which a young boy and his mother successfully outwit the Hairy Man three times, sending him into the land of "never to be seen again."

Barthes, Roland. 1989. "The Death of the Author." *Contemporary Critical Theory,* ed. Dan Latimer, 53–59. San Diego: Harcourt Brace. This article suggests that the traditional concept of "author" is a positivistic outgrowth of capitalism. Text does not yield a single meaning, reminiscent of a single author, but instead several meanings, all of which result from cultural sources. Writers do not write texts; language writes texts.

Bartlett, Frederic C. 1932. *Remembering: A Study in Experimental and Social Psychology.* London: Cambridge UP. This book presents the results of over 2,000 experiments conducted over a number of years concerning the conditions and functions of remembering. Bartlett presents the theory of schemata as the means human beings use to organize and recall stimuli.

Beard, John D. 1990. "Principles of Business Communication: A Departure from Academic Writing." *The Writing Instructor* (9) 101–108. Beard discusses four principles that often pose problems for students making the transition from academic to business writing: goodwill building, course of action, bottom line, and most important first.

Beck, Aaron. 1972. *Cognitive Psychology.* New Haven: Yale University. Contending that the practice of psychotherapy relies extensively on the foundations of rhetoric, Beck presents innovative ideas for helping patients revise potentially destructive narratives of their past into more healing accounts.

Beck, Charlotte Joko. 1989. *Everyday Zen: Love and Work.* New York: Harper and Row. Beck presents a down-to-earth account of using Zen in daily life.

Benson, Herbert H. 1975. *The Relaxation Response.* New York: William Morrow. The book offers a simple meditation that can help lower blood pressure.

————. 1984. *Beyond the Relaxation Response.* New York: Times Books. Benson gives a popular account of his research into the "faith factor," which is a combination of meditation and one's deepest held beliefs, whether they be religious or philosophical.

Berger, Peter L. 1967. *The Sacred Canopy: Elements of a Sociological Theory of Religion.* Garden City, NY: Doubleday. This book examines the phenomenon of religion from the perspective of the sociology of knowledge. Berger builds on his premise that human beings are products and producers of society. Religion, as an institutionalized aspect of society, thus is both a sociohistorical construct and a coercive force maintaining societal status quo.

Berman, M. 1990. *Coming to Our Senses: Body and Spirit in the Hidden History of the West.* New York: Simon & Schuster. This book reinterprets history from a somatic perspective. Berman contends that human beings ontogenetically and phylogenetically apprehend their universe somatically (through bodily awareness) and intellectually. However, with the rise of rationality and empiricism, emphasizing a mind-body duality, an "alienated consciousness" evolved. Berman asserts the need to reevoke a "participating consciousness."

Berthoff, Ann E. 1972. "From Problem-Solving to a Theory of Imagination." *College English* (33): 636–649. Intent on reclaiming "imagination" as the active mind engaged in the rhetorical formation of ideas, this article argues the need for teaching the composing process by devising assignments appropriate to the different phases of writing: forming concepts and seeing relationships.

————. 1981. *The Making of Meaning.* Portsmouth, NH: Boynton/Cook. Berthoff's definitive book is a broad-ranging synthesis of trends in philosophy, pedagogy, literary criticism, and composition theory. Berthoff concludes that composing is inevitably a matter of managing chaos, a process that demands a well-honed and creative imagination more than any particular technique. Since language is at once both a representational and an interpretational phenomenon, though, pragmatic interrogation and reinterpretation of one's own language is suggested as uniquely powerful work for applying and refining creative imagination.

————. 1994. "Spiritual Sites of Composing: Introduction." *College Composition and Communication* (45): 237–38. Berthoff briefly summarizes Freire's religious convictions in terms of what he conceptualizes as the prophetic church and its mission of transforming cultural practices. She suggests this concept serves as a corrective to antifoundationalism.

Bickerton, Derek. 1990. *Language and Species.* Chicago and London: University of Chicago Press. Drawing upon investigations into such diverse matters as language development in children, ape language experiments, aphasia studies, fossil records, evolutionary theory, and linguistic analysis of language structures, Bickerton investigates the relationship between human language and other biological representational systems. He demonstrates with great thoroughness the likelihood that the evolution of human language is continuous with the general evolution of representational systems in general, such as those that represent physical territories. The great and explosive power resulting from human development of syntactically hierarchical language is, hence, less a function of special qualities of such language itself and more a function of the great value of having two complex representational systems (sensory and linguistic) cross-referenced with each other. Bickerton also establishes the probability that incremental gains in language ability drove the evolution of greater brain capacity rather than the reverse.

Bishop, Wendy. 1991. "Jo'al." *Teaching English in the Two-Year College* (18.1): 4. The author's poem was published in this journal.

Bizzell, Patricia. 1991. "Marxist Ideas in Composition Studies." *Contending with Words: Composition and Rhetoric in a Postmodern Age*, eds. Patricia Harkin and John Schilb. New York: The Modern Language Association of America. 52–68. The argument centers on acknowledging Freire's Marxist influences and their impact on American educational philosophy. Bizzell's emphasis on the necessity of political consciousness in developing literacy pedagogies further clarifies her ethical concerns.

———. 1992. *Academic Discourse and Critical Consciousness.* Pittsburgh: University of Pittsburgh Press. The problem of devising an ethical system within an antifoundational approach is addressed. The series of essays in this book chronologically documents Bizzell's own movement towards conscientization.

Bleich, David. 1989. "Reconceiving Literacy: Language Use and Social Relations." *Writing and Response: Theory, Practice, and Research*, ed. Chris Anson. Urbana, IL: National Council of Teachers of English. 15–36. Bleich critiques the tendency to associate literacy pedagogies with remedial techniques, ignoring them as a means of transforming society and cultivating—rather than merely preserving—social (and, hence, spiritual) legacies.

Booth, Wayne C. 1974. *A Rhetoric of Irony.* Chicago: University of Chicago Press. Booth presents a comprehensive and authoritative study of the abstract concept of irony in its various rhetorical forms, including the distinction between stable and unstable ironies.

Bradley, David. 1988. "Bringing Down the Fire." In *Spiritual Quests: The Art and Craft of Religious Writing*, ed. William Zinsser, 55–82. Boston: Houghton Mifflin Company. Bradley discusses the ways religious preaching as it occurred in his childhood background influenced his spiritual connections to writing.

Brand, Alice Glarden. 1989. *The Psychology of Writing.* New York: Greenwood. Contributions in *Psychology* 13. Working within an admittedly underdeveloped area of research, Brand attempts both to create a speculative framework for including emotional factors within rhetorical and cognitive analyses and to encourage further development of this body of knowledge. The scholarly discussion is followed by extensive case studies illustrating and extending the concepts being addressed.

Brand, Alice Glarden and Richard L. Graves. 1994. *Presence of Mind.* Portsmouth: Boynton/Cook Publishers. This collection of essays breaks ground in composition studies by compiling numerous approaches to teaching that go beyond the cognitive approaches now practiced.

Brent, Joseph. 1993. *Charles Sanders Peirce: A Life.* Bloomington and Indianapolis: Indiana UP. This ambitious intellectual biography succeeds about as well as can be imagined at clarifying Peirce's enigmatic life and his sometimes elusive thought in light of each other. Extraordinarily well documented, it reveals above all the extent to which factors having nothing to do with the quality of Peirce's astute and unique philosophy of semiotics impeded its production and reception—a phenomenon that continues to distort current philosophical discussions of meaning. Peirce's central concept, that we can trust a "contritely fallible" but pragmatic community of investigators to gain at least some actual knowledge about a more fundamental reality, is explored and validated in an unusually accessible form.

Britton, James, et al. 1975. *The Development of Writing Abilities.* London: MacMillan. This book examines the development of writing abilities of students within the British school system by analyzing writing samples taken from a range of grades. Britton presents his categories of writing functions (transactional, expressive, and poetic), which are based on participant and spectator roles.

Brooke, Robert. 1991. *Writing and Sense of Self: Identity Negotiation in Writing Workshops.* Urbana: National Council of Teachers of English. Brooke argues that the roles writers experience in the workshop classroom are as important as the writings they produce. He uses identity negotiation theory, based on the work of Erving Goffman, and an analysis of several writing classroom models—sequential, Piagetian-based, and writing workshop–based—to explore the ways students develop writers' identities.

Bruffee, Kenneth A. 1984. "Collaborative Learning and the Conversation of Mankind." *College English* (46.7): 635–652. "This essay [encourages] other teachers to try collaborative learning and to help them use collaborative learning appropriately and effectively.... It is written ... on the assumption that understanding both the history and the complex ideas that underlie collaborative learning can improve its practice and demonstrate its educational value."

———. 1986. "Social Construction, Language, and the Authority of Knowledge: A Bibliographical Essay." *College English* (48.8): 773–790. This article provides a bibliographical guide to work done in social constructionist theory in a variety of fields, synthesizing these texts to present a coherent view of a complex theory of knowing.

Buechner, Frederick. 1988. "Faith and Fiction." In *Spiritual Quests: The Art and Craft of Religious Writing,* ed. William Zinsser, 103–130. Boston: Houghton Mifflin Company. Buechner illustrates ways in which faith and fiction are similar and are connected to spirituality.

Burke, Kenneth. 1968. *Language as Symbolic Action: Essays on Life, Literature and Method.* Berkeley: University of California Press. This collection of essays is an authoritative and innovative study of the negative and positive dimensions of thought processes that employ language for clarity.

Burroway, Janet, ed. 1987. *Writing Fiction.* New York: Harper Collins, 1987. Intended for creative writing students, this book includes advice, exercises, and a strong selection of short fiction to help open discussion on such writing techniques as point-of-view, setting, and plot.

Calinescue, Matei. 1993. *Rereading.* New Haven, Connecticut: Yale University Press. The book analyzes the concept of rereading as an integral part of reading with understanding. It is an excellent source for recent scholarship in the study of the processes of rereading.

Campbell, Joann. 1994. "Writing to Heal: Using Meditation in the Writing Process." *College Composition and Communication* (45): 246–251. Campbell defines spirituality and describes ways in which women participants in a twelve-step program connect spirituality, meditation, healing, and writing in the workshop setting.

Campbell, Joseph. 1972. *Myths to Live By.* New York: Bantam Books. Tracing the way ancient myths have been transformed through myriad cultures over the ages, this work shows how myth reconciles human beings to the mysteries of life.

————. 1988. *Masks of Eternity.* Videocassette, ed. Bill Moyers. Prod. WNET New York, 60 min. Bill Moyers interviews Joseph Campbell about spiritual beliefs and practices he has observed from around the world.

Capra, Fritjof. 1983. *The Turning Point: Science, Society, and the Rising Culture.* London: Fontana. Capra manages to explain very clearly an extremely ambitious and scientifically grounded vision of a holistic universe operating similarly at all levels of universal processes and human experience. Finding that virtually all phenomena are best understood as systemically embedded ecologies of information, Capra calls for a corresponding adjustment in social systems of belief at every level. Capra has helped popularize the parallels between Eastern philosophy and quantum physics. Because the observer's participation helps to evoke observed reality, Capra argues that the observer's perspective comprises the only truth. This controversial view seems to deny the possible realities inherent within the universe, such as the properties of subatomic particles.

Charkrabarti, Tarapada. 1971. *Indian Aesthetics and Science of Language.* Calcutta, India: Sanskrit Pustak Bhandar. This work provides a comprehensive introduction to Indian aesthetics and literary criticism. Charkrabarti discusses the basic principles of the major schools of criticism in relation to higher consciousness, explaining the notions of *rasa* or divine rapture, *dhvani* or suggestion, and the four levels of language. It also defines Indian axiology in terms of poetry.

Cleary, J. C. 1992. *Meditating with Koans.* Berkeley: Asian Humanities Press. This work provides an introduction to koan study, focusing on the history of koans, stories, and instruction on koan study from ancient masters, and includes a brief appendix with some of the more famous koans.

Cleary, Thomas. 1989. *Book of Equanimity.* Trans. Cleary, Thomas. San Francisco: North Point Press. One of the most famous classic koan collections.

————. 1992. *The Blue Cliff Record.* Trans. Cleary, Thomas and J. C. Cleary. Boston: Shambhala.

————. 1993. *Gateless Barrier.* Trans. Cleary, Thomas. London: Aquarian/ Thorsons. This is a standard text for koan study.

Coward, Harold. 1980. *The Sphota Theory of Language.* Columbia, Missouri: South Asia Books. This book presents a survey of different theories on the nature of the word in Indian philosophy. Coward deals with speculations about the relationship between knowledge of ourselves and language. He focuses on sphota as the highest level of language as derived from Bhartrhari.

————. 1990. *Derrida and Indian Philosophy.* New York: State University of New York Press. This book is an excellent introduction to philosophy of both East and West. Coward compares Derrida with four Indian philosophers: Bhartrhari, Shankara, Aurobindo, and Nagarjuna. He builds a bridge between the Eastern view of language and consciousness and Western thought.

Crow Dog, Mary and Richard Erdoes. 1990. *Lakota Woman.* New York: Harper Perennial. This autobiography recounts how Crow Dog reclaims her native spirituality by joining the American Indian Movement. In particular, her descriptions of the sun dance, peyote use, sweat lodges, and yuwipi ceremonies help readers to reconceptualize Christian ritual and belief.

Cszikszentmihalyi, Mihaly. 1990. *Flow: The Psychology of Optimal Experience.* New York: Harper & Row. This book presents for a general audience the results of decades of research on "flow," the experience of total involvement with an endeavor. It specifically examines its contribution to joy and creativity in life.

Daly, John A. and Joy Lynn Hailey. 1984. "Putting the Situation into Writing Research: State and Disposition as Parameter of Writing Apprehension." *New Directions in Composition Research,* ed. Richard Beach and Lillian S. Bridwell, 259–73. New York: Guilford. This article reports on research investigating the situational dimension, as opposed to the dispositional dimension, of writing apprehension. Results indicate the need to examine the relationship between situational variables and actual writing performance.

Daniell, Beth. 1994. "Spiritual Sites of Composing: Composing (as) Power." *College Composition and Communication* (45): 238–246. In her study of the influence of writing on women in an Al-Anon program, Daniell examines how journals, letter writing, dream recording, and other forms of writing help the subjects to attain spiritual growth in dealing with or resolving personal conflicts.

Dantrell, Jan Johnson. 1993. *Healing Hearts: Meditations for Women Living with Divorce.* New York: Bantam. "When we divorce, we always become someone else. . . . Most of us have any number of people in our lives telling us what our lives should be. The trick is to listen to ourselves. . . . Daily reading and meditation with this book can help you discover who you are and create a space in which to nurture yourself in the present moment."

Dasgupta, Surendranath. 1988. *A History of Indian Philosophy*, Vol. 1. New Delhi, India: Motilal Banarsidass. This work is part of a definitive five-volume history of Indian philosophy that includes a full discussion of Shankara's nondual Vedanta. Dasgupta provides clear access to the arcana of Indian philosophy in a balanced and objective way. His style is clear and enjoyable.

de Beaugrande, Robert. 1984. *Text Production: Toward a Science of Composition.* Advances in Discourse Processes 11. Norwood: Ablex. This book, drawing heavily on cognitive theory and linguistics, presents a theory of composition that includes the production and processing of text. de Beaugrande presents his parallel stage interaction model of text processing, which involves eight recursive processes simultaneously interacting.

Di Cesare, Mario, ed. 1978. *George Herbert and the Seventeenth-Century Religious Poets.* New York: Norton. This collection of poetry by Herbert and his contemporaries includes helpful background information on the poets as well as critical essays by noted scholars.

Dickinson, Emily. 1956. "There's a Certain Slant of Light." In *The American Tradition in Literature,* ed. Sculley Bradley et al. New York: Norton, 153. This poem appears in many standard anthologies of American literature.

Dillard, Annie. 1974. *Pilgrim at Tinker Creek.* New York: Harper Perennial. Dillard presents meditations on the natural world where she lives, on the banks of Tinker Creek in the Blue Ridge Mountains of Virginia.

————. 1988. "Sight into Insight." *Norton Reader*, ed. Arthur M. Eastman. New York: Norton, 1182–1193. An intimate knowledge of nature leads one to a world of mystical wonder.

Edwards, Betty. 1979. *Drawing on the Right Side of the Brain.* Los Angeles: Tarcher. Edwards reviews brain research as well as drawing.

————. 1987. *Drawing on the Artist Within.* New York: Fireside. This is the companion volume to *Drawing on the Right Side of the Brain.*

Elbow, Peter. 1986. *Embracing Contraries: Explorations in Learning and Teaching.* New York: Oxford University Press. Presenting a collection of essays on the processes of learning, teaching, and evaluation and on the nature of inquiry, Elbow has written his insights for teachers, students, and administrators. The essays argue for a reconceptualization of how people learn and thus how teachers should teach and grade.

————. 1993. "Ranking, Evaluating, and Liking: Sorting Out Three Forms of Judgment." *College English* (55): 187–206. The idea of being able to say I "like" a piece of student writing is liberating. To be assured that the glimpses I see in students are really what I ought to be looking for is assuring. But the article has much more: an analytical grid for evaluating student papers, for instance, and thoughtful commentary about students, writing, and teaching.

Elias, John L. 1976. *Conscientization and Deschooling: Freire's and Illich's Proposals for Reshaping Society.* Philadelphia: Westminster. Elias gives an early examination and critique of Paulo Freire's and Ivan Illich's radical pedagogies.

Erikson, Erik. 1968. *Identity, Youth, and Crisis.* New York: Norton. Erikson describes how adolescents and young adults discover and shape their identity.

Estes, Clarissa P. 1991. *The Creative Fire.* Sounds True Recording. Using a mythological base, Estes describes the roles of such inner forces as the "critic" who would thwart our creativity. The author gives advice as to how we might overcome these forces to allow our creative powers to flourish.

Fisher, Walter. 1984. "Narration as a Communication Paradigm." *Communication Monographs* (51): 1–22. Distinguishing a "rational world paradigm," which privileges logic, from a "narrative paradigm," which privileges myth over logic, this article discusses the importance of the narrative model for understanding ourselves as storytellers.

Fleckenstein, Kristie S. 1991. "Inner Sight: Imagery and Emotion in Writing Engagement." *Teaching English in the Two-Year College* 18 (210–16). This article examines empirically a possible relationship between the vividness of cued mental imagery and the degree of writing engagement in an expressive writing experience. The students involved in the study were freshmen in a regular composition program. Results suggest a statistically significant relationship between the vividness of a writer's mental imagery and the degree of writing engagement during expressive writing.

Flynn, Elizabeth A. 1990. "Composing As a Woman." *Gender in the Classroom: Power and Pedagogy,* eds. Susan L. Gabriel and Isaiah Smithson. Urbana, IL: University of Illinois Press. This work provides a survey of recent feminist research on gender differences in social and psychological development. Flynn examines student writing in light of research and suggests directions in which composition as a discipline can go with feminist investigation.

Foehr, Regina and Susan A. Schiller, Richard Graves, and James Moffett. *Live To Learn: Spiritually Open Pedagogy.* NCTE Audiotape, Allied Vision, TE 94–36. Exploring spirituality within the academy, this four-member panel presentation was recorded live at the November 1994 NCTE convention in Orlando, FL.

Fox, Matthew. 1993. "Stories That Need Telling Today." In *Sacred Stories: A Celebration of the Power of Stories to Transform and Heal,* eds. Charles Simpkinson and Anne Simpkinson, 243–250. San Francisco: Harper Collins. Fox discusses the kinds of stories humanity needs to tell in order to reclaim its connection to the natural world. The article ties in with Fox's theology of "Creation Spirituality."

Frankl, Victor. 1975. *The Unconscious God.* New York: Simon and Schuster. Frankl presents an existential-hermeneutical approach to meaning production and non-rational regions of subjectivity.

Freire, Paulo. 1972. "Education, Liberation, and the Church." *Risk* (9): 34–48. Freire shows connections between models of the Roman Catholic Church and models of education. He argues for liberatory models of both.

———. 1973. *Education for Critical Consciousness.* New York: The Seabury Press. Freire argues that one must become actively engaged in the shaping of history. If one reads Freire together with Hanh, one may discover possibilities for nonviolent social and personal change.

————. 1985. *The Politics of Education.* Trans. Donaldo Macedo. New York: Bergin & Garvey. This volume explicates the fusion of Marxist theory and liberation theology, which so deeply informs Freire's pedagogical philosophy. Of special interest are his lucid definitions of conscientization and the prophetic church.

————. 1990a. "Conscientizing as a Way of Liberating." *Liberation Theology: A Documentary History,* ed. Alfred T. Hennelly, 5–13. Maryknoll, NY: Orbis. Freire discusses the role of the church in Latin America and his own Christian commitments.

————. 1990b. *The Pedagogy of the Oppressed.* New York: The Continuum Publishing Company. Part of Freire's evolving educational philosophy, this book presents the conviction that all people are capable of dialogical encounter with others while looking critically at the world. Becoming subjects, people in dialogue transform the world because they refuse to be objects for manipulation by others.

————. "The Third World and Theology." USCC 13–14. This article examines the relationship between Roman Catholic theology and Third World reality.

Furnish, Dorothy Jean. 1990. *Experiencing the Bible with Children.* Nashville: Abingdon Press. This book presents a pedagogy that is interactive, often utilizing creative drama and always starting where the learner is. The understandings about children's growth and development underscore the importance of all teachers knowing the souls of their hearers. The appendix is useful in understanding how a larger educational objective is met by providing smaller, sequential learning experiences.

Gablik, Suzi. 1991. *The Reenchantment of Art.* New York: Thames and Hudson. Gablik distinguishes between deconstructive postmodernism and a reconstructive postmodernism based on "an aesthetics of interconnectedness." She argues that modernism and deconstructive postmodernism have lost their relevance in an age of "social responsibility and ecological attunement." It is an excellent work that supports spiritual empowerment through the reenchantment of art.

Gadamer, Hans-Georg. 1993. *Truth and Method.* 2nd revised edition. Trans. Joel Weinsheimer and Donald G. Marshall. New York: The Continuum Publishing Company. The is a philosophical enquiry into the concept of truth that includes a chapter on the relationship between prejudices and hermeneutics.

Gallehr, Donald R. 1994. "Wait, and the Writing Will Come: Meditation and the Composing Process." *Presence of Mind: Writing and the Domain Beyond the Cognitive,* ed. Alice Glarden Brand and Richard Graves, 21–29. Portsmouth, NH: Boynton/Cook. This article discusses the connections between writing and meditation and presents a classroom approach to joining the richness of a meditative tradition with students' writing processes.

Gardner, Howard. 1993. *Multiple Intelligences.* New York: Basic Books. Gardner explains the theory of the seven multiple intelligences, identifying them as Linguistic, Logical-Mathematical, Spatial, Musical, Bodily-Kinesthetic, Interpersonal, and Intrapersonal. He discusses how to educate them and how to assess them.

Ginsberg, Allen. 1988. "Meditation and Poetics." In *Spiritual Quests: The Art and Craft of Religious Writing,* ed. William Zinsser, 143–166. Boston: Houghton

Mifflin Company. Ginsberg brings Buddhist ideas of renunciation and meditative practice to the study of poetry and writing.

Goffman, Erving. 1963. *Stigma: Notes on the Management of Spoiled Identity.* New Jersey: Prentice-Hall. This work studies the devastating effects of stigma and "spoiled identity" on those deviating from the customary attributes possessed by the so-called "normals" in any given society.

Goldberg, Natalie. 1986. *Writing Down the Bones.* Boston: Shambhala. This is a popular book that has inspired many beginning writers to let go of their inhibitions and just write.

————. 1990. *Wild Mind.* New York: Bantam Books. Goldberg gives compassionate, practical, and humorous advice on writing.

————. 1993. *Long Quiet Highway: Waking Up in America.* New York: Bantam Books. This is Goldberg's spiritual autobiography that includes her years of study with Zen master Dainin Katagiri in Minneapolis.

Goldstein, Joseph. 1987. *The Experience of Insight.* Boston: Shambhala. A simple and direct guide to Buddhist insight meditation, the book presents Goldstein's understanding of mind, which arises from our direct confrontation with those thought patterns that bind us. Through this direct confrontation, we experience liberation.

Goleman, Daniel. 1988. *The Meditative Mind.* Los Angeles: Tarcher. Goleman describes the range of meditative techniques.

————. 1995. *Emotional Intelligence.* New York: Bantam. Drawing on brain and behavior research, Goleman illuminates the crucial role of emotion in clear thnking and wise decision making. Both IQ and emotional intelligence determine how we do in life.

Gore, Al. 1992. *Earth in the Balance: Ecology and the Human Spirit.* This is a political and cultural examination of the human implications of the environmental crisis.

Graff, Gerald. 1994. "Disliking Books at an Early Age." *Falling into Theory: Conflicting Views on Reading Literature,* ed. David H. Richter. Boston: St. Martin's Press. Graff argues that reading always involves interpretation, and that theory provides one with a language for discussing literature. This collection of essays covers many aspects of why, what, and how we read.

Graves, Richard L. 1994. "Writing Is Like Breathing." *Conference on College Composition and Communication.* Nashville, 18 Mar. Graves discusses silence in the classroom.

Gray, Jeffrey A. 1990. "Brain Systems That Mediate Both Emotion and Cognition." *Cognition and Emotion* (4): 269–88. Gray demonstrates that, on an anatomical basis, cognition and emotion may be so deeply and thoroughly intertwined that studying each as if it were severable from the other is counterproductive.

Gruchow, Paul. 1991. *Journal of a Prairie Year.* Minneapolis: University of Minnesota Press. Gruchow presents his appreciation of the prairie landscape of southwestern Minnesota.

Gutierrez, Gustavo. 1973, 1988. *A Theology of Liberation.* Trans. Sister Caridad Inda and John Eagleson. Rev. ed. Maryknoll, NY: Orbis. Many believe that his is the most important text in liberation theology. Gutierrez is one of the movement's founders and this is his definitive work.

Hagelin, John. 1987. "Is Consciousness the Unified Field? A Field Theorist's Perspective." *Modern Science and Vedic Science* (1): 29–89. This is a two-part study of the relationship between consciousness and the unified field. The first part is purely mathematical, while the second draws a parallel between quantum physics and Indian philosophy as formulated by Maharishi Mahesh Yogi. Hagelin argues that the proposed parallel between consciousness and the unified field is consistent with all known physical principles.

Hairston, Maxine. 1984. "The Winds of Change: Thomas Kuhn and the Revolution in the Teaching of Writing." *Rhetoric and Composition: A Sourcebook for Teachers and Writers,* ed. Richard L. Graves. 14–26. Upper Montclair, NJ: Boynton/ Cook Publishers, Inc. Hairston briefly summarizes Kuhn's work on paradigm shifts and then discusses the product/process shift in composition theory.

Haney II, William S. 1993. *Literary Theory and Sanskrit Poetics.* Lewiston, New York: The Edwin Mellen Press. A two-part study of Western literary theory in the light of Sanskrit literary criticism, its first part deals with the concepts of Derrida, Barthes, Hillis Miller, and others in terms of basic principles of Indian theory, while the second part applies these concepts to an analysis of works by Joyce, Faulkner, Pynchon, and Soyinka.

Hanh, Thich Nhat. 1990. *Present Moment, Wonderful Moment.* Berkeley: Parallax. Hanh offers mindfulness verses for daily living as ways to experience each moment clearly and with loving-kindness.

————. 1993. *Love in Action.* Berkeley: Parallax Press. This work is a collection of Hanh's writings on nonviolent social change.

Harding, D. E. 1986. *On Having No Head: Zen and the Re-Discovery of the Obvious.* London: Arkana. Harding presents an account of transcending the ego.

Harre, Rom, ed. 1986. *The Social Construction of Emotions.* Oxford, NY: Blackwell. The articles in this book elaborate the methodology of a social constructionist theory of emotion, based on the contention that the experience of emotions involves cognition-based evaluations and, thus, depends on an individual's cultural orientation.

Harris, Joseph. 1994. "Writing from the Moon." *College Composition and Communication* (45): 161–162. Harris urges compositionists to let go of old arguments, explore new, and to use narratives for a purpose rather than just for their own sake.

Harris, Maria. 1988. *Women and Teaching: Themes for a Spirituality of Pedagogy.* New York: Paulist Press. Harris discusses her understanding of spirituality as a way of life and a way to affirm ourselves and our world.

Hawkins, Anne. 1993. *Reconstructing Illness: Studies in Pathography.* West Lafayette: Purdue University. As a study of the myths, attitudes, and assumptions that inform the way we deal with illness, this work argues the therapeutic value of illness narratives and looks at important issues in contemporary medical practice.

Heath, Shirley Brice. 1983. *Ways with Words: Language, Life, and Work in Communities and Classrooms.* New York: Cambridge University Press. An analysis of literacy as a product of regional socialization, this study is probably one of the best we have in suggesting the influence of what Freire would call the traditional church upon children whose Piedmont Carolinian communities are historically differentiated by racial, economic, familial, and religious factors.

Henderson, Randi. July/August 1994. "Our Evolving Selves." *Common Boundary.* 36–40. This article features an interview with psychologist Mihaly Csikszentmihalyi, author of *Flow* (1990) and *The Evolving Self* (1993), both published by HarperCollins. It explores his opinions on human development, happiness and personal experience, optimal experience, flow, education, religion, culture, and spirituality.

Hershusius, Lous. 1994. "Freeing Ourselves from Objectivity: Managing Subjectivity or Turning Toward a Participatory Mode of Consciousness?" *Educational Researcher* (23): 15–22. This article suggests the need to reconceptualize current theories of knowing to center on Morris Berman's "participating consciousness," a theory that involves the body as well as the mind in the act of knowing. Hershusius asserts that such a recentering will resolve the debate concerning subjectivity in qualitative research.

Hoffman, Martin. 1984. "Interaction of Affect and Cognition in Empathy." *Emotion, Cognitions, and Behavior,* ed. Carroll E. Izard, Jerome Kagan, Robert B. Zajonc, 103–31. Cambridge: Cambridge University Press. This article describes the interaction of affect and cognition in six developmental modes of empathy, ranging from the circular responses of newborns to the cognitive sense of other, which is necessary for increasingly mature empathetic responses.

Hoffman, Yoel, trans. 1975. *The Sound of One Hand.* New York: Basic Books. This book presents koans Zen students use to train their minds.

Holman, Elizabeth. 1994. "Behind the Screen of Consciousness: Intuition, Insight, and Inspiration in the Writing Process." *Presence of Mind: Writing and the Domain Beyond the Cognitive,* ed. Alice Glarden Brand and Richard Graves, 65–76. Portsmouth, NH: Boynton/Cook. This article examines intuition and suggests that it is innate and preconscious, linked both to emotion and to physical experiences, and that it is beyond the territory of reason but not unreasonable.

Holstein, Alexander, trans. 1993. *Pointing at the Moon: 100 Zen Koans from Chinese Masters.* Rutland, Vermont: Charles E. Tuttle Company. Each koan is followed by the author's commentary and accompanied by 85 Chinese brush paintings.

Hopcke, Robert H. 1992. *A Guided Tour of the Collected Works of C.G. Jung.* Boston: Shambhala. In readable prose this concise book summarizes major topics in the works of C. G. Jung. It treats topics such as the Psyche, the Unconscious, Dreams, Eros and Logos, Synchronicity, Archetypes, Anima/Animus, Trickster, Love and Marriage Esoterica, and many others.

Houston, Jean. 1987. *The Search for the Beloved.* New York: Putnam Publishing Group. Houston defines sacred psychology, frames her argument in practical methodology, and urges us to accept the idea of a whole-system transition.

Hughes, Elaine. 1991. *Writing from the Inner Self.* New York: HarperCollins. This book contains a rich collection of easy-to-use creative writing exercises suitable for writers at the college, secondary, or adult level. Many of them are based on silence and imagery.

James, William. 1961. *The Varieties of Religious Experience.* New York: Macmillan Publishing Co. James's book, now a classic, is a collection of lectures known as the Gifford Lectures, which he gave in Edinburgh at the turn of the century. He combines a nondogmatic yet empirical approach to understanding religion and what it means to be a spiritual being.

Jauss, Hans Robert. 1989. *Question and Answer: Forms of Dialogic Understanding.* Trans. Michael Hays. Minneapolis: University of Minnesota Press. Jauss's theoretical investigation of the literary evolution and impact of question/answer paradigms provides a valuable tool for imagining a pedagogy of spiritual literacy. His emphasis on the socially transformative potential of the magistral discussion is especially useful.

Johnson, Willard. 1982. *Riding the Ox Home.* Boston: Beacon Press. Johnson provides a historical survey of meditative practice, exploring the development of Eastern meditation and examining similar meditative practices in the West.

Johnston, William. 1970. *The Still Point.* New York: Fordham University Press. Simply written but with a deep perspective, this book seeks the experiential groundings of spirituality.

Kalamaras, George. 1994. *Reclaiming the Tacit Dimension.* Albany: State University of New York Press. Kalamaras gives a detailed discussion of meditative silence as a means of knowing in the context of pedagogical practice.

Kane, Sean. 1994. *Wisdom of the Mythtellers.* Ontario: Broadview Press. This work is a study of the relationships between story, myth, and human relationships with the earth, examined from the perspective of the indigenous thought of Native Australians and Native Americans, together with ancient Celtic and Greek mythology.

Kantrowitz, Barbara, et. al. 1994. "In Search of the Sacred." *Newsweek*, 28 Nov., 52–55. This article describes the current upsurge in Americans' quest for spiritual meaning.

Kapleau, Philip. 1965. *The Three Pillars of Zen.* Garden City, New York: Anchor Books. Kapleau provides instruction on how to begin meditating.

————. 1980. *Zen: Dawn in the West.* Garden City, New York: Anchor Books. This companion volume has stories and a question and answer section.

Katagiri, Dainin. 1988. *Returning to Silence.* Boston: Shambhala. The late Zen master who taught Natalie Goldberg is the author.

Keller, Evelyn Fox. 1983. *A Feeling for the Organism.* New York: W. H. Freeman and Company. This biography discusses McClintock's development of meditative concentration.

Kelsey, Morton. 1972. *Encounter with God.* New Jersey: Paulist Press. Dreams and meditation play a role in the experiential discovery of spirituality and of communicating spirituality.

Khan, Hazrat Inayat. 1982. *A Meditation Theme for Each Day,* ed. Pir Vilayat Khan. New Lebanon, N.Y.: Omega Publications. Khan is credited with bringing

Sufism to America. This meditation booklet offers a range of topics suitable for daily contemplation and guidance.

Khema, Ayya. 1987. *Being Nobody, Going Nowhere.* Boston: Wisdom Publications. Introducing Buddhist teachings on insight and loving-kindness, Khema offers an English version of the Buddha's discourse on loving-kindness.

Klein, Karen and Linda Hecker. 1994. "The Write Moves: Cultivating Kinesthetic and Spatial Intelligences in the Writing Process." *Presence of Mind: Writing and the Domain beyond the Cognitive,* ed. Alice Glarden Brand and Richard Graves, 89–98. Portsmouth, NH: Boynton/Cook. This article describes an approach to teaching composition that taps spatial and kinesthetic ways of knowing to supplement linguistic knowledge by envisioning an essay as a three-dimensional process.

Lacan, Jacques. 1979. *The Four Fundamental Concepts of Psychoanalysis.* Trans. A. Sheridan. Harmondsworth: Penguin. The book presents Lacan's arcane analysis of the mind as a field of difference. Lacan reinterprets Freudian psychology in light of the linguistic turn through which the transcendental signified, such as the self, is infinitely deferred along a chain of signifiers. His theories are contradicted by Shankara's Vedanta and the direct experience of expanded consciousness.

Lakoff, George and Mark Johnson. 1980. *Metaphors We Live By.* Chicago: The University of Chicago Press. This book contends that our fundamental conceptual system is metaphorically structured and our thought processes themselves are largely metaphorical in nature.

Langer, Suzanne K. 1957. *Problems of Art.* New York: Charles Scribner's Sons. Langer defines the domains of art, identifies the boundaries and qualities of each domain, and describes the relationships among the arts. Langer discusses poetic creation, dance as the dynamic image, the art symbol and the symbol in art, musical hearing, and abstraction in science and art.

Langston, M. Diane. 1989. "Engagement in Writing: How Experts and Novices Peruse Personal Agendas While Drafting New Texts." Conference on College Composition and Communication, 17 March, at Seattle. This presentation reviews the tentative results of research in progress. After examining the texts and composing processes of freshmen, Langston contends that the writer's ability to evolve and instantiate personal goals relates to the writer's ability to experience writing engagement.

Larsen, Earnie and Carol Hegarty. 1991. *Believing in Myself: Daily Meditations for Healing and Building Self-Esteem.* New York: Simon and Schuster. The authors advocate that a solid sense of self-worth is the single most important factor in determining happiness in life and success in work and relationships. With it, virtually all things are possible. Without it, even victories can feel like defeats.

Lazear, Jonathon. 1992. *Meditations for Men Who Do Too Much.* New York: Simon and Schuster. Written to fill the need for "a companion volume" to *Meditations for Women Who Do Too Much,* this book is one "that came from a man and spoke directly to men about the unique issues that men face in their lives," one that could thus "offer doors of options from the self-abuse and self-destructive patterns" characterizing the lives of many men.

Lazear, Jonathon and Wendy Lazear. 1993. *Meditations for Parents Who Do Too Much.* New York: Simon and Schuster. "Parents who do too much may try to do more for their children than there are hours in the day. . . . Our children need us as more than just 'doers'. . . . What our children need from us is companionship. If we forget this we will lose more than just hours and days."

Leder, Drew. 1990. *The Absent Body.* Chicago: University of Chicago Press. Leder explores the profound consequences of a simple phenomenon: When the body functions well it disappears from consciousness but is noticed whenever it is functioning poorly. Hence the body, given credit for little of its good work but blame for all of its bad work, seems like a "problem" from which "spirit" ought to seek to free itself. Since, though, we do not *have* bodies but rather *are* bodies, "spirit" is never able to be as free of the generative body as it thinks it ought to be. Leder urges that phenomenology holds great promise as a way to reintegrate body and spirit.

Levin, David Michael. 1988. *The Opening of Vision: Nihilism and the Postmodern Condition.* New York. Drawing on Eastern thought, Levin argues that modernist aesthetics is being superseded by a new paradigm. Whereas modernism emphasizes noninteraction and the freedom from community, the new paradigm involves relationality and social participation. As opposed to difference and isolation, Levin advocates wholeness, openness, and contact.

Lewin, Roger. 1983. "A Naturalist of the Genome." *Science* (222): 402–405. Science writer Lewin reports on Barbara McClintock's winning the Nobel Prize for Physiology or Medicine in 1983. He includes interesting commentaries on McClintock's description of herself as a "mystic."

Lindbergh, Anne Morrow. 1978. *Gift from the Sea.* New York: Vintage Books. A Nebraska friend reads this book once a year. The call to contemplation and to claim one's own time and space is important for both women and men.

Longinus. 1899. *On the Sublime.* Trans. W. Rhys Roberts. Cambridge: Cambridge University Press. Attributed for many years to Longinus, a third-century Neo-Platonist, this essentially anonymous work may date from the first century of the Common Era. The author seeks to uncover the key to the "universal" power of certain authors (Homer, Plato, Sappho, and others) to move audiences profoundly. Finding some of this effect in devices of style, the author nevertheless concludes that even greater importance must be attributed to a greatness of vision and purport, which is claimed by the author to have declined since the days of Greek and early Roman civilization.

Lynch, William F. 1975. *Images of Faith: An Exploration of the Ironic Imagination.* Notre Dame, Indiana: Notre Dame Press. Lynch establishes the inevitable connection between faith and irony by relating both to the human faculty of imagination. His discussion includes many specific examples from the Bible to validate his theory.

Maharaj, Nisargadatta. 1982. *I Am That.* Durham, North Carolina: The Acorn Press, 1982. This book is an account of transcending the ego.

Maharishi Mahesh Yogi. 1969. *On the Bhagavad-Gita: A New Translation and Commentary, Chapter 1.* New York: Penguin. Providing a clear translation and commentary of *The Bhagavad-Gita* that emphasizes the experience of higher states of consciousness, Maharishi approaches the text in terms of the six systems of Indian philosophy and analyzes the nature of transcendental consciousness and its development into cosmic and unity consciousness. This is a basic handbook for the Transcendental Meditation Technique.

————. "Inaugural Address." 1986. *Life Supported by Natural Law: Lectures by Maharishi Mahesh Yogi.* Washington, D.C.: Age of Enlightenment Press. Presenting an introduction to Maharishi's Vedic Science as an aspect of his Science of Creative Intelligence, Maharishi analyzes the nature of transcendental consciousness in terms of self-referral. He defines this state as a perfect administrator that displays the organizing power of natural law.

Mairs, Nancy. 1990. *Carnal Acts.* New York: Harper Collins. A series of personal essays, many previously published as "Hers" columns in the *New York Times,* documents the difficult life of a woman with multiple sclerosis, struggling for psychological balance amid her progressively deteriorating disease.

McCleary, Dick. 1993. *The Logic of Imaginative Education.* New York: Teachers College Press. McCleary discusses imaginative thinking, teaching, and learning through insightful discussions of the work of Sophocles, Jerome Bruner, Erik Erikson, R. D. Laing, George Dennison, Paolo Freire, Seymour Papert, Ira Shor, and others. He interweaves themes such as artificial intelligence, synectics, metaphor, critical theory, and multiculturalism.

Meadow, Mary Jo. 1994a. *Gentling the Heart.* New York: Crossroad. Giving directions on Buddhist loving-kindness meditation for Christians, Meadow shows that Buddhist practice can be useful in cultivating Christian virtues. A clinical psychologist, Meadow also recognizes the benefits of meditation that are nonsectarian.

————. 1994b. "Preparing for Insight Practice" and "The Buddhist Tradition of Insight Meditation" in Culligan, Kevin, Mary Jo Meadow, and Daniel Chowning, *Purifying the Heart.* New York: Crossroad. Meadow presents background on and instructions for Buddhist insight meditation for Christians in a book cowritten with Carmelites Culligan (also a psychologist) and Chowning. Culligan, Meadow, and Chowning have led meditation retreats together.

Menchù, Rigoberta. 1984. *I, Rigoberta Mench: An Indian Woman in Guatemala,* ed. Elisabeth Burgos-Debray. Trans. Ann Wright. New York: Verso. An account of Menchù's emergence as a national leader of Indian resistance in Guatemala, this autobiography articulates a praxis of liberation theology and its complementary relationship to Indian spirituality.

Merton, Thomas. 1969. *The Way of Chuang Tzu.* New York: New Directions. Merton includes readings from Chuang Tzu, the leading thinker of Taoism.

Meyer, Michael, ed. 1993. *The Bedford Introduction to Literature.* Boston: St. Martin's Press. An anthology introducing students to the basic elements of poetry, fiction, and drama, this work includes a large selection of culturally diverse authors, critical essays and perspectives, student examples, and a more in-depth examination of such writers as Hawthorne, Joyce, O'Connor, Keats, Dickinson, Frost, and Shakespeare.

Miller, Caroline Adams. 1994. *Bright Words for Dark Days: Meditations for Women Who Get the Blues.* New York: Bantam. "This book addresses the serious and increasingly recognized problem of depression, which strikes 25 percent of all woman at some point in their lives." This book was written "to help the millions of women who experience various forms of depression—from run-of-the-mill blahs, or 'the blues,' to chronic depression, to postpartum depression . . . [but] is not meant to replace therapy or medication."

Miller, Hildy. 1994. "Sites of Inspiration: Where Writing Is Embodied in Image and Emotion." *Presence of Mind: Writing and the Domain Beyond the Cognitive,* ed. Alice Glarden Brand and Richard Graves, 113–24. Portsmouth, NH: Boynton/Cook. This article reports on research involving 148 college students. It examines the three ways in which images affect writers emotionally: conceptual images, self-images, and bodily sensations.

Moffett, James. 1981. *Coming on Center.* Portsmouth, NH: Boynton/Cook. Focused on ways of achieving a student-centered curriculum in which writing is explored not only as the descent into the self but also as the "ascent from chaos to cosmos," this book contains the essay "Writing, Inner Speech, and Meditation," Moffett's seminal work on the allied practices of writing and meditation.

————. 1992. "Responses to Interchanges: Spiritual Sites of Composing." *College Composition and Communication.* May: 258–263. James Moffet introduces a CCC interchange whose authors consider spiritual sites of composing. Long a proponent of meditative and spiritual connections between writing, teaching, and learning, Moffett argues that institutions need to pay attention to spirituality and should welcome those concerned with these issues.

————. 1994. *The Universal Schoolhouse: Spiritual Awakening Through Education.* San Francisco: Jossey-Bass. Moffett argues that we should look at the personal development and enrichment of the whole child to transform society and education. He further suggests that a spirituality-based educational system will awaken the culture and offer solutions to very serious economic, cultural, and educational problems.

Moore, Thomas. 1992. *Care of the Soul: A Guide for Cultivating Depth and Sacredness in Everyday Life.* New York: HarperPerennial. Care for the soul, Moore writes, has to do with "modest care and not miraculous cure" (5). As regards the writing classroom, it is not the teacher's task to try to "cure" her students by marking and correcting their work or by insisting on particular writing assignments, for example. Rather, it is the writing teacher's task to care for the students, to care about what is going on among them, and to nurture and encourage them in doing their work.

Morrison, Toni. 1990. *Playing in the Dark.* New York: Vintage Books. In this major work that opens up new perspectives in literary criticism, Morrison claims a fresh vantage point that is uninhibited by the traditional cultural biases in a "genderized and a wholly racialized world."

Muecke, D. C. 1969. *The Compass of Irony*. London: Methuen. Muecke provides a global definition of irony, examining the concept in its totality. Wayne C. Booth lauds Muecke's study as a complementary work to his own work, with some additional insights.

Murphy, Robert. 1987. *The Body Silent*. New York: Henry Holt. Narrating its author's experience of paralysis from a disease of the spinal cord, this work by an anthropologist explores the social circumstances of the physically impaired and the meaning of this condition as an allegory of all life in society.

Murray, Donald M. 1990. *Write to Learn*, 3rd ed. Chicago: Holt, Rinehart and Winston Inc. Donald Murray's text is full of good writing instruction, including generating writing, ways to begin and end writing, titles, and ways to read a paper to edit and revise. This book is a useful source for minilessons.

Neeld, Elizabeth Harper. 1990. *Seven Choices*. New York: Clarkston N. Potter. Following the untimely death of her husband, the author is drawn through seven stages of grief. She give a moving account of a painful journey whose ultimate goal is light and healing.

Norris, Kathleen. 1993. *Dakota: A Spiritual Geography*. New York: Ticknor & Fields. An autobiography of Norris's life on the Dakota plains, the book describes her relationships with the landscape, her ancestral home, and the Benedictine community that often inspired her.

O'Keefe, John. 1985. "Is consciousness the gateway to the hippocampal cognitive map? A speculative essay on the neural basis of mind." *Brain and Mind*, ed. David A. Oakley. New York: Methuen. O'Keefe, a coauthor of what remains the landmark treatment of the role of the hippocampus in mapping real and symbolic territories, marshalls considerable support for a view that hippocampal function generates much of what is thought to make up the criteria for conscious thought. Hippocampal function is explained in concise (and perhaps dense) technical terms, revealing most centrally the extent to which the hippocampus functions holographically and engages in special problem solving as opposed to habitual problem solving. As one consequence, the spatial "feel" of conscious thought may simply indicate fresh hippocampal "mapping."

O'Reilley, Mary Rose. 1993. *The Peaceable Classroom*. Portsmouth, NH: Boynton/Cook Heinemann. Starting with the question, How can we teach a class in a way that would encourage no more wars? O'Reilley takes readers on a narrative journey of her development of a peaceable classroom, one that honors learners and teachers alike. This journey was not without difficulties, and O'Reilley explores her own interactions with a rare honesty as she develops her understanding(s) of spiritual and ethical teaching and invites readers to do the same.

Orme-Johnson, Rhoda. 1987. "A Unified Field Theory of Literature." *Modern Science and Vedic Science* (1): 322–73. This essay proposes a unified field theory of literature based on Maharishi's Vedic Science, physiological research on consciousness, and the quantum unified field theory. Orme-Johnson gives a clear exposition of how literary techniques affect the reader's consciousness. She breaks new ground on the relationship between Western literary studies and Eastern thought.

Paivio, Allan. 1986. *Mental Representations: A Dual Coding Approach.* Oxford Psychology Series 9. Oxford: Oxford University Press. This book presents an updated version of the dual-coding theory. Dual coding suggests that knowledge is constructed via two systems: visual and verbal. The visual system encodes and stores concrete information; the verbal encodes and stores abstract information.

Palmer, Parker J. 1983. *To Know as We Are Known: Education as a Spiritual Journey.* San Francisco: HarperCollins Publishers. Palmer outlines and describes a system for developing personal and professional spirituality.

Payne, David. 1989. *Coping with Failure: The Therapeutic Uses of Rhetoric.* Columbia: University of South Carolina. This work explores the importance of "compensation" and "consolation" in ameliorating feelings of loss, failure, and inadequacy and it stresses the therapeutic value of writing that aims to discover consoling trade-offs for such feelings.

Peirce, Charles Sanders. 1982. "Grounds of Validity of the Laws of Logic: Further Consequences of the Four Incapacities." *Writings of Charles S. Peirce,* 242–73. This is the third (and most technical in terms of philosophical logic) in a series of three articles written by Peirce for the *Journal of Speculative Philosophy* in the late 1860s. This article is important only to the extent that it clarifies and refines certain points expressed in the two articles that follow below. More important, a reader of the second article alone might infer that Peirce believed reality to be "epistemic," created by discourse communities. Here Peirce demonstrates how his conception of reality as semiotic and his emphasis on the value of a community of enquirers is rooted in an underlying, objectively based logic of discovery that is even more fundamental than the community of human enquirers. This article is also a valuable early statement of Peirce's important concept of "abduction," the principle by which human beings seem more or less capable of guessing at those hypotheses that are more likely to be verified out of what would seem to be inadequate information.

————. 1982. "Questions concerning [sic] Certain Faculties Claimed for Man." *Writings of Charles S. Peirce,* 193–211. This is the first in a series of three articles written by Peirce for the *Journal of Speculative Philosophy* in the late 1860s. Peirce's central claim here is that since all thought is essentially interpretive, there is no such thing as plain apperception of an idea or a phenomenon itself—meaning especially that introspection is no more likely to be reliable than any other form of inspection and interpretation. Peirce demonstrates his claim with references to various perceptual illusions, pointing out that even the knowledge of their illusivenesss does not prevent us from perceiving "wrongly." Peirce means neither to deny that there are "things themselves" nor that there is such a thing as a private view of one's own thoughts, but he does mean to insist that the most that can be perceived is the interpretive *sign* of things or ideas, not things or ideas themselves.

————. 1982. "Some Consequences of the Four Incapacities." *Writings of Charles S. Peirce,* 211–42. This is the second in a series of three articles written by Peirce for the *Journal of Speculative Philosophy* in the late 1860s. Possibly the one writing that best presents Peirce's entire early conception of semiotics, this article is dense and provocative enough to defy meaningful condensation. Superficially, one could say that here Peirce demonstrates the superiority of realism over nominalism as a means for humankind as a whole to approach improving our interpretations of an objective reality that is itself most essentially semiotic in nature.

————. *Writings of Charles S. Peirce: A Chronological Edition.* 1982–until completed, ed. Peirce Edition Project. Vol. 2. Bloomington and Indianapolis: Indiana University Press. Projected 30 vols. This is included solely as a bibliographic reference for the preceding articles.

Perl, Sondra. 1994. "A Writer's Way of Knowing: Guidelines for Composing." In *Presence of Mind: Writing and the Domain Beyond the Cognitive,* ed. Alice Glarden Brand and Richard Graves, 77–88. Portsmouth, NH: Boynton/Cook. This article describes a method of helping writers attend to their "felt sense" of an idea, a term referring to the somatic manifestation of evolving concepts.

Planas, Ricardo. 1986. *Liberation Theology: The Political Expression of Religion.* Kansas City, MO: Sheed & Ward. Planas presents a useful and fairly comprehensive summary of liberation theology's major themes.

Price, Reynolds. 1994. *A Whole New Life.* New York: Atheneum. As a spiritual autobiography of its author's battle with spinal cancer, paralysis, and long-term disability, this work describes the intimate daily struggles that such a life entails without overlooking the redemptive side of such illness.

Progoff, Ira. 1975. *At a Journal Workshop.* New York: Dialogue House Library. Exploring the use of profound, self-integrating diary-feedback techniques, this work illustrates creative ways for overcoming inhibitions before moving on to other stages in life.

Radhakrishnan, S., ed. and trans. 1989. "Mandukya Upanishad." *The Principle Upanishads.* New Dehli: Oxford University Press. An excellent translation and commentary of the principle Upanishads with a clear introduction, this work includes Indian translation of the text but not the Sanskrit. The Upanishads express the basic religious spirit of Indian culture as contained in Vedanta.

Rich, Adrienne. 1979. "Taking Women Students Seriously." *On Lies, Secrets, and Silence.* New York: W. W. Norton & Company. Rich creates a context to talk about women as students and students as women. Her questions on the teaching/learning connection, the literary canon, and classroom practices that exemplify the male as the norm force us to reexamine our classroom stances and practices.

Rico, Gabriele. 1991. *Pain and Possibility: Writing Your Way Through Personal Crisis.* Los Angeles: J. P. Tarcher/Putnam. Focused on strategies for educating the emotions and developing receptivity to our feelings, this work explores the uses of writing as a therapeutic tool for healing.

————. 1994. "The Heart of the Matter." In *Presence of Mind,* ed., Alice Brand & Richard Graves. Portsmouth: Boynton/Cook. Analyzing the relationships between language, feeling, stories, and healing, this article validates the efficacy of healing through writing and argues that such writing may be the ultimate creative act.

Roberts, Bernadette. 1984. *The Experience of No-Self.* Boulder: Shambhala. Roberts gives yet another account of transcending the ego.

————. 1985. *The Path to No-Self.* Boston: Shambhala. Roberts describes how she transcended the ego.

Ronald, Kate and Hepzibah Roskelly, eds. 1990. *Farther Along: Transforming Dichotomies in Rhetoric and Composition.* Portsmouth, NH: Boynton. This collection of articles by various authors is a truly heroic effort to mediate most of the major contentious dichotomies found within the field of composition studies (such as those that artificially divide personal and private writing, reading and writing, and secondary and postsecondary instruction). Peirce's concept of interpreting dualities together from a third perspective forms the philosophical touchstone of the collection, and this mediating principle is thoroughly illuminated both in the editor's introduction and in the leading article on "Killer Dichotomies" by Ann E. Berthoff. Given the comprehensive nature of the issues addressed, the collection serves as an interesting overview of the field of composition and rhetoric as a whole.

Rorty, Richard. 1989. *Contingency, Irony, and Solidarity.* Cambridge: Cambridge University Press. Rorty attempts to provide a nonfoundational basis (irony intended, both by Rorty and at a different level by this writer) for a kinder, gentler society. Intentionally engaging remorse in painting the picture of his vision than in arguing it, Rorty seems to urge that given a presumption of the contingent and social nature of all meaning (a presumption he seems to accept on faith as a universal truth), a collective spirit of ironic distance from truth claims should permit humanity to develop ways of working together more peacefully than we do now.

Rose, Mike. 1984. *Writer's Block: The Cognitive Dimension.* Carbondale: Southern Illinois University Press. This book examines through a cognitive framework students' difficulty in producing text. While acknowledging the range of other affective and motivational factors at work, this study focuses specifically on the cognitive variables at work.

————. 1989. *Lives on the Boundary.* New York: The Free Press. Rose describes the life of the educationally underprepared students in his classes and the story of his own personal journey from a Los Angelos ghetto to a major research university. He describes the stigmas of intellectual deficiency that haunt students whose lives are on the boundary; he gives hope and offers challenge to those who teach them.

Rosenblatt, Louise. 1978. *The Reader, the Text, the Poem.* Carbondale: Southern Illinois University Press. This book presents a transactional theory of reading, suggesting that neither text nor reader "exists" as such until each is mutually constituted in the act of reading. Rosenblatt contends that all reading transactions are either predominantly efferent (reading for information) or aesthetic (reading for the experience).

Sachs, Oliver. 1984. *A Leg to Stand On.* New York: Summit Books. Describing the aftermath of a leg injury that left its author unable to feel sensation or even register that the leg belonged to him, this work presents the story of his recovery as a spiritual conversion.

Sadoski, Mark, Allan Paivio, and Ernest T. Goetz. 1991. "Commentary: A Critique of Schema Theory in Reading and a Dual Coding Alternative." *Reading*

Research Quarterly (26): 463–84. This article examines the problematic gaps in current schema theory and asserts the greater explanatory value of dual-coding theory. Dual-coding theory contends that stimuli are encoded and stored in long-term memory imagistically and linguistically in structurally distinct ways.

Sams, Jamie. 1993. *The 13 Original Clan Mothers.* HarperSanFrancisco. Sams presents Native American feminine wisdom that can help cultivate daily spiritual living.

Schaef, Anne Wilson. 1990. *Meditations for Women Who Do Too Much.* New York: HarperCollins. "[T]here are many of us who do too much, keep too busy, spend all our time taking care of others and, in general, do not take care of ourselves. Many of us have crossed over the line to compulsive, addictive, self-defeating behavior and need to make major changes in our lives. . . . These meditations . . . are intended to stir up some feelings, get you thinking, and precipitate possibilities for change which will add to the quality and vitality of your life."

Schumacher, Michael. 1992. *Dharma Lion: A Biography of Allen Ginsberg.* New York: St. Martin's Press. Schumacher presents a current biography of Ginsberg.

Schweickart, Patrocinio P. 1986. "Reading Ourselves: Toward a Feminist Theory of Reading." In *Gender and Reading—Essays on Readers, Texts, and Contexts,* ed. Elizabeth A. Flynn and Patrocinio P. Schweickart, 31-62. Baltimore: The Johns Hopkins University Press. This article is part of a collection of essays that consider a feminist approach to reading a meritorious process. Schweickart's essay proposes a feminist revision of the androcentric canon that imposes androcentric constraints on critical theory and the literary canon.

Shankara. 1988. *Vivekacudamani.* Commentary by Sri Candrasekhara Bharati of Srngeri; trans. Sankaranarayanan. Bombay, India: Bharatiya Vidya Bhavan. Also known as "The Crest Jewel of Discrimination," this work simplifies Shankara's Vedanta for the nonspecialist. Shankara discriminates between the self and the nonself, analyzing the basic attributes of the self as a unified state of consciousness. The goal of Vedanta is the experience of unity.

Shibayama, Zenkei. 1974. *Zen Comments on the Mumonkan.* San Francisco: Harper and Row. This is an advanced book of koan study.

Shor, Ira. 1980, 1987. *Critical Teaching and Everyday Life.* Chicago: University of Chicago Press. The theory and practice of critical teaching is developed by an American leftist.

Shor, Ira and Paulo Freire. 1987. "What is the 'Dialogic Method' of Teaching?" *Journal of Education* (169) 3: 11–31. This is Freire and Shor's "talking article" about dialogic teaching.

Silko, Leslie Marmon. 1981. *Storyteller.* New York: Arcade/Little, Brown. This work is a compilation of Laguna Pueblo myth, contemporary fiction and poetry, autobiography, and photography.

————. 1986. "Landscape, History, and the Pueblo Imagination." *Antaeus* (57): 83–94. Making a major statement on the relationships between nature, culture, and story, Silko illustrates how her Laguna Pueblo culture's stories and beliefs are indissolvably connected to the natural features of the landscape that her people inhabit.

Sing, Tara. 1985. *A Course in Miracles—A Gift for All Mankind.* Los Angeles: Life Action Press. Sing describes spiritual practices by which to live life.

Smith, Craig R. 1993. "Finding the Spiritual Dimension in Rhetoric." *Western Journal of Communication* (57): 266–271. This article explores how the spiritual dimension of rhetoric has been frequently overlooked or ignored by academic bias. By calling for a poetization of critical language, the author seeks to remind us of the spiritual dimension of any art form, including rhetoric.

Solly, Richard and Roseann Lloyd. 1991. *Journey Notes.* New York: Hazelden Books, Ballantine Books. Solly and Lloyd look at various genres such as fiction and letter writing as tools for reflection and self-discovery.

Solomon, Robert C. 1993. *Introducing Philosophy: A Text with Integrated Readings.* 5th ed. New York: Harcourt Brace. Solomon provides a thematic approach to philosophy with a reading from original texts. Each theme is traced from the classical period to the present. The book covers non-Western philosophy and is excellent.

St. Augustine. 1990. *De Doctrina Christiana.* In *The Rhetorical Tradition: Readings from Classical Times to the Present,* ed. Patricia Bizzell and Bruce Herzberg. Boston: Bedford Books of St. Martin's Press. This text, St. Augustine's most important rhetorical work, is written for the Christian pastor. By correctly interpreting the Christian truth of the Scriptures and informing diverse audiences of this truth, St. Augustine intended to foster both psychological and social order. He emphasizes pleasing, teaching, and persuading, or moving to action, as the three offices of rhetoric.

Suhor, Charles. 1991. "Surprised by Bird, Bard, and Bach: Language, Silence, and Transcendence." *English Journal* 21–26. Suhor discusses the transcendent nature of peak experiences in literary works and other arts, music in particular. To achieve transcendence, he calls for a fertile language environment that encourages a dynamic interaction between talk and silence in this thought-provoking essay.

Suzuki, D. T. 1956. *Zen Buddhism: Selected Writings of D. T. Suzuki,* ed. William Barrett. New York: Anchor Books. This is a more advanced book on the finer points of Zen.

———. 1964. *An Introduction to Zen Buddhism.* New York: Grove Press. Suzuki provides both a philosophical and a practical description of Zen.

Suzuki, Shunryu. 1970. *Zen Mind, Beginner's Mind.* New York: Weatherhill. The book presents talks given by the Soto Zen master.

Swearingen, C. Jan. 1994. "Women's Ways of Writing, or, Images, Self-Images, and Graven Images." *College Composition and Communication.* (45): 251–258. Swearingen and two others conducted summer workshops in a week-long format that invoked religious faith and spirituality as a means to stimulate creativity.

Teich, Nathaniel. 1994. "Teaching Empathy Through Cooperative Learning." *Presence of Mind: Writing and the Domain Beyond the Cognitive,* ed. Alice Glarden Brand and Richard Graves, 143–54. Portsmouth, NH: Boynton/Cook. This article argues that the writing and reading classroom is a natural environment in which to teach empathy as a human response to personal and social problems because those language activities already rely on empathy.

Tenneson, Joyce. 1992. *Transformations.* Boston: Bulfinch Press. This work contains 70 color photos and an interview with Tenneson.

Tobin, Lad. 1993. *Writing Relationships: What Really Happens in the Composition Classroom.* Portsmouth, NH: Boynton Cook. Tobin takes a refreshingly honest look at important yet seldom discussed areas of teaching: student and teacher relationships, teachers' fears, students' relationships to each other, and teachers' interactions. He argues that we need to develop better understandings of these complex relationships and the ways they affect curriculum design, evaluation and response, and the general success and tone of classrooms.

Tompkins, Jane. 1990. "Pedagogy of the Distressed." *College English.* Oct., 653–660. Tompkins presents a nonspiritual interpretation and adaptation of Freire's work.

Tremmel, Robert. 1993. "Zen and the Art of Reflective Practice in Teacher Education." *Harvard Education Review* 63: 434–457. Tremmel recommends incorporating non-Western theories of reflection, particularly Zen "mindfulness," in teacher education programs. He uses his personal experience as a teacher educator to teach his students the art of "paying attention" in order to nurture reflective practice.

Underhill, Evelyn. 1994. "A Hold on the Eternal." *Weavings* (IX): 18–19. Adapted from Underhill's *The Spiritual Life,* this excerpt concisely provides the rationale for developing a pedagogy of spiritual literacy from the perspective that spirituality is deeply essential to, and an integral part of, human development.

United States Catholic Conference. Paulo Freire. The LADOC "Keyhole" Series 1. Washington, D.C.: USCC, Division for Latin America, n.d. These early major religious writings by Paulo Freire were collected by the United States Catholic Conference.

van de Wetering, Janwillem. 1973. *The Empty Mirror: Experiences in a Japanese Zen Monastery.* New York: Washington Square Press. The Dutch novelist gives an account of his year in a Kyoto Zen monastery.

————. 1975. *A Glimpse of Nothingness: Experiences in an American Zen Community.* New York: Washington Square Press. This companion volume describes experiences in an American Zen community.

Vygotsky, Lev. 1962. *Thought and Language,* ed. and trans. E. Hanfmann and G. Vakar. Cambridge: MIT Press. This book examines the interrelationship of thought and language, concluding that the internalization of action creates thought and the internalization of external dialogue brings language to bear on thought.

Wakefield, Dan. 1990. *The Story of Your Life: Writing a Spiritual Autobiography.* Boston: Beacon Press. What Wakefield says about writing the spiritual journal is what makes for good writing anywhere: writing details of encounters with persons and places, reading aloud in a community of writers where all are accepted, and working toward a completed piece of writing that is received as gift and celebrated by the readers and listeners. His underscoring of acceptance and community is what makes for an inclusive classroom

Wallace, Robert Keith. 1993. *The Physiology of Consciousness.* Fairfield, IA: MIU Press. Wallace studies how Maharishi Ayur-Ved can improve individual and collective health. This holistic approach to health is a new paradigm based on the quantum unified field and the experience of higher consciousness and is an important source of knowledge for new levels of fulfillment provided by twentieth-century science.

Wallace, Ron. 1989. "Cognitive Mapping and the Origin of Language and Mind." *Current Anthropology* (30): 518–26. Though Wallace's main aim seems to be aiding researchers in modeling language more accurately on computers, his article is a superior collection and explanation of various research on the role of the hippocampus and its mapping utilities in the construction of human language and consciousness. Presented to an audience of anthropologists and linguists rather than brain scientists, it has the virtue of being written in a manner accessible to humanities scholars even though it is well versed in the technical background.

Warner, Gertrude C. 1977. *The Boxcar Children.* New York: Scholastic. Four orphaned children set out on an adventure to find their only remaining relative, an aging grandfather. In this children's novel, the characters happen upon an old boxcar, which they make into a home using dishes and pieces of furnishings found along the roadside.

Watson, Burton, trans. 1994. *Selected Poems of Su Tung-p'o.* Port Townsend, WA: Copper Canyon Press. This translation of poems by the tenth-century Chinese poet Su Tung-p'o illustrates how poetry was an essential part of the life of an educated individual of that time.

Willeford, Lynn Murray. 1993. "Who Will Rule the Schools?" *New Age Journal* November/December 76–81+. Murray carefully balances an exposé of the problems created by so-called New Age religions and protests raised by the religious right. While the article argues in favor of diversity and innovation in teaching methodology, it also sympathizes with concerns held by the religious right. The complexity of the educational conflict is clearly presented with numerous examples and references to cases.

Wolpert, Lewis. 1992. *The Unnatural Nature of Science.* Cambridge: Harvard. A passionate defender of science, Wolpert indicates that he would be opposed to the view that meditation can help develop scientific clarity. Wolpert describes McClintock's scientific method differently from the way McClintock herself describes it. Wolpert also views holistic philosophy as inherently antiscientific.

Worley, Demetrice. 1994. "Visual Imagery Training and College Writing Students." In *Presence of Mind: Writing and the Domain Beyond the Cognitive,* ed. Alice Glarden Brand and Richard Graves, 133–142. Portsmouth, NH: Boynton/Cook. This article describes a classroom approach that uses visual imagery training to help students hone and connect their visual and verbal abilities.

The Writer's Life. 1993. *New Age Journal.* Nov–Dec., 82+. This work presents interviews with Walker, Bolen, and Allende about creativity, spirituality, passion, and what it means to be a writer.

Yampolsky, Philip B., trans. 1971. *The Zen Master Hakuin: Selected Writings.* New York: Columbia University Press. This book contains the writings of the Rinzai Zen master.

Yeats, William Butler. 1962. "The Second Coming." In *Selected Poems and Two Plays by William Butler Yeats.*, ed. M. L. Rosenthal, 91. New York: Macmillan. Annotating a poem is an oxymoron.

Yokoi, Yuho. 1976. *Zen Master Dogen: An Introduction with Selected Writings.* New York: Weatherhill. Yokoi introduces writings of Dogen (AD1200–1253), founder of the Soto sect of Zen meditation.

Zajonc, Robert B. 1980. "Feeling and Thinking: Preferences Need No Inferences." *American Psychologist* (33): 151–75. This article contends that cognition and affect are essentially two systems that are inextricably connected. However, Zajonc asserts that affect precedes cognition and that cognition never occurs without affect, although affect can occur without cognition.

Zohar, Danah. 1991. *The Quantum Self.* London: Flamingo. Zohar provides a clear study of subatomic physics and how it has led to a paradigm shift in psychology. Zohar argues for a more participative view of our relation with society and the universe. Like the physicist John Hagelin, she defines the quantum self as a state of consciousness that parallels the unified field.

Zweig, Connie and Jeremiah Abrams, eds. 1991. *Meeting the Shadow.* Los Angeles: J. P. Tarcher. Containing short, potent, new, and original classic essays by renowned experts in psychology, spiritual growth, and healing, this collection investigates the hidden power of the dark side of human nature found in the archetypal shadow. It explores the shadow side of envy, anger, deceit, work, achievement, religion, spirituality, healing of the disowned body and self, and other topics. It features essays by C. Jung, J. Campbell, S. Peck, J. Hillman, L. Dossey, S. Keen, R. May, and others.

Contributors

Herbert John Benally, a Navajo, lives on a Navajo reservation in Sweet Water, Arizona, and teaches at Navajo Community College, Shiprock, NM. He teaches courses in Navajo culture, Navajo history, Navajo philosophy, bilingual and bicultural curriculum, and oral Navajo tradition and style. He uses Navajo epistemology as a basis for curriculum reform on the reservation. Herb also pursues his interest in the historical and anthropological origins and commonalities of diverse tribes within the Indian Nation. He has published many articles featuring Navajo epistemology and culture. He and his wife have seven grown children.

Wendy Bishop teaches writing at Florida State University. Her recent books include two edited collections: *Colors of a Different Horse: Rethinking Creative Writing, Theory and Pedagogy* (1994), coedited with Hans Ostrom, and *The Subject Is Writing: Essays by Teachers and Students* (1993). She's working on a collection of nonfiction works, titled *The Shape of Fact,* and she's also taking time for her second and third a/vocations: spending time with her children, Morgan and Tait, and writing poems with her poetry group each week.

John Bradshaw, a leading figure in the field of recovery and dysfunctional families, combines the roles of author, counselor, theologian, consultant, and public speaker. He earned three degrees from the University of Toronto and studied for the Roman Catholic priesthood but left just prior to being ordained. Bradshaw's books have been *New York Times* bestsellers. They include *Bradshaw on the Family* (1988), *Creating Love* (1992), *Homecoming* (1992), and his latest book *Family Secrets* (1995). Bradshaw and his work have been featured on public television: *Bradshaw on the Family,* a series; *Bradshaw on Homecoming,* a series; and *Healing the Shame That Binds You,* a 90-minute special. He lives in Houston, Texas.

Thomas K. Dean is an assistant professor of English at Cardinal Stritch College in Milwaukee, Wisconsin, where he teaches composition, introductory literature, American literature, and world literature. His dissertation examined the work of Frank Norris, and he has published articles and presented papers on this American author. His interests in nature writing have also allowed him to publish and deliver papers on such authors as Sigurd Olson, Gerald Vizenor, Leslie Marmon Silko, Ray Young Bear, and William Least Heat-Moon. He enjoys the wilderness of northern Minnesota with his wife and son, as well as the tamer wilds of the local Audubon Center.

Larry Dossey, M.D., former Chief of Staff of Dallas Medical City Hospital, cochairs the Panel on Mind/Body Interventions, Office of Alternative Medicine, National Institutes of Health. Dossey has published numerous articles and six books including *Space, Time & Medicine* (1982) and *Beyond Illness* (1984), which have been translated into several languages and which explore human consciousness and the possibility of a Universal Mind. His *New York Times* bestseller *Healing Words* (1993) and his *Prayer Is Good Medicine* (1996) examines the role of prayer and healing from the perspective of a scientifically trained physician. Dossey is also executive editor of the journal *Alternative Therapies*. His goal in all of his publications is to anchor the so-called holistic health movement in a model that is scientifically respectable and that, at the same time, answers to individual spiritual needs. In 1988 he delivered the annual Mahatma Gandhi Memorial Lecture in New Delhi, India, the only physician ever invited to do so. Dossey served as a battalion surgeon in Vietnam. He lives with his wife, Barbara, an award-winning author, in Santa Fe.

Christopher Ferry is an assistant professor of English at Clarion University of Pennsylvania. He teaches writing, rhetorical and critical theories, and cultural studies.

Kristie S. Fleckenstein teaches composition at the University of Missouri, Kansas City. Her research interests include imagery and affect and reading and writing. She is currently examining liberation pedagogy from the stance of feminist ethics.

Regina Paxton Foehr teaches The Teaching of Literature and writing at Illinois State University. She is Chair of the NCTE Assembly for Expanded Perspectives on Learning. Her research interests include literacy, transformative writing, and psychoanalytical dimensions of reading and writing. Her forthcoming edited collection *The Writer as Hero: Archetypes, Creativity, and the Unconscious* investigates the effects of archetypal power from the personal and collective unconscious upon the act of writing. She is a former championship debate coach.

Donald R. Gallehr teaches nonfiction writing at George Mason University, where he is director of the Northern Virginia Writing Project. His most recent articles include "Portfolio Assessment in the College Writing Classroom," in *Process and Portfolios in Writing Instruction*, NCTE, 1993, and "Wait and the Writing Will Come: Meditation and the Composing Process," in *Presence of Mind: Writing and the Domain Beyond the Cognitive,* Boynton/Cook, 1994. Interested in learning beyond the cognitive since 1973 and its application to the classroom since the middle 1980s, he currently serves as associate chairman of NCTE's Assembly for Expanded Perspectives on Learning.

Richard L. Graves is professor of English education at Auburn University. He has edited *Rhetoric and Composition: A Sourcebook for Teachers and Writers,* now in its third edition, and with Alice G. Brand, *Presence of Mind: Writing and the Domain Beyond the Cognitive.* His professional interests center around writing and holistic learning, particularly the ways in which learning is rooted in mystical, nonlogical processes. A student of folk culture, he enjoys folk art, music, and dancing.

William S. Haney II teaches English at Easter Mediterranean University in the Turkish Republic of Northern Cyprus. His articles on American, British, and postcolonial literary theory have appeared in journals such as *Semiotica, Research in African Literatures,* and *Mosaic.* In his book *Literary Theory and Sanscrit Poetics,* he compares Eastern and Western strategies of interpretation in the attempt to formulate an approach to literature that incorporates higher consciousness.

Paul Heilker teaches courses in the theory and practice of rhetoric, writing, and the teaching of composition at Virginia Tech, where he serves as an assistant professor and codirector of writing programs. His work has appeared in such journals as *Rhetoric Review, Composition Studies, The Writing Instructor, Computers and Composition,* and *Issues in Writing.* His most recent publication is "Critical Thinking, the Thesis/

Support Form, and the Essay," in *Reading and Writing Nonfiction,* ed. Philip Anderson. Schenectady: New York State English Council, 1994.

Marianthe Karanikas teaches scientific and technical writing at Southwest Missouri State University. She holds an A.B. cum laude in biochemistry from Smith College, an M.A. in biophysics from Brandeis University, and a Ph.D. in Language Literacy and Rhetoric from the University of Illinois at Chicago. For ten years she has practiced meditation. She is currently writing a collection of essays on science, metaphor, rhetoric, traditional Chinese medicine, and meditation.

James Moffett is an author and consultant in education. He has been on the faculties of Phillips Exeter Academy, the Harvard Graduate School of Education, the University of California at Berkeley, San Diego State University, and the Middlebury College Bread Loaf School of English. A long-time reformer of English teaching at all levels, he has recently focused on the total learning environment, especially from the spiritual point of view. This shift is reflected in his two latest books, *Harmonic Learning: Keynoting School Reform,* Boynton/Cook, and *The Universal Schoolhouse: Spiritual Awakening Through Education,* Jossey Bass.

Thomas Moore, author of *New York Times* bestselling books *Care of the Soul,* 1992, *Soul Mates,* 1994, and *Re-enchantment of Everyday Life* (1996), has published many articles and lectured widely on spirituality, archetypal and Jungian psychology, mythology, and the arts. A former psychotherapist and university professor, Moore has become a leading figure in the field of archetypal psychology. In 1987 he founded the Institute for the Study of Imagination, a forum for seminars, lectures, and workshops on the history and practice of imagination. Moore studied for the priesthood, spending twelve years in a Roman Catholic religious order. Shortly before he was to be ordained, he left the order. Moore has a Ph.D. in religion and degrees in music and theology. His other books include *The Planets Within, Rituals of the Imagination, Dark Eros,* and the recently published *Meditations.* He also edited *A Blue Fire.* He lives with his wife and children in Massachusetts, where he enjoys woodworking and music composition.

Jacqueline Rinaldi is director of the University Learning Center at Sacred Heart University in Fairfield, Connecticut, where she teaches courses in rhetoric and literature. She has published essays in *College English* and the *New York Times* and is currently completing her dissertation at the University of Connecticut on "The Therapeutic Uses of Rhetoric in Contemporary American Lifewriting About Disability."

Susan A. Schiller is an associate professor at Central Michigan University where she teaches composition and literature. She serves as director of composition and was for three years coeditor of *Literacy Networks: A Journal of Literacy Providers.* She currently serves on the advisory board of JAEPL. Her research interests are in spirituality, affect, and imagery.

Sherry Seale Swain, a first-grade teacher at heart, is currently director of the Mississippi State University Writing/Thinking Project. In addition to spirituality in education, her areas of interest include professional empowerment for teachers, teacher research, writing process, writing across the curriculum, performance assessment, at-risk students, and integrated curriculum. Her book *I Can Write What's on My Mind: Theresa Finds Her Voice,* published by the National Writing Project, explores one child's journey into literacy within a community of supportive parents and classmates. She currently serves on the advisory board of JAEPL.

Notes:

People who would be great to have write for us —

- Peter Elbow — what does he think about spiritual applications, implications of things like freewriting, authentic voice?

- Irene Papoulis — she's written about grading and responding in terms of immanence vs. transcendence.